ALAIN BADIOU

ALAIN BADIOU

BETWEEN THEOLOGY AND ANTI-THEOLOGY

Hollis Phelps

ACUMEN

First published in 2013 by Acumen

Acumen Publishing Limited
4 Saddler Street
Durham
DH1 3NP

ISD, 70 Enterprise Drive
Bristol, CT 06010, USA

www.acumenpublishing.com

ISBN: 978-1-84465-553-3 (hardcover)
ISBN: 978-1-84465-554-0 (paperback)

British Library Cataloguing-in-Publication Data
A catalogue record for this book is available from the British Library.

Typeset in Warnock Pro and Myriad Pro.
Printed and bound in the UK by MPG Books Group.

CONTENTS

ACKNOWLEDGEMENTS

I'd like to thank Tristan Palmer at Acumen for taking this project on. Thanks also goes to Ellen Ott Marshall, Marc Redfield, Henry Krips, and Justin Clemens, all of whom read and commented on this project at various stages of its production. Roland Faber deserves special mention. His guidance, criticism and, most importantly, friendship, have been indispensible. I've benefited immensely from discussions with numerous friends and colleagues, too many to mention here. Although we have quite different interests, Will Schanbacher and Katy Scrogin, in particular, have been invaluable partners in dialogue and a constant source of encouragement. My colleagues at Mount Olive College, especially David Hines, Tyanna Yonkers, Neal Cox, Carla Williamson and Christopher Skinner, have provided me with the flexibility and resources necessary to finish this project in a timely manner. Christopher Skinner, especially, has consistently motivated me to become better at what I do. I could not ask for a better colleague and friend. My parents, Hollis and Susan, have given me their unwavering support, and for that I am most thankful. My son Alden is young enough to not really understand what I do, but his simple presence provides me with all the joy I need to continue doing what I do. Last, but certainly not least, is my wife Catherine. She has been with me from this project's inception to its conclusion. It's hard to express how much her patience, confidence and love mean to me, but for her I am eternally grateful.

ABBREVIATIONS

BE   *Being and Event* (2005a)
C   *The Communist Hypothesis* (2010a)
CH   continuum hypothesis
D   *Deleuze: The Clamor of Being* (2000)
E   *Ethics* (2001)
HI   *Handbook of Inaesthetics* (2005b)
IT   *Infinite Thought: Truth and the Return of Philosophy* (2004a)
LW   *Logics of Worlds* (2009c)
M   *Metapolitics* (2005c)
MP   *Manifesto for Philosophy* (1999c)
MS   *The Meaning of Sarkozy* (2008b)
NN   *Number and Numbers* (2008c)
OB   *On Beckett* (2003c)
P   *Polemics* (2006d)
PP   *Pocket Pantheon* (2009d)
SP   *Saint Paul: The Foundation of Universalism* (2003a)
TC   *The Century* (2007a)
TO   *Briefings on Existence: A Short Treatise on Transitory Ontology* (2006b)
TS   *Theory of the Subject* (2009e)
TW   *Theoretical Writings* (2004g)
WA   *L'antiphilosophie de Wittgenstein* (2009b)
WL   "What is Love?" (1996)

INTRODUCTION

The French philosopher Alain Badiou has emerged as one of the most recognizable voices in contemporary philosophy, although it is relatively recently that his work has begun to receive considerable attention in the English-speaking world. Over the past ten to fifteen years, many of his most significant texts have been translated into English, and his philosophy as a whole has been the subject of a growing body of commentary and criticism, including several book-length introductions and edited volumes devoted to his thought. The scope of Badiou's philosophy is vast, encompassing and incorporating various topics, disciplines, perspectives and schools of thought. Given the range that Badiou's corpus covers, any number of approaches to his philosophy can be taken.

The approach adopted here is to focus on the relationship that Badiou's philosophy maintains with Christian theology. Like any tradition, the Christian theological tradition is extremely diverse, constituted through a multitude of various, and often conflicting, perspectives. Despite the differences, as the term suggests, what all theology shares is a concern with God and the major tenets of the Christian faith. Theology is, at its most basic level, discourse about God, which includes a deliberate, conceptual articulation of faith in God. Such an understanding of theology, of course, presupposes faith, meaning that the practice of theology has normally been understood as reserved for those who already share the faith theology expresses. That is, theology is done by and for those who already have a stake in the enterprise. It would be wrong, however, to limit the scope of theology to this seemingly closed circle of faith. A discourse can remain theological to the extent that it relies on the apparatus of faith itself, even if belief in the God that underpins it is lacking or actively opposed. Nietzsche understood this all too well when he noted the following: "After Buddha was dead, his shadow was still shown for centuries in a cave – a tremendous, gruesome shadow. God is dead; but given the way of men, there may still be caves for thousands of years in which his shadow will be shown" (1974: 167).

To approach Badiou's philosophy from the perspective of theology is, how-ever, not entirely self-evident, at least if we follow the lead of Badiou himself and many of his most well-known interpreters. Although it is clear from even the most cursory reading of Badiou that he often references theology, such references are often taken as epiphenomenal to his philosophy as a whole, so much so that a sustained investigation of the role that theology plays in his philosophy hardly warrants any serious consideration. When Badiou does rely on certain theological themes, it is only to provide an example of a more essential philosophical point, a point that could have been made without an appeal to theology. Such estimations are seemingly consistent with the over-all thrust of Badiou's philosophy, which grounds ontology in mathematics and understands the categories of truth and the subject in formal terms, and his explicit, and often highly polemical, statements against theology.

Yet this focus tends to obscure the fact that theology remains an essential element of Badiou's philosophy, and its presence extends well beyond his most obvious foray into the land of theology, *Saint Paul: The Foundation of Universalism*. The goal of this book is to show how theological language, concepts, themes and forms inform the shape of Badiou's philosophy as a whole, so much so that we can speak of a theological core and eschatologi-cal form that animate Badiou's philosophy, despite claims to the contrary. Working out this claim entails a careful consideration of the basic elements of Badiou's philosophy in the chapters that follow. Before turning to these, it is helpful to situate the focus of this book in light of the basic concerns of Badiou's philosophy.

It is common to divide Badiou's philosophy into two major periods, the division between them marked by the publication of *Being and Event* in 1988. Badiou's philosophy prior to *Being and Event* was largely determined in both theory and practice by an explicitly Marxist framework of analy-sis. Generally speaking, Badiou's work in this period, from his attempt to develop a materialist epistemology of mathematics in *The Concept of Model*, written in 1968, to his concern with the dialectic and the subject in his Maoist phase that culminates in the publication of *Theory of the Subject* in 1982, has as its concern the question of structural and historical change in light of radical political practice. Although many of the concerns and con-cepts from this period of Badiou's philosophy clearly inform and influence the shape of his later thought, a clear turning point occurs in the mid-1980s. Declaring in 1985 in *Peut-on penser la politique?* the end or completion of Marxism, Badiou begins to develop a new framework for analysis. Although articulated in nascent form in *Peut-on penser la politique?*, this new frame-work is worked out fully in *Being and Event*, initially published in 1988. The chapters that follow discuss the main features of this framework in light of the theological problematic mentioned above, but for now we can note that, in the most general terms, Badiou's project since *Being and Event* can be understood as an attempt to construct a contemporary systematic philosophy, the parameters of which revolve around the articulation of a mathematical, and hence rational and deductive, ontology and a non-objective or generic theory of truth and the subject.

In the opening pages of *Being and Event*, Badiou situates his thought in light of various calls for the end of philosophy, against what appears to be a "general agreement that speculative systems are inconceivable and that the epoch has passed in which a doctrine of the knot *being/non-being/thought* (if one allows that this knot, since Parmenides, has been the origin of what is called 'philosophy') can be proposed in the form of a complete discourse" (BE 2, original emphasis). Badiou notes that the theme of philosophy's demise is common to various, and often divergent, schools. For instance, Heidegger, along with his progeny, attempts to think being before and after metaphysics, that epoch ruled by the forgetting of being; the Anglo-American or "analytic" school of philosophy, in conserving scientific rationality as a paradigm for thought, pits science against philosophy, reducing the latter to so many senseless propositions and/or language games; and Marx declares philosophy's end and realization in practice, while Lacan reduces "speculative totalization to the imaginary" (*ibid.*). In *Being and Event* and his subsequent work, Badiou takes it as his task to work through the assumptions that animate these calls for the end of philosophy, drawing a "diagonal" through them by taking their claims seriously without, however, abandoning philosophy as such (*ibid.*).

Thus, following Heidegger, Badiou maintains the priority of the ontological question for philosophy, but seeks to interrogate it through the resources that "analytic" philosophy has preserved. Specifically, along with "analytic" philosophy, Badiou holds that "the mathematico-logical revolution of Frege-Cantor sets new orientations for thought" (*ibid.*), orientations that coincide with the ontological question. The combination of the priority of the question of being and mathematical rationality, then, provides a way through the impasses that taking either individually creates, providing the framework for speculative thought. It is in this sense that Badiou will attempt to re-ground philosophy after its apparent dissolution in the identification of mathematics as ontology.

If the basic ontological framework that Badiou proposes and deploys cuts a diagonal through the assumptions that animate the Heideggerian and Anglo-American calls for philosophy's end, Badiou also attempts to take seriously the dismantling of the Cartesian idea of the subject, a dismantling present in Marx, Lacan, and many of the philosophers who have followed in their wake. Along with the latter, Badiou assumes that the "founding subject, centered and reflexive" (BE 3), a subject that constitutes the theme of much modern philosophical reflection, is no longer a viable category. For Badiou, however, this does not entail an end to the subject itself. The subject that we must now deal with is, rather, "void, cleaved, a-substantial, and ir-reflexive" (*ibid.*). Rather than being an external, substantial vantage point, then, the contemporary subject is a theoretico-practical category, whose existence can only be understood from within "the context of particular processes whose conditions are rigorous" (*ibid.*). Badiou will refer to these processes as truths, meaning that a renewed theory of the subject implies a "*new departure* in the doctrine of truth, following the dissolution of its relation of organic connection to knowledge" (*ibid.*, original emphasis).

Implied in Badiou's renewal of speculative philosophy around the categories of being, truth and the subject is also, however, a concerted effort to effect this renewal by taking seriously the idea of God's death. Peter Hallward, author of what is widely regarded as the most comprehensive introduction to Badiou's philosophy available to date, has suggested that "[n]o one, perhaps, has taken the death of God as seriously as Badiou" (Hallward 2003: 7). Hallward goes on to state that Badiou "aims to take Nietzsche's familiar idea to its absolute conclusion, to eliminate any notion of an originally divine or creative presence (however 'inaccessible' this presence might remain to the creatures it creates), and with it, to abolish any intuition of Life or Power" (*ibid.*). Although there are certainly many ways to interpret Badiou's philosophy, then, Hallward's claim suggests that one fruitful approach is to take the notion of the death of God as fundamental, using the idea as a lens through which to understand the whole. Badiou's mature philosophy, in this sense, from its use of mathematics and logic to inscribe being and appearance to its formal interrogation and organization of various truth procedures and the subjective consequences that follow from these, represents a consistent and concerted effort to think through God's death. Badiou says so much himself, when he suggests that his thought "should be conceived as in a meditation, in the clearing of God's death, of what must be thought in the word: 'here'" (TO 32). Since Badiou's insistence that we understand his philosophy "in the clearing of God's death" is fundamental for the argument developed in this book, it is worth detailing how this should be understood.

The clearest statement of how Badiou understands the death of God in relation to his own philosophy is found in his essay "God is Dead". Badiou begins the essay by asking a fundamental question: "What is God the name of in the formula 'God is dead'?" (TO 21). In order to provide an answer to this question, Badiou goes on to note the "complete difference between the theoretical formula 'God does not exist,' and the historical or factual statement 'God is dead'" (*ibid.*). The difference between these two statements basically corresponds to the often-made theological distinction between Athens and Jerusalem, between the God of the philosophers and the God of Abraham, Isaac and Jacob.[1] Badiou glosses this common theological distinction as that between the God of metaphysics or, following Heidegger, onto-theology and the God of religion. Badiou points out that the former posits "God" as a concept, as a principle that gives sense to and guarantees the consistency of thought and what thought thinks. For instance, whether understood along the lines of Aristotle's unmoved mover or Descartes' perfect being, the metaphysical or onto-theological God primarily functions as a presupposition for thinking the necessity of being as one or whole. However, since the God of metaphysics only gains meaning through its position in a proof, it remains indifferent to history, to the concerns of life and death. Because of this, the metaphysical God cannot be said to have died in any literal sense. In Badiou's words, "When you consider a concept, a symbol, a signifying function, you can say that they have become obsolete, contradicted, and inefficient. They cannot be said to have died" (TO 22).

In contrast, to claim that "God is dead" turns "God into a name, a proper name" (TO 21). According to Badiou:

> The living God is always *somebody's* God. The God with whom somebody – Isaac, Jacob, Paul, or Pascal – shares the power of living in the pure present of His subjective unfolding. Only this living God nourishes a properly religious conviction. The subject must deal with him as with an experienced power in the present. He must be *encountered*, and encountered on one's own.
>
> (TO 23, original emphasis)

To claim that this God, the God of religion, is dead, is thus to assert that this God was once alive, present in and to life, but is no longer. Badiou follows Nietzsche, here, at least when it comes to endorsing Nietzsche's proclamation of God's death. Recall that for Nietzsche, the statement "God is dead" means, among other things, that belief in the Christian God has become unbelievable. The traditional theological ideas that assume, in one way or another, God's relation to the world and the creatures in it – for instance, God's providential and beneficent governance of the world, the existence of an objective moral order that secures divine justice and mercy, the authority of the church – no longer directly inform human affairs. The slow and uneven march towards secularization, even Christianity itself, has gradually rendered such ideas unnecessary and irrelevant, transforming faith into dishonesty. God, for Nietzsche, no longer directly correlates to life, a sentiment well expressed in his equation of nihilism with the auto-devaluation of our highest values (Nietzsche 1967: 9). Badiou makes a similar claim without, however, necessarily adopting full force the nihilistic framework that encapsulates Nietzsche's proclamation.[2] Although Badiou acknowledges that the God of religion did at one time belong to the dimension of life, this is no longer the case in a post-Enlightenment world.[3] In Badiou's words:

> God is dead means that He is no longer the living being who can be encountered when existence breaks the ice of its own

> transparency. That so and so declares to the press that He was
> encountered under a tree, or in a provincial chapel, changes
> nothing. For we know that from such an encounter no thought
> can use its rights to advantage any longer, let alone do we grant
> someone claiming to see specters more than the positive consid-
> eration of a symptomatic manifestation. (TO 24)

Badiou leaves no room for argument on this point: "I take the formula 'God
is dead' literally. It *has* happened. Or, as Rimbaud said, it has passed. God is
finished. And religion is finished, too" (*ibid.*, original emphasis).

Badiou's insistence that "religion is finished" appears counter-intuitive on
the surface, especially since the idea of secularization that Badiou adopts
has fallen on hard times as of late. Although it was once common to assume
without much hesitation that increasing modernization spells the decline of
religious belief, that assumption now seems less persuasive than it once was.
According to the sociologist Peter L. Berger, "the relation between religion
and modernity is rather complicated" (Berger 1999: 3), much more complicated than was previously assumed. Indeed, whether overtly or not, and
despite – or perhaps because of – the effects of modernization, religion continues to play a vital role at both the individual and social level, as seen at its
most extreme in the rise of various fundamentalisms and religious violence
(see Juergensmeyer 2003). Thus, far from going away, religion has seemingly
shown a remarkable persistence, even something of a return, above and
beyond the various prophecies and proclamations of its demise, Badiou's
included.

Badiou, to be sure, does not necessarily deny that, at least empirically
speaking, something of religion seems to persist in the present, either as an
anchor for meaning in the world or as a political force in various forms of
fundamentalisms. Nevertheless, in line with Nietzsche, who claims that the
event of God's death has not yet fully arrived, Badiou rejects that the apparent persistence of religion has any bearing on the "motif of the living God's
real death" (TO 24). Badiou's claim that "religion is finished", then, should
be taken in a more normative or axiomatic sense. Concerning religion as a
locus of meaning for individuals, Badiou acknowledges that religion can and
does give sense to life, but the sense that it offers is by no means irreducible. If religion does, in fact, endow life with meaning, it does not follow that
"all kinds of donation of sense are religious, that is, requiring the living God
and thus the God who is historically able to die" (*ibid.*). Indeed, to acknowledge other forms of sense in addition to the religious is already an argument against the irreducibility of religion, in so far as the latter claims to
be all-encompassing. The multiplication of kinds of sense, Badiou observes,
"deeply severs the religious allocation of sense from the disposition of the
living God" (TO 26).

Rather than taking the seeming persistence of religion at face value, in line with modern critiques of religion Badiou prefers to explain the "subjective mechanism" through which religion "prospers" or "returns" (TO 23). It is along these lines that Badiou understands contemporary fundamentalisms. Far from being manifestations of the vitality of the religious, they are "contemporary formations, the political and state-based phenomena of our time" (TO 26). Contemporary fundamentalisms fall under the category of what Badiou calls "the obscure subject". We will analyse this category in detail in Chapter 2, but for now we can simply note that the obscure subject attempts to occult or abolish the present by appealing to some fixed, transcendent point that subsists beyond the "uncertain becoming" of the present, a point that Badiou describes as "an atemporal fetish: the incorruptible and indivisible over-body, be it City, God, or Race" (LW 60). Contrary to its stated claims, the obscure subject of fundamentalism ironically bears witness to God's death, as the unconscious principle animating its violent fetishism. It is a political "return of the repressed", which "is something about which no psychoanalyst should be surprised. Hence the desperate and bloody affirmation of a mortified religion, whose subjectively burrowed real principle is, from end to end, that God is dead" (TO 27). Badiou thus concludes, "What subsists is no longer religion, but its theater" (TO 24).

The death of the God of religion, however, does not immediately lead to the end of the God of metaphysics, the onto-theological God. Because, as we have said, the metaphysical God takes its position outside the sphere of life and death, it proves more resilient, as Heidegger knew all too well in his labelling of the history of philosophy an onto-theology (see Heidegger 1969). According to Badiou, the God of metaphysics maintains itself in the link it establishes between the infinite and the one. Thus in order to break the hold that the God of metaphysics continues to exert on and in thought, it is necessary to cut the link between the infinite and the one, thereby releasing the infinite from imposed metaphysical constraints. Badiou writes, "The key point is to unseal the infinite from its millenary collusion with the One. It is to restitute the infinite to the banality of manifold-being, as mathematics has invited us to do since Cantor. For it is as a suture of the infinite and the One that the supposed transcendence of the metaphysical God is constructed" (TO 30). We will discuss Badiou's attempt to de-suture the infinite from the one in detail in Chapter 1. For now we can simply note that the rending of the infinite from the one entails the following axiom: "There is no God. Which also means: the One is not" (E 25).

So far we have discussed Badiou's insistence on the death of the God of religion and the end of the God of metaphysics. Particularities aside, the basic substance of Badiou's insistence of these two issues puts him in line with the concerns of much continental thought since Nietzsche. What Badiou adds to the discussion is the way in which he links the two gods to a third: the God of the poets. Badiou describes this God in the following terms:

> It is neither the living Subject of religion, although it is certainly about living close to Him. Nor is it the Principle of metaphysics, although it is all about finding in His proximity the fleeing sense of Totality. It is that from which, for the poet, there is the enchantment of the world. As there is also its loss, which exposes one to idleness. About this God, we can say that It is neither dead nor alive. And It cannot be deconstructed as a tired, saturated, or sedimented concept. The central poetic expression concerning It is as follows: this God has withdrawn and left the world as prey to idleness. The question of the poem is thus that of the retreat of the gods. It coincides neither with the philosophical question of God nor with the religious one. (TO 28)

Emblematic of this insistence of what Badiou calls the God of the poets is Heidegger. Badiou, to be sure, credits Heidegger with re-establishing the priority of the ontological question for philosophy, and even refers to him as "the last universally recognizable philosopher" (BE 1). What Badiou takes issue with is the way in which Heidegger frames the question of being in light of the epochal forgetting of being in *Being and Time* and, in his later works, along the lines of the oscillation between withdrawal and unveiling. Although Heidegger thinks that thinking being in this way gestures towards an opening beyond nihilism, a nihilism that goes hand in hand with the theme of the technological end or completion of metaphysics, Badiou rejects this framework, and faults him for allowing his philosophy to be dominated by the form of the poem. Far from moving beyond metaphysics, Heidegger remains "enslaved" to what Badiou takes as "the essence of metaphysics; that is, the figure of being as endowment and gift, as presence and opening, and the figure of ontology as the offering of a trajectory of proximity" (BE 9). Heidegger's "poetic ontology", coupled with the theme of nihilism, lapses into a quasi-mythical discourse "haunted by the dissipation of Presence and the loss of origin" (BE 9–10). So much is evident, for Badiou, in Heidegger's posthumously published *Der Spiegel* interview, in which he claims that "philosophy will not be able to effect an immediate transformation of the present condition of the world. This is not only true of philosophy, but of all merely human thought and endeavour. Only a god can save us" (Heidegger 1988: 107). Taken in light of Heidegger's attempt to gesture towards an opening beyond nihilism, this statement for Badiou represents nothing more than a nostalgic longing for the "re-enchantment of the world" (TO 29). According to Badiou, "To say 'only a God can save us' means: the thinking that poets teach – educated by cognition of the Platonic turning, renewed by interpretation of the Presocratic Greeks – may uphold at the heart of nihilism the possibility, devoid of any way or means open to utterance, of a resacralization of the Earth" (MP 51).

Although Heidegger is the ostensible target here, the disposition itself extends well beyond the confines of his philosophy. As Justin Clemens points out, for Badiou the name "Heidegger" functions "as a synecdoche for late Romantic theory in general" (Clemens 2003b: 195). At the most basic level, the disposition that Badiou identifies with the God of the poets coincides with Romanticism, understood broadly as "any disposition of thinking which determines the infinite within the Open, or as a historical correlate for a historicity of finitude" (TW 25). Although articulated variously, the fundamental feature of Romanticism is, then, an emphasis on historicism and finitude. If and when the infinite does come into play, it "only manifests itself as a horizontal structure *for the historicity of the finitude of existence*" (TW 24, original emphasis). Badiou understands this emphasis on the temporal nature of the concept and the finitude of existence in philosophical thought as the direct result of too closely aligning philosophy to poetic form at the expense of mathematics. Badiou's problem with this disposition, it is important to emphasize, is not poetic form as such. Badiou generally has nothing but praise for the poets he is fond of citing, such as Hölderlin, Mallarmé, Rimbaud, Trakl, Pessoa, Mandelstam and Celan. Moreover, he is clear that poetry, and art in general, is an irreducible condition for philosophy, occupying its rightful place alongside science, love and politics. Badiou even credits the poets with thinking through, in their own way, "the destitution of the category of the object, and of objectivity, as necessary forms of presentation" (MP 72). The problem, rather, lies in taking poetry as either the main or sole condition for philosophy or mistaking it for philosophy itself, in effect exaggerating its importance. The Romantic disposition, as Badiou identifies it, "sutures" philosophy to poetry, "handing over the whole of thought to *one* generic condition" (MP 61, original emphasis).

Although Romanticism, as a distinct historical phenomenon and movement, is over, at a structural level the disposition itself continues to influence, even determine, much contemporary philosophy, serving as the common yet unacknowledged presupposition behind hermeneutic, postmodern and analytic philosophies (IT 39–57).[4] For Badiou, "The Romantic gesture still holds sway over us insofar as the infinite continues to function as a horizonal correlative and opening for the historicity of finitude. Our modernity is Romantic to the extent that it remains caught up in the temporal identification of the concept" (TW 25). The upshot of this emphasis on finitude, whether it is expressed speculatively in Hegel's reading of the incarnation, poetically in Heidegger's ontology, or linked to the interplay of language and sense in hermeneutic and linguistic philosophy, is a continuation of religion by other means, even if only in a negative guise. The God of the poets thus brings us back full circle. "As long as finitude remains the ultimate determination of existence," Badiou writes, "God abides. He abides as that whose disappearance continues to hold sway over us, in the form of the abandonment, the dereliction, or the leaving-behind of Being" (TO 25). Indeed, "Finitude is like the trace of an afterlife in the movement that entrusts the overcoming of the religion-God and the metaphysics-God to the poem-God" (TO 29). Against this disposition, Badiou calls for a "contemporary atheism": "It is about no longer entrusting the nostalgic God of the return with the joint balance consisting of the death of the living God and the deconstruction of the metaphysical God. All in all, it is about finishing up with promises" (ibid.). What such an atheism requires is the abandonment of the theme of finitude as the fundamental horizon of philosophical thought, an abandonment that coincides with the restitution of mathematics as a foundational discourse for philosophy. Mathematics is particularly suited to this task, since it alone thinks the infinite, in both form and content, as infinite. Moreover, it does so in a resolutely secular manner, against any explicit or implicit theological assumptions. Badiou writes, "Only by relating the infinite back to a neutral banality, by inscribing eternity in the matheme alone, by simultaneously abandoning historicism and finitude, does it become possible to think within a radically deconsecrated realm" (TW 27).

I argue in the chapters that follow that Badiou's concern to situate thought within a "radically deconsecrated realm" constitutes Badiou's philosophy as an anti-theology. I use the term "anti-theology" to describe Badiou's philosophy to emphasize the polemical stance it adopts with respect to theological forms of thought. Badiou's philosophy is not merely non-theological, in the sense that it remains indifferent to theology and its concerns. Badiou's philosophy comes out explicitly against theology, and in doing so attempts to provide an anti-theological alternative.

The first two chapters of this book focus on Badiou's anti-theology, in an attempt to assess the extent to which Badiou claims to depart from theology. Chapter 1 focuses on how Badiou's identification of mathematics and ontology constitutes an anti-theology in both form and content. In contrast to the lawlessness of poetic speech and its focus on meaning and sense, mathematics provides a rigorously deductive form of thought that subtracts itself from empirical, linguistic and subjective concerns. Mathematics functions as a language of secularization against re-enchantment and, ultimately, theology. The form of ontology directly informs its content, as the basic elements of Badiou's ontology function as secularized alternatives to theology: the decision for the pure multiple or multiple-without-one as primary displaces the one of onto-theology; the void, the subtractive suture of a situation to its being and the initial point of presentation, displaces the name of God as the ground of presence; the transfinite unbinds being from the one, releasing the infinite from its designation as an inscrutable attribute of supreme being towards multiplicities of infinities transmissible in knowledge.

Although certainly foundational for his thought, ontology is not an end in itself. For Badiou ontology serves as a propaedeutic for philosophy proper, whose main concern is the construction of a theory of truth and the subject. Chapter 2 discusses the formal elements that constitute Badiou's theory of truth and the subject, beginning in the first part with Badiou's doctrine of the event. Events are ruptures that have the potential to force absolutely new trajectories in situations, trajectories that correspond to the production of truths. The conceptual apparatus that supports the passage from events to truths, specifically the interrelated notions of intervention, nomination, evental recurrence, resurrection, fidelity and forcing, constitute a subject as the local configuration of a procedure of truth. So understood, Badiou's theory of truth and the subject continues the anti-theological emphasis of his ontology in regard to historical situations: truths, and the subjects that correspond to them, are local, historical productions.

Nevertheless, although Badiou ostensibly uses mathematical deduction as the model for the production of truths, he consistently relies both implicitly and explicitly on theological notions to articulate his theory. Such reliance, I will suggest, complicates the anti-theological trajectory of his thought, and leaves open the question of the role of theology in it.

In order to consider the role that theology plays in Badiou's philosophy, Chapter 3 begins with a more detailed discussion of truths, specifically how science, art, politics and love function as conditions for philosophy. On Badiou's account, each of these four truth procedures, understood as irreducibly singular, must be in play for philosophy to be possible. Nevertheless, I argue that Badiou's emphasis on the uniqueness of each truth procedure leaves unaddressed how science, art, politics and love might be more substantially interrelated. I thus provide a way to understand the interrelation among the four truth procedures without nullifying the singularity of each. Drawing primarily on Badiou's theory of intervention, I argue that each truth procedure, whether scientific, artistic, political or amorous, incorporates the formal elements of the other truth procedures, irrespective of content.

In negotiating its conditions, philosophy also has to deal with sophistry and anti-philosophy. Although it is common to distance Badiou's philosophy from the latter, the relationship is more complex. Whereas sophistry conditions philosophy by limiting the latter's pretensions towards dogmatic totalization, anti-philosophy plays a more constructive role, to the extent that the philosopher must pass through anti-philosophy before doing philosophy. Anti-philosophy shares with sophistry a suspicion of truth, but it identifies the philosophical desire for truth with an act that conceals hidden, misdirected motivations. Against this philosophical act, the anti-philosopher appeals to another act, an act of radical novelty that breaks through the limits of thought, speech and experience. I argue, however, that this anti-philosophical act, constitutive of all anti-philosophy, brings anti-philosophy into the realm of religion and theology.

The identification of anti-philosophy with a theological impulse serves as the foundation for the argument made in Chapter 4. After discussing and criticizing how interpreters have understood the role of theology in Badiou's philosophy, this chapter analyses Badiou's use of theological language in the construction of many of his key ideas. Although when pressed, Badiou claims that his use of theological language is metaphorical, such an explanation is unconvincing, given Badiou's own understanding of the relationship between language and truths. Badiou's use of theological language, in this sense, implicates him formally in the discourse of theology. This implication, however, is also conceptual. So much is most clearly on display in *Saint Paul: The Foundation of Universalism*, in which Badiou reads Paul as an anti-philosophical thinker of the event. The implication, however, extends to the event itself. Although it is common among interpreters to separate Badiou's philosophy from anti-philosophy, I suggest that the event functions in an anti-philosophical, and thus theological, register in Badiou's philosophy. There is thus a theological element at work in Badiou's philosophy.

Although Badiou does attempt to avoid the anti-philosophical bent of his theory by dialecticizing the event, this dialecticization itself adopts a theological form, one that is eschatological in orientation. Such a claim certainly goes against the grain of many interpretations of Badiou. Nevertheless, to support this claim, I focus on Badiou's notion of periodization as found in *Theory of the Subject*, a notion that is meant to replace a circular and idealist dialectic with a materialist dialectic that emphasizes the passage between contingent historical sequences. I then link the notion of periodization to the notions of intervention and eventual recurrence, as found in *Being and Event*, and the resurrection of truths, as found in *Logics of Worlds*. When combined with forcing as the knowledge of truth in the future anterior and the eternality of truths, these notions construct a time that is eschatological, a time constructed through retroaction and anticipation. Simply put, this time requires belief or faith in the "yet to come" of truths.

1. BADIOU'S ANTI-THEOLOGY

As we discussed in the Introduction, Badiou calls for a contemporary atheism, an atheism that breaks with the three Gods that continue to hold thought captive: the God of religion, the God of metaphysics and the God of the poem. Since the influence of these gods ultimately rests on the persistence of the theme of finitude, we must take leave of the latter as the horizon of philosophical speculation. Put more positively, we must unseal the infinite from the one, restoring it to the banal multiplicity that it is. This chapter discusses Badiou's attempt to unbind the infinite from its collusion with the one, by discussing the main elements of Badiou's ontology. However, to be clear, no attempt will be made to provide a copious overview of Badiou's ontology in its entirety, examining all the twists and turns involved in its complex presentation. There are already numerous good introductions to Badiou's ontology and critical discussions of its particular elements already in print, and there is no need to repeat the work of others on these issues. Rather, in keeping with the focus of this book, the goal of this chapter is to read Badiou's ontology and its main themes as an anti-theology, an anti-theology that takes its departure from the main thesis of *Being and Event*: "mathematics *is* ontology" (BE 4, original emphasis). Since Badiou's mathematical ontology constitutes the main challenge of his thought for theology, in so far as it ostensibly allows for philosophy finally to separate itself from theology (cf. Depoortere 2009), understanding and taking seriously the anti-theological intent of his ontology serves as a necessary propaedeutic to the argument that follows in later chapters. Accordingly, the discussion that follows is divided into two main sections. The first section focuses in detail on Badiou's equation of mathematics and ontology, since grasping the sense of Badiou's claim that mathematics is ontology is foundational for any attempt to read his ontology as an anti-theology. The second section focuses on the main elements of Badiou's ontology, in particular multiplicity without one, the void and the infinite, as these constitute an anti-theology.

"MATHEMATICS *IS* ONTOLOGY"

Crucial for any understanding of Badiou's philosophical system, especially its anti-theological dimensions, is a grasp of the fundamental role of mathematics in the deployment of his thought. Badiou's interest in mathematics as integrally related to philosophical speculation goes back to the beginning of his intellectual career, as seen for instance in his attempt to develop a materialist epistemology of mathematics in articles published in the late 1960s and in his lecture given in Louis Althusser's Philosophy Course for Scientists at the École Normale Supérieure in 1968, published as *The Concept of Model* in 1970.[1] Badiou's explicit use of mathematics largely drops out of his Maoist phase in the 1970s, during which time his main concern was with questions concerning the dialectical practice of militant politics. Although we can find piecemeal use of set-theoretical concepts in *Theory of the Subject*, mathematics returns to the centre of his reflections in *Being and Event*, published in 1988. Badiou tells us in the Introduction to *Being and Event* that, while doing research into the paradoxes associated with the continuum hypothesis, he "arrived at the certainty that it was necessary to posit that mathematics writes that which, of being itself, is pronounceable in the field of a pure theory of the Multiple" (BE 5). In other words, he came to the conclusion that "mathematics *is* ontology" (BE 4, original emphasis).

Before analysing this claim in detail, it is worth pointing out its contentious nature, of which Badiou is well aware. It is of course one thing to claim that mathematics is in some way important to philosophy; it is another thing altogether to claim that it is ontology. Indeed, it is safe to say that the equation of mathematics and ontology is one that is not recognized by the majority of working mathematicians or philosophers. On the one hand, as Badiou points out, mathematicians do mathematics perfectly well without ever giving any thought to the question of being qua being, meaning that advances in mathematics do not at all require posing the ontological question. Even if it were required, the highly technical and specialized language of mathematical discourse would seem to elude the grasp of many philosophers, making the ontological status of mathematics a moot point. As Badiou says, "Empirically, the mathematician always suspects the philosopher of not knowing enough about mathematics to have earned the right to speak" (BE 11). On the other hand, with few exceptions the mainstream of the continental philosophical tradition from which Badiou works has for the most part downplayed or ignored the significance of mathematics for philosophy. Such is the continuing influence of the Romantic disposition in philosophy, a disposition that often manifests itself as a generalized suspicion of science as a merely technical enterprise. For Badiou, such suspicion, especially when it comes to the relationship between science or, more specifically, mathematics and ontology, has more to do with fear than anything else: "At base, affirming that mathematics accomplishes ontology unsettles philosophers because this thesis absolutely discharges them of what remained the centre of gravity of their discourse, the ultimate refuge of their identity" (BE 10).

What, then, does it mean to say that mathematics completes ontology, that "mathematics *is* ontology"? We can begin to analyse this thesis, fundamental to Badiou's whole enterprise, by first delineating what it does not mean. In his essay "Mathematics and Philosophy: The Grand Style and the Little Style", Badiou discusses the relationship between mathematics and philosophy. Badiou distinguishes his own deployment of mathematics as ontology from an attempt to provide a philosophy of mathematics, which would construct "mathematics as an *object* for philosophical scrutiny" (TW 3, original emphasis). According to Badiou, differences aside, what most philosophies of mathematics share is the attempt to adjudicate the relationship between mathematics and philosophy by assigning "mathematics a subservient role [to philosophy], as something whose only function seems to consist in helping to perpetuate a well-defined area of philosophical *specialization*" (TW 3, original emphasis). When understood in this way, the relationship between philosophy and mathematics is ultimately epistemological in nature, in that philosophy attempts to shoehorn the unbounded creativity of mathematical construction into predetermined philosophical categories. Badiou refers to such an approach to the relationship between the two as representative of "the little style" (*ibid.*). By subordinating mathematics to philosophy, however, "the little style" can only present "a neutered mathematics", in that it "strives to dissolve the ontological sovereignty of mathematics, its aristocratic self-sufficiency, its unrivalled mastery, by confining its dramatic, almost baffling existence to a stale compartment of academic specialization" (*ibid.*).

Against the subordination of mathematics to philosophy according to "the little style", Badiou seeks to understand the relationship between mathematics and philosophy according to what he calls "the grand style", which "stipulates that mathematics provides a direct illumination of philosophy" (TW 7). As we will see in Chapter 3, the stipulation that mathematics should directly and immediately illuminate philosophy is in line with Badiou's more general claims regarding the relationship between truths and philosophy. For now, we can simply note that Badiou cites Descartes, Spinoza, Kant, Hegel and Lautréamont as "five majestic examples of the grand style" (*ibid.*). Although Badiou has substantial philosophical disagreements with each of these thinkers, at the most basic level what each shares is the recognition that mathematics "is at once descriptively external and prescriptively immanent for philosophy" (*ibid.*). Badiou's primary source for thinking the relationship between mathematics and philosophy in this manner is, however, Plato, "who deployed a fundamental entanglement of mathematics and philosophy in all its ramifications" (TW 28).

A key passage for Badiou is Glaucon's summation of the relationship between mathematics and dialectics, in Book 6 of *The Republic*:

> The theorizing concerning being and the intelligible which is sustained by the science [*episteme*] of the dialectic is clearer than that sustained by what are known as the sciences [*techné*]. It is certainly the case that those who theorize according to these sciences, which have hypotheses as their principles, are obliged to proceed discursively rather than empirically. But because their intuiting remains dependent on these hypotheses and has no means of accessing the principle, they do not seem to you to possess the intellection of what they theorize, which nevertheless, in so far as it is illuminated by the principle, concerns the intelligibility of the entity. It seems to me you characterize the procedures of geometers and their ilk as discursive [*dianoia*], which is not how you characterize intellection. This lies midway between [*metaxu*] opinion [*doxa*] and intellect [*nous*].
>
> (Quoted in TW 28–9)[2]

Badiou draws out four points from this passage, points that are essential to his own understanding of the relationship between mathematics and philosophy. First, as an actual practice, mathematics, which in the passage cited above is associated with "the sciences" and the "geometers and their ilk", institutes "a paradigm for the *possibility* of breaking with opinion" (TW 29, original emphasis). Precisely because its subject matter and operations are atemporal and universal, mathematics constitutes itself in a break with the empirical, which, when taken on its own terms, remains confined to the interplay of competing and often contradictory perspectives. Badiou's second point, however, is that the mathematical break with *doxa* or opinion "is, to some extent, involuntary, unapparent to itself, and above all devoid of freedom" (TW 30). That is, because mathematics necessarily proceeds in its own work on the basis of hypotheses or axioms that cannot be legitimated from outside its own operations, mathematics cannot on its own terms bring to light the principle or reason behind the break that it effectuates. In Badiou's words, "The mathematical rupture is carried out under the constraint of deductive chains that are themselves dependent upon a fixed point which is stipulated in authoritarian fashion" (*ibid.*). Because of this involuntary constraint – and this is Badiou's third point – the mathematical break must be supplemented with a second break, an additional break that allows for the illumination of the first. The locus of this break is dialectics or philosophy, which alone has access to the principle of intelligibility that goes unnoticed in the mathematical gesture. "Although mathematics genuinely encapsulates the discontinuity with *doxa*," Badiou writes, "only philosophy can allow thought to establish itself in such a way as to assert the principle of this discontinuity" (TW 31). Fourth, this means that mathematics as such remains insufficient, since it is *metaxu*, between opinion and intellect; mathematics, in order to grasp the substance of this break, needs philosophy. Mathematics thus belongs on the side of truth, but only "to a constrained form of it. Above and beyond this constrained figure of truth stands its free figure which elucidates discontinuity: philosophy" (*ibid.*).

Although Badiou criticizes Plato's assignation of mathematics to a "constrained form" of truth – as we will see, it is precisely the "authoritarian" nature of mathematics that allows it to function in an ontological register – the upshot of the passage is clear: mathematics is a form of thought in its own right, a form of thought that has direct implications for philosophy. Indeed, if these implications are not taken seriously, philosophy cannot help but become a mere shell of its true self: "if there is no grand style in the way philosophy relates to mathematics, then there is no grand style in philosophy full stop" (TW 14).

Returning to the claim that "mathematics is ontology", if it should not be taken as an attempt to construct a philosophy of mathematics but in the mode of "the grand style", it is also important to avoid taking the claim as indicative of some sort of neo-Pythagoreanism, which would understand being as mathematical. Although Badiou stresses that the claim "mathematics is ontology" should be taken literally, he is quick to point out that the statement "does not in any way declare that being is mathematical, which is to say composed of mathematical objectivities" (BE 8). He goes on to state, "It is not a thesis about the world but about discourse. It affirms that mathematics, throughout the entirety of its historical becoming, pronounces what is expressible of being qua being" (*ibid.*). The claim that "mathematics is ontology" names mathematics as the "language" of being. Mathematics thus grasps and inscribes being, but what it grasps and inscribes is not itself mathematical. Another way to put the matter is to say that "mathematics writes that which, of being itself, is pronounceable in the field of the pure theory of the Multiple" (BE 5).

Badiou's insistence that the claim "mathematics is ontology" is a claim about discourse should also caution against ascribing to him a particular stance on the nature of mathematical objects. Given Badiou's own characterization of his philosophy as a "Platonic gesture" (MP 97–101), it is of course tempting to ascribe to him the position that mathematical objects and structures exist independently of actual mathematical operations.[3] Attributing this type of ontological idealism to Badiou, however, misses the sense of his restitution of Plato and, ultimately, turns him into a representative of "the little style". What interests Badiou in Plato is not the commonly held view that Plato assigns independent existence to mathematical objects and structures, a view that, in separating subject from object, seems more indebted to

17

an empiricist epistemology than "the genuine Platonic framework" (TW 49). Indeed, for Badiou the nature of mathematical objects and structures is an "entirely relative" or "secondary" concern for Plato: Plato's main point, evident in the passage from Book 6 of *The Republic* discussed above, is that "mathematics intrinsically thinks" (TW 50). In Badiou's words:

> Plato's fundamental concern is to declare the immanent identity, the co-belonging, of the knowing mind and the known, their essential ontological commensurability … In so far as it touches on being, mathematics intrinsically thinks. By the same token, if mathematics thinks, it accesses being intrinsically. (TW 49–50)

The thinking proper to mathematics in regard to being is indissolubly linked to the manner in which mathematics thinks. Although Badiou's use of mathematics cannot be reduced to its form, he does stress that the form of mathematical language is essential for ontology, in that it allows mathematics to think the general structure of any situation. Mathematics and, as we will see below, set theory in particular, "*formalizes* any situation whatsoever insofar as it reflects the latter's being as such; that is, the multiple of multiples which makes up any presentation" (BE 130, original emphasis). Mathematics is able to think what it thinks – being qua being – precisely because of its ability to attain complete abstraction in the realm of thought, an abstraction whose potential is universal in scope. Mathematics is, to use the words of Justin Clemens and Jon Roffe, "as pure as reason gets, i.e., mathematics is at once non-empirical, axiomatic, deductive, extra-linguistic, non-definitional, universalizing" (Clemens & Roffe 2008: 350). Because of this, mathematics is able to access being as such, to think being as "*the presentation of presentation*" (BE 27, original emphasis).

Another way to put the matter is to say that mathematics – and mathematics alone, on Badiou's account – is a thinking of the infinite. It is a thinking of *the infinite* or, more specifically, infinities, in that the latter is its proper subject, as we will discuss in detail below. But it is also a *thinking* of the infinite in its form: it is not limited to the empirical, the linguistic, the definitional, the experiential or the particular. In so far as it abstracts itself from these and other limitations, mathematics avoids admitting the finite into its thought in both form and content. Mathematics is, to borrow the title from one of Badiou's collections of essays, "infinite thought". It is precisely this characteristic that, in Badiou's estimation, makes mathematics the perfect – indeed, only – vehicle for ontology.

In order to deploy mathematics as ontology, Badiou specifically draws from contemporary set theory, as axiomatized in the Zermelo–Fraenkel (ZF) system.[4] It is important to point out, however, that Badiou's choice to utilize set theory does not limit ontological speculation to set theory to one particular domain of mathematics. Nevertheless, the decision to deploy set theory as ontology is by no means insignificant or arbitrary, either. There is general agreement that set theory is "that branch of mathematics which expressly considers the nature of its objects and terms, that is, what they *are* or how they are made" (Hallward 2003: 82–3, original emphasis). In this sense, set theory, as the mathematician Keith Devlin says, "provides a unified framework for the whole of mathematics" (quoted in *ibid.*: 366 n5), making it particularly suited for the work of ontology.

We will see how this is the case in the next section, but to sum up: the thesis that "mathematics is ontology" is not a statement about being; rather, it positions mathematics as the discursive vehicle through which being qua being can be thought and expressed. Mathematics and, in particular, set theory, inscribes being qua being through its axiomatic decisions and operations. For this reason, mathematics really is ontology, the science or study of being as such. However, this is not to deny that the question of being is a philosophical problem, at least historically speaking, in that it has fallen primarily to the discipline of philosophy to provide answers to the question of being. Badiou acknowledges as much, but claims that it is now mathematics that provides answers to the question. Such a claim is in keeping with the priority Badiou gives to "the grand style" over "the little style" that we discussed above. If "the little style" ultimately subordinates mathematics to philosophy, "the grand style" holds that mathematics directly illuminates philosophy, which in this instance concerns providing the means through which being qua being can be thought and expressed. "All that we know, and can ever know of being qua being," Badiou writes, "is set out, through the mediation of a theory of the pure multiple, by the historical discursivity of mathematics" (BE 8). Mathematics is, in this sense, "a *condition* for philosophy" (TW 21, original emphasis).

What are the consequences of the claim that "mathematics is ontology", the science of being qua being? First, to claim that mathematics as ontology functions as a condition for philosophy is also to state that "*philosophy is originally separated from ontology*" (BE 13, original emphasis). That is, what can be said "of being qua being does not in any manner arise from the discourse of philosophy" (*ibid.*). The equation of ontology and mathematics thus takes ontology out of the realm of philosophy proper, but in so doing it frees philosophy for what Badiou considers to be its true task: "the care of truths" (BE 4). The thesis that "mathematics is ontology" is certainly radical, but from another angle it is designed to "*delimit* the proper space of philosophy" (BE 14, original emphasis). We can of course assign value to ontology in its own right (cf. Brassier 2007: 97–117), but Badiou himself appears to understand the entanglement of ontology with mathematics as a propaedeutic to the real concern of philosophy, the problem of "what-is-not-being-qua-being". Otherwise put, ontology clears the ground for the philosophical articulation of a theory of truth and the subject, which we will discuss in the next chapter. The guiding question of *Being and Event* and the mathematical-ontological formulations that occupy a good portion of it is, then: "pure mathematics being the science of being, how is a subject possible?" (BE 6).

Nevertheless, if the thesis "mathematics is ontology" delimits the respective tasks of ontology and philosophy, the thesis itself is meta-ontological, that is, philosophical. In Badiou's words, "The demonstration of the thesis [ontology = mathematics] prescribes the usage of certain mathematical fragments, yet they are commanded by philosophical rules, and not by those of contemporary mathematics" (BE 13). This is an important point to emphasize since, as we stated above, most mathematicians go about their work without the slightest bit of concern for ontological questions. Although mathematical knowledge is "certainly worthwhile in itself, however difficult to conquer", the "ontological dignity" of that knowledge is for the most part "constrained to blindness with respect to itself" (TW 12, 14). The meta-ontological identification of ontology with mathematics, then, is meant to bring this largely unrecognized knowledge to light, to deploy it in the service of constructing a science of being qua being. In this respect, the philosophical deployment of mathematics as ontology is in line with Plato's discussion of the relationship between mathematics and philosophy in Book 6 of *The Republic*. Recall from our discussion of this passage above that mathematics constitutes a break with *doxa*, but this break remains unrecognized from within the purview of mathematics itself, in the actual practice of mathematics by mathematicians. What is needed, as Badiou emphasizes, is an illumination of this break, an illumination that falls to the practice of dialectics or philosophy. The meta-ontological identification of ontology with mathematics thus repeats this Platonic gesture: mathematics is actually ontology, but it falls to philosophy to bring its ontological destiny to the surface, to deploy it as ontology.

Second, if the deployment of mathematics as ontology separates ontology from philosophy, in effect limiting the scope of philosophical reflection proper to truth and the subject, the thesis also puts strong limitations on ontology in regard to what can be said of being qua being and how it can be said. Specifically, the location of ontology in the domain of mathematics dispels poetic form and speech – indeed, language in general – from ontology. This is an important point, and it goes to the heart of the way in which Badiou's ontology functions as an anti-theology.

Recall from the Introduction that taking the death of God to its ultimate conclusion requires abandoning not only the God of religion and the God of metaphysics, but also the God of the poem. Although in *Being and Event* he suggests that "Heidegger is the last universally recognized philosopher" (BE 1), Badiou goes on to argue that, by suturing ontology to the form of the poem, Heidegger remains "enslaved" to "the essence of metaphysics: that is, the figure of being as endowment and gift, as presence and opening; and the figure of ontology as the offering of a trajectory of proximity" (BE 9). Heidegger's "poetic ontology" lapses into a quasi-mythical discourse "haunted by the dissipation of Presence and the loss of origin" (BE 9–10). Referring to Heidegger's statement in his posthumously published *Der Spiegel* interview, Badiou writes:

> To say "only a God can save us" means: the thinking that poets teach – educated by cognition of the Platonic turning, renewed by interpretation of the Presocratic Greeks – may uphold at the heart of nihilism the possibility, devoid of any way or means open to utterance, of a resacralization of the Earth.   (MP 51)

Heidegger's ontology is thus wrapped up with a nostalgic longing for or anticipation of re-enchantment, a re-enchantment that goes hand in hand with the form that his ontology takes. For this reason, Heidegger's insistence on the relationship between ontology and the poem ultimately conceals a religious impulse; more precisely, it allows for "the return of the religious" (PP 71). Suturing the thinking of being to the poem ties being to the circulation of sense, which in Badiou's estimation can only lead to a quasi-mythical and mystifying desire for presence within the finitude of existence. But, as Badiou suggests, "As long as finitude remains the ultimate determination of existence, God abides. He abides as that whose disappearance continues to hold sway over us, in the form of the abandonment, the dereliction, or the leaving behind of being" (TO 26).

Badiou's grounding of ontology in mathematics is a direct attempt to subvert this ostensible theological tendency at the heart of poetic ontologies. If poetic ontologies tend to lapse into a quasi-mythical discourse of withdrawal and unveiling, endowment and gift – in short, if they unwittingly preserve religion through other means, even the theme of being's absence – it is mathematics, and mathematics alone, that allows for a "break with superstition and ignorance" (TW 22). On Badiou's account, mathematics is "that singular form of thinking which has *interrupted the sovereignty of myth*. We owe to it the first form of self-sufficient thinking, independent of any sacred form of enunciation; in other words, the first form of an entirely secularized thinking" (*ibid.*, original emphasis). Moreover, mathematics instantiates a secularized thinking not through the establishment of some neutral domain, but in direct opposition to those forms of thought that seek to preserve the sovereignty of myth. Mathematics goes on the attack against the latter, attempting to dispel any remaining forms of ignorance and superstition and refusing the claim that something lies beyond the limits of thought. "Mathematics", Badiou says, "provides philosophy with a weapon, a fearsome

machine of thought, a catapult aimed at the bastions of ignorance, superstition, and mental servitude" (TW 16). To use another metaphor, mathematics thus clears the ground much as a bulldozer, pushing away the worn
out myths that shore up our putative limitations so as to clear a space for
the construction of something new (TW 16–17). Against "the seduction of
poetic proximity", then, Badiou opposes:

> the radically subtractive dimension of being, foreclosed not only
> from representation but from all presentation. I will say that
> being qua being does not in any manner let itself be approached,
> but solely allows itself to be *sutured* in its void to the brutality
> of a deductive consistency without aura. Being does not diffuse
> itself in rhythm and image, it does not reign over metaphor, it is
> the null sovereign of inference. For poetic ontology, which – like
> History – finds itself in an impasse of an excess of presence, one
> in which being conceals itself, it is necessary to substitute math-
> ematical ontology, in which dis-qualification and unpresentation
> are realized through writing. Whatever the subjective price may
> be, philosophy must designate, insofar as it is a matter of being
> qua being, the genealogy of the discourse on being – and the
> reflection on its possible essence – in Cantor, Gödel, and Cohen
> rather than in Hölderlin, Trakl and Celan.   (BE 10)

To sum up, Badiou's recourse to mathematics guards against the lawlessness of poetic speech. According to Badiou, grounding ontology in the cold,
deductive rigour of the matheme alone wards of the potential theological
contamination of the science of being qua being. Mathematics, then, "is an
essentially de-mystificatory screen designed to prevent us from becoming
fascinated by the luxuriant plenitude of what there is" (Brassier 2007: 114).

Third, and directly related to the second point, to claim that "mathematics is ontology" is also to claim "*ontology is a situation*" (BE 27, original emphasis). What Badiou means by "situation" will become clearer in
the next section, where we discuss the main features of Badiou's ontology.
Suffice it to say at this point that Badiou defines a "situation" as "any presented multiplicity … a situation is the place of taking-place, whatever the
terms of the multiplicity in question" (BE 24). A situation or, in the language of *Logics of Worlds*, world is, in turn, always structured in a particular
way, according to a specific logic or count that organizes it. The structure
of a situation is "what prescribes, for a presented multiple, the regime of
its count-as-one" (*ibid.*). Given the relationship between a situation and its
structure, things *are* only in so far as they are presented in situations, meaning that there is literally "nothing apart from situations" (BE 25). If there is
nothing apart from situations, then ontology must also be a situation, with

its own one-count or structure that determines its manner of presentation and what it presents.

Badiou's insistence on the situated character of ontology sets his ontology against those ontologies that take an opposite route, working from the assumption that "there is no structure of being" (BE 26). To say that being lacks structure "is to signify that being cannot be signified within a structured multiple, and that only an experience situated beyond all structure will afford us an access to the veiling of being's presence" (*ibid.*). We can see this tendency in Plato, for instance, when he posits that the Idea of the Good is "beyond substance", and thus incapable of being grasped through discursive means. Plato, despite his emphasis on the importance of mathematics for *dianoia*, in the end holds that the "donation in thought of this supreme principle – which is the donation in thought of a Being beyond beings – does not let itself be traversed by any kind of *dianoia*" (HI 19). Indeed, when attempting to approach this unsignified beyond, Plato falls back on images, myths and metaphors, that is, "the power of poetic speech" (HI 20). The tendency is also found, as Badiou points out, in negative or apophatic theologies, which in general understand God or the One as the inscrutable negation of all presentation and signification, as the beyond of all sense. But the insistence that being lacks structure is also a feature of many philosophies associated with the linguistic turn, in so far as these rely upon the dialectic of the said and the unsaid to secure meaning. Wittgenstein's words are telling in this respect: "There is indeed the inexpressible. This *shows* itself; it is the mystical" (Wittgenstein 1955: 6.522; cf. WA 22).

Now, it is worth pointing out that Badiou's main problem with such "ontologies of presence", as he calls them, concerns the structure of ontological thought, whether the one is involved or not. For instance, we can read the apophatic tradition in theology in general as concerned with what we could call, for lack of a better word, the hyper-one, the one beyond being (see Derrida 1995). From this perspective, the apophatic dis-identification of God with the powers of speech and knowledge, with beings and being as such, serves to reintroduce a one beyond being, a one more magnificent than the one of being. We can see such dis-identification at work in the writings of Pseudo-Dionysius, for instance, who in *The Divine Names* posits the divine one beyond the grasp of all rational processes (1987: 49–50). It is also possible, however, to read the apophatic tradition in general as a refusal of the priority of the being of the one. From this perspective, apophatic dis-identification grounds the priority of difference over identity, thereby interrupting the rigidity and stasis of the one with multiplicity, so much so that it calls into question the one as such. As Catherine Keller puts it in her reading of Nicholas of Cusa, "apophatic logic performs an infinite deconstruction, spun from the negativity of the in/finite itself" (Keller 2010: 33; see also Faber 2010). Indeed, on Keller's reading, Nicholas of Cusa's apophasis, his "learned ignorance", "lets the universe be read as a finite 'image' of the infinite – not a faceless totality but a mysterious infinity" (Keller 2010: 39).

Badiou seems to recognize this dual potentiality of the apophatic tradition, when he notes that the apophatic or "mystical" path leads to "an annihilation in which, on the basis of an interruption of all presentative situations, and at the end of a negative spiritual exercise, a Presence is gained, a presence which is exactly that of the being of the One as non-being, thus the annulment of all functions of the One" (BE 26). However we understand the role of the one in the apophatic tradition, Badiou's main issue lies in the limitations it puts on the thinking of being. For Badiou, the problem with the apophatic tradition, and all "ontologies of presence", is the insistence on some surplus or remainder that can only be experienced, not thought. That is, for Badiou the problem comes down to rationality: being must be "fully transmissible in knowledge" (BE 27) if we are to avoid lapsing back into a religious or quasi-religious stance in regard to ontology.

Thus, in contrast to such "ontologies of presence", Badiou opposes "the rigor of the subtractive, in which being is said solely as that which cannot be supposed on the basis of any presence or experience" (*ibid.*). What, however, is the situation proper to ontology? If, as we mentioned above, we only have access to being in so far as it is presented in situations, ontology, for Badiou, will be that unique situation concerned with the general form of presentation itself: "the ontological situation" is "*the presentation of presentation*" (*ibid.*, original emphasis). As the presentation of presentation, ontology has no concern with the supposed indication of a presence situated at the limits of thought, a meaning revealed through experience; the concern of ontology is rather with the rational articulation of the structure of being, the manner in which inconsistent multiplicity becomes consistent. Naming ontology a situation, as a general theory of situations, allows Badiou to "refuse the traditional ontotheological conclusion that what is 'revealed' in the pure presentation of presentation is only a quasi-divine beyond – inconceivable plenitude, or creativity, the clearing or letting be of Being – which defies structured, systematic exploration" (Hallward 2003: 93). It is in this sense that Badiou's mathematical ontology qua the presentation of presentation is strictly anti-theological in orientation (cf. Clemens & Roffe 2008). Badiou's aim, as Ray Brassier affirms, is to construct a "disenchanted ontology: 'being' is insignificant, it means, quite literally, nothing" (Brassier 2007: 116). As we will see in the next section, what the major tenets of Badiou's ontology point to is this: "God is dead at the heart of presentation" (TW 37).

BADIOU'S ONTOLOGY

Having discussed the anti-theological thrust of Badiou's claim that "mathematics is ontology", we can now go on to work out how the location of ontology in mathematics allows Badiou specifically to construct an ontology in the wake of the death of the God of religion, the God of metaphysics and the God of the poem. Badiou insists that the basic task of any contemporary ontology is to unseal "the infinite from its millenary collusion with the One. It is to restitute the infinite to the banality of manifold-being, as mathematics has invited us to do since Cantor" (TO 30). What we are interested in in this section, then, is discussing the main features of Badiou's ontology – in particular, multiplicity without one, the void, and the infinite – as these relate to the anti-theological dimensions of Badiou's programme.

If we are to leave behind the God of metaphysics, then according to Badiou ontology must accomplish its task in thinking being qua being on the assumption of the inexistence of the one. Badiou's ontology thus begins and ends in a decision, a decision that makes the following wager: "the one is *not*" (BE 23, original emphasis). Or as Badiou puts it in his *Ethics*, "Let us posit *our* axioms. There is no God. Which also means: the One is not. The multiple 'without-one' – every multiple being in its turn nothing other than a multiple of multiples – is the law of being" (E 25, original emphasis). Although Badiou maintains that the inexistence of the one is the result of a decision, it is not simply a "mere decision" (Milbank 2007: 132), as if it lacked support. Badiou's decision against the one is, of course, in line with the critique of metaphysics installed by Nietzsche, a critique that remains fundamental, albeit in different forms, to much contemporary philosophy. In addition to this, Badiou holds that modern science, particularly in its recognition of the infinity of nature and the mathematical theory of the infinite, liquidates the need to posit any substantial, metaphysical notion of the one. To presuppose the existence of the one or the whole is, in the end, to recall "those outdated conceptions of the cosmos which envisaged it as the beautiful and finite totality of the world", conceptions which, under the pressure of the scientific revolution, simply lack "physical or phenomenological evidence" (LW 111).

Moreover, and directly related to Badiou's deployment of set theory, the positing of the one as primary results in a seemingly intractable paradox, first detected by Bertrand Russell in reference to the work of Gottlob Frege.[5] Take, for instance, as does Russell, the property "a is a set which is not an element of itself". As Badiou points out, all mathematical sets possess this property, for instance "the set of whole numbers is not itself a whole number, etc" (BE 40). The same could be said of the one: the one, as the set of its elements, is not itself an element of the set. However, if this set does not contain itself as an element, then it possesses the property of the set in question, meaning that it is, in fact, an element of itself. But if it is an element of itself, then it possesses the property in question, meaning that it is not an element of itself. The paradox, here, is the coincidence of a statement with its negation. There are two ways out of this apparent impasse. One way out is to shove off this impasse into a realm beyond all signification and predication, into an inconsistent realm beyond thought. Such is the path taken by the "ontologies of presence" discussed in the previous section, and also, as we will see below, by Cantor himself. The upshot of this move, however, is the onto-theological reintroduction of the one: it is "the decision to declare that beyond the multiple, even in the metaphor of its inconsistent grandeur, the one is" (BE 42). The other path, taken by axiomatic set theory and Badiou himself, is to prohibit such paradoxical multiples, multiples that belong to themselves, from ontological exposition. Badiou contends that this constraint is not "an artifice of exposition, but an intrinsic necessity" (BE 43). For, if it is the multiple-without-one that is truly at stake in ontology, axiomatization, including the prohibition of paradoxical multiples, "is required such that the multiple left to the implicitness of its counting rule, be delivered *without concept*, that is, *without implying the being-of-the-one*" (*ibid.*, original emphasis).

The ontological inexistence of the one does not, however, mean that the one – or, more exactly, oneness – is completely lacking, at least at the level of appearance. We do, of course, experience oneness regularly, and to deny that experience would be counter-intuitive in the worst possible way. However, for Badiou oneness is always a result, the outcome of an operational procedure that organizes and counts a region of multiple-being as one. In Badiou's words, "What has to be declared is that the one, which is not, solely exists as *operation*. In other words: there is no one, only the count-as-one. The one, being an operation, is never a presentation" (BE 24, original emphasis). The "what" of presentation, then, is the multiple-without-one, meaning that the one only ever emerges as a result, a result of counting the multiple-without-one into one.

Such a division, however, between the multiple-without-one and oneness as a result or, to use the terminology that Badiou borrows from Cantor, between inconsistent multiplicity and consistent multiplicity, immediately raises a problem. Although being qua being resides on the side of inconsistent multiplicity, that is, multiplicity that has yet to be submitted to the law of the count-as-one, we almost never experience or confront this pure multiplicity as such. Rather, we always confront multiplicity in situations as presented or consistent, already structured according to a count-as-one. If we always find ourselves on the side of consistent multiplicity, then how is it possible to discern the regime of pure multiplicity, of being qua being? Strictly speaking, we cannot grasp inconsistent multiplicity as such in non-ontological or non-mathematical situations. Badiou explains, "In a non-ontological (thus non-mathematical) situation, the multiple is possible only insofar as it is explicitly ordered by the law according to the one of the count. Inside the situation there is no graspable inconsistency which would be subtracted from the count and thus a-structured" (BE 52).

However, precisely because the mathematical or ontological situation is the presentation of presentation, it allows being to be grasped or exhibited as inconsistent through a process of retroaction or subtraction:

> [T]he multiple is the inertia which can be retroactively discerned starting from the fact that the operation of the count-as-one must effectively operate in order for there to be Oneness. The multiple is the inevitable predicate of what is structured because the structuration – in other words, the count-as-one – is an effect. The one, which is not, cannot present itself; it can only operate. As such it founds, "behind" its operation, the status of presentation – it is of the order of the multiple. (BE 25)

According to Badiou, inconsistent multiplicity can be discerned because it has been made consistent, submitted to the structuring operation of a count-as-one. Because the structure of a situation, its one-count, is a result of the organization of inconsistent multiplicity, the latter remains in the situation as its latent content. So much is entailed by Badiou's thesis on the non-existence of the one. "Insofar as the one is a result," writes Badiou, "by necessity 'something' of the multiple does not absolutely coincide with the result" (BE 53). Inconsistency, then, is not presented as such; it is rather presented as "the presupposition that prior to the count the one is not" (BE 52).

It is important to emphasize, however, at least two ways in which the manner of Badiou's invocation of inconsistency as the presupposition of consistency departs from a more theological or quasi-theological understanding of inconsistency, as found in ontologies of presence. First, contrary to how the latter equate inconsistency with the non-rational, Badiou's notion of inconsistency is, to a certain extent, rational or rationalizable, in the sense that it is logically entailed by the existence of consistent multiplicity. Although inconsistency is in part irrational, since it "exists" prior to its count-as-one, the procedure through which it becomes rational can be grasped through ontology. Strictly speaking, irrationality is the effect of rationality, since the former is only known retroactively through the latter, which is what it means to ground ontology as "the presentation of presentation". Second, it is important to emphasize that inconsistent multiplicity is for Badiou entirely banal, lacking any essential meaning, value or vitality, no matter how weakly conceived. So much is in keeping with Badiou's criticism of the Romantic disposition, and it is on this point that Badiou can be said to

ALAIN BADIOU

depart most fully from the legacy of theology, in so far as the latter endows the multiplicity of the world with meaning. Badiou himself makes this distinction, when he defines religion as "everything that presupposes continuity between truths and the circulation of sense" (MP 143).

Given what we have said so far, Badiou's ontology thus proceeds on the basis of two conditions:

1. The multiple from which ontology makes up its situation is composed solely of multiplicities. There is no one. In other words, every multiple is a multiple of multiples.
2. The count-as-one is no more than the system of conditions through which the multiple can be recognized as multiple. (BE 29).

It is in light of these two requirements that set theory becomes important as the discourse supporting Badiou's ontology. If, as we said above, we always find ourselves in situations, then ontology too must be a situation, meaning that "it must admit a mode of the count-as-one, that is, a structure" (BE 26). If ontology, understood in terms of mathematics, is not immune from the count-as-one, then how is it the case that it is uniquely positioned to discern the regime of inconsistent multiplicity? How is it that ontology can position itself as "the science of the multiple qua multiple" (BE 28) if it is always and already structured, submitted to the operation of the one? One way out of this apparent conundrum is, we have said, to deny that ontology is a situation, but this would lead us back to positing a one beyond all structure, as is the case in various ontologies of presence. Badiou's own way out is to affirm that ontology is indeed situation, but one governed by the axioms of set theory, which provide its structure: the axiom of extensionality, the axiom of the power set, the axiom of union, the axiom of infinity, the axiom of the void or null set, the axiom of foundation, the axiom of replacement, the axiom of separation and the axiom of choice.[6] Since it is not our purpose to provide a copious discussion of every detail of Badiou's ontology, we can deal with these axioms in more detail individually as necessary. Suffice it to say that the use of these axioms in the ontological situation allows for the subtractive presentation of inconsistent multiplicity without reference to the one, in so far as the operational structure of ontology, its count-as-one, does not admit anything other than the multiple. Badiou's set-theoretical ontology legislates what can be said of being qua being without falling back on the one because "what is presented in the ontological situation is the multiple without any other predicate than its multiplicity" (ibid.). What this means is that Badiou's ontology precludes any attempt to pin down what a multiple is or to specify the objects of which a multiple is composed, since to do so would be to reintroduce the one through means of definition. As Badiou puts it:

28

> Strictly speaking, mathematics *presents nothing*, without for all
> that constituting an empty game, because not having anything to
> present, besides presentation itself – which is to say the Multiple
> – and thereby never adopting the form of the ob-ject, such is
> certainly a condition of all discourse on being *qua being*.
>
> (BE 7, original emphasis)

Rather than being the presentation of something, ontology, as the mathematically determined discourse of the pure multiple, is simply "*the presentation of presentation*" (BE 27, original emphasis).

As the presentation of presentation, as a general theory of situations,
Badiou's ontology thus seeks to subtract itself from all questions concerning the explicit properties of any multiple. Otherwise put, in order to subtract itself from the reign of the one, Badiou's ontology proceeds without
an explicit definition of a set, since, as we discussed in reference to Russell's
paradox, the definition of what a set is leads to the introduction of paradoxical sets and risks reintroducing the one. Badiou writes:

> Neither intuition nor language are capable of supporting the
> pure multiple ... By consequence, it is of the very essence of set
> theory to only possess an implicit mastery of its "objects" (mul-
> tiplicities, sets): these multiples are deployed in an axiom system
> in which the property "to be a set" does not figure.   (BE 42)

Badiou's understanding of a set is, in this sense, extensional instead of inten-
sional: a set is the result of a procedure of counting its elements from the
ground up; it is not determined in advance through the application of a concept (Hallward 2003: 333).

Instead of proceeding conceptually, then, Badiou's ontology proceeds axi-
omatically. Following ZF, Badiou reduces and fixes the question of what a
set is to the elementary relation of belonging, denoted $\in$. Quoting Badiou:

> The multiple is implicitly designated here in the form of a logic
> of belonging, that is, in a mode in which the "something = a" in
> general is presented according to a multiplicity b. This will be
> inscribed as $\alpha \in \beta$, a is an element of b. What is counted as *one*
> is not the concept of the multiple; there is no inscribable thought
> of what *one*-multiple is. The one is assigned to the sign $\in$ alone;
> that is, to the operator of denotation for the relation between the
> "something" in general and the multiple. The sign $\in$, *unbeing* of
> any one, determines, in a uniform manner the presentation of
> "something" as indexed to the multiple.
>
> (BE 44, original emphasis)

What this means, in effect, is that Badiou's set-theoretical ontology only and always aims at presenting the multiple-without-one, since the elementary relation of belonging assures that "what belongs to a multiple is always a multiple; and that being an 'element' is not a status of being, an intrinsic quality, but the simple relation, to-be-element-of, through which a multiplicity can be presented by another multiplicity" (BE 45). To state the matter in clearer terms, what the relation of belonging establishes at the ontological level is that "inasmuch as a multiple exists, we can only declare its existence inasmuch as it belongs to another multiple. To exist as a multiple is always to belong to a multiplicity. To exist is to be an element *of*. There is no other possible predicate of existence as such" (Badiou & Hallward 1998: 130, original emphasis).[7] From within set theory and Badiou's own ontology, what matters are not the various properties that we may be able to assign a set and its elements but the procedure of counting itself, understood according to the relation of belonging. The upshot of this is that Badiou's set-theoretical ontology, as a formal theory of being qua being, remains indifferent to what is being counted, and it is this indifference that allows set theory to function as ontology, as a general theory of the pure multiple.

Although belonging constitutes the elementary relation and only form of predication in Badiou's set-theoretical ontology, there is another possible relation implicit in, but distinct from, the former, that of inclusion, written $\subset$. If, as we have said, belonging fixes the relation between sets by indicating the manner in which a multiple is counted or presented by another multiple as its element, inclusion refers strictly to the relation that obtains between the parts or subsets of multiples. Both relations have to do with pure multiplicity, so the difference between them does not have to do with any specific property of the multiple involved. The difference lies in the position of the count in regard to the multiple in question. Badiou writes, "In one case (the case $\in$), the multiple falls under the count-as-one which is the other multiple. In the other case (the case $\subset$), every element presented by the first multiple is also presented by the second. But being-multiple remains completely unaffected by these distinctions of relative position" (BE 82). Belonging and inclusion thus refer to "two distinct operators of counting, and not two different ways to think the being of the multiple" (BE 83). That there are two distinct counting operations is a consequence of the power set axiom, which "guarantees that *if* a set exists, *then* another set also exists that counts as one all the subsets of the first" (*ibid.*, original emphasis).[8]

Since inclusion refers to the parts or subsets of multiples, inclusion is always in excess over belonging. More specifically, taking the set of the subsets of a given multiple, that is, the power set of that multiple, will always produce a set larger than the initial set in question. This seems undeniable at an intuitive level, but this excess of inclusion over belonging is crucial to Badiou's entire ontological edifice, since it implies that "it is literally impossible to assign a 'measure' to this superiority in size. In other words, the 'passage' to the set of subsets is an operation in *absolute* excess of the situation itself" (BE 84, original emphasis).

We will return to this "theorem of the point of excess", which Badiou calls "a real impasse" for ontology (*ibid.*), below. For now we can note that the relationship between belonging and inclusion implies not one but two counts operative in any situation. As mentioned above, every situation is submitted to a count-as-one, which provides the structure for that situation. The structure of a situation is solely concerned with providing a degree of order to the elements that belong to the situation in question. However, counting the elements of a situation as one is not enough to produce consistency. It is also necessary to fix the parts or subsets that are included in the elements of the situation, to re-present them in the situation. Badiou refers to this second, re-presentative count as the state of the situation or its metastructure, which he defines as follows:

> *The domain of metastructure is parts*: metastructure guarantees that the one holds for inclusion, just as the initial structure holds for belonging. Put more precisely, given a situation whose structure delivers consistent one-multiples, there is always a metastructure – the state of the situation – which counts as one *any* composition of these consistent multiplicities.   (BE 97, original emphasis)

In other words, the state of the situation or its metastructure assures that what "is *included* in a situation *belongs* to its state" (*ibid.*, original emphasis). Ultimately what this double count – the initial count-as-one and the count of this count at the level of metastructure – attempts to foreclose is the errancy of the void in any situation.

In order to understand the fundamental place of the void in Badiou's ontology, recall the distinction between inconsistent multiplicity and consistent multiplicity. In a normal, that is, non-ontological, situation, the structure of a situation, the domain of its one-count, divides the situation into inconsistent multiplicity and consistent multiplicity, that is, multiplicity before the count and multiplicity as counted. However, since a situation is, by definition, always structured, it is impossible for inconsistent multiplicity to be presented as inconsistent multiplicity therein, since presentation is nothing other than being submitted to the operation of the count. Otherwise put, from the perspective of a situation, multiplicity can only be grasped as consistent, in that it is always and already submitted to the law of its count-as-one. In Badiou's words:

> Nothing is presentable in a situation otherwise than under the effect of structure, that is, under the form of the one and its

> composition in consistent multiplicities. The one is thereby not only the regime of structured presentation but also the regime of the possible of presentation itself. (BE 52)

Nevertheless, in so far as the one exists only through the operation of the count-as-one, it is impossible for the one as result to coincide completely with that of which it is the result, the multiple. That is, even if the structure of a situation forecloses the presentation of inconsistent multiplicity as such, the one as result remains "discernible as operation" (BE 53). As Badiou explains, "[O]ne has to admit that if the one results, then 'something' – which is not an in-situation-term, and which is thus nothing – has not been counted, this 'something' being that it was necessary that the operation of the count-as-one operate" (BE 55). Precisely because it is the result of an operation and discernible as such, the one-count marks inconsistent multiplicity as its own latent content, as that which, prior to the count, must be subsumed as consistent under the count. Inconsistent multiplicity is, in this sense, retroactively or subtractively discernible in the mode of the future anterior, "as-what-will-have-been-presented" (BE 54). All situations thus harbour within themselves a "phantom of inconsistency" or "phantom remainder", which is nothing other than "the unperceivable gap, cancelled then renewed, between presentation as structure and structured-presentation, between the one as result and the one as operation, between presented consistency and inconsistency as what-will-have-been-presented" (BE 53, 54).

Badiou designates this gap between consistency and inconsistency the void, which names the "suture" of a situation "to its being" (BE 55). As Hallward explains:

> The void is what connects any particular counting operation (any particular situation) to the ungraspable situation that it counts. Or again, the void is the normally inaccessible access to the pure inconsistent being of a situation, an access that can never normally be presented within the situation, never identified, one-ified, or located. (2003: 65)

As the anchor of a situation to the inconsistent multiplicity that it is, the void serves as the original existential term from which the multiples of a situation are composed. This is an important point. Belonging, inclusion and the axioms that determine the composition of multiples – the axioms of extensionality, union, separation, replacement and the power set axiom – presuppose that a multiple has already been presented, that a multiple exists. In order for the composition of multiples to even begin, however, the positing of an original existential position is required, a first count, to bind the compositions in question to being. In set-theoretical terms, this is the axiom of the empty set or the void, the purpose of which is to inscribe existence. The place of the void, then, decides on the traditional question of ontology: "Is there something rather than nothing?" (BE 66).

Nevertheless, in order to avoid the possible reintroduction of the one through the existential seal of the void, two things are necessary. First, the positing of existence must be an axiomatic decision rather than a deduction. This requirement is at the heart of Badiou's criticisms of Gottlob Frege in *Number and Numbers*. Frege had sought to generate a definition of the individual numbers through purely logical means. Number, in this sense, is thought primarily as the extension of a concept. Important for Badiou is how Frege attempts to establish the individual numbers from the deduction of zero. Frege defines zero as "the Number which belongs to the concept 'not identical with itself'" (Frege 1960: 74).[9] Following Leibniz's principle of identity, which asserts the identity of objects with themselves based on the notion that two objects are the same as each other if they can be substituted for each other without a loss of truth, zero can thus be said to have an empty extension, in that no object falls under its concept. Although the choice for this definition of zero seems somewhat arbitrary, since there are numerous other concepts under which no object falls (i.e. a square circle), Frege notes that he has "made a point of choosing one which can be proved to be such on purely logical grounds; and for this purpose 'not identical with itself' is the most convenient that offers, taking for the definition of 'identical' the one from Leibniz … which is in purely logical terms" (*ibid.*). Based on this definition, Frege then proceeds to examine the concept "identical with zero", under which one object falls, namely the number zero (*ibid.*: 77). Frege labels this new number that corresponds to the concept "identical with zero" the number 1. As Anthony Kenny summarizes, "There is a concept, *identical with zero*, and an object falling under it, zero, such that the number which belongs to the concept *identical with zero* is 1, and the number which belongs to the concept *identical with zero but not identical with zero* is 0" (Kenny 2000: 94, original emphasis). From this simple deduction, it is relatively easy to generate the procession of individual numbers.[10]

As Badiou points out, however, despite Frege's claim to have recourse to pure logic alone, his deduction of the individual numbers from the concept of zero rests on an unexamined ontological presupposition, namely "that we can unproblematically move from concept to existence, given that the extension of a concept brings into play the 'objects' that fall under this concept" (NN 127). According to Badiou, this is the upshot of the paradox that Russell detected in Frege's system. For instance, take the concept "to be a set that is not an element of itself", which Badiou discusses in *Number and Numbers* and *Being and Event*. Subsuming under this concept all the sets that possess this property results in an impasse, as we mentioned above. If the set belongs to itself, then it violates its own definition; conversely, if the set does not belong to itself, then, based on the same definition, it belongs to itself.[11] As Badiou points out, "to admit the existence of a set of all those sets that do not belong to themselves undermines deductive language by introducing a *formal* contradiction (the equivalence between a proposition and its negation)" (NN 20, original emphasis). Axiomatic set theory attempts to bypass this logical problem by prohibiting the introduction of paradoxical sets, that is, sets that belong to themselves, into its formal language. However, the price to be paid for this is the dissolution of Frege's notion that we can pass directly from a concept to the existence of its extension, a dissolution that serves as the foundation for Zermelo's axiom of separation. As Badiou explains, the axiom of separation holds "that we can conclude from the concept the existence of its extension *on condition that we operate within an already given existence*" (*ibid.*, original emphasis). From the perspective of the axiom of separation, Badiou concludes that Russell's paradox "is not paradoxical in the slightest. It is a materialist argument, because it *demonstrates* that multiple-being is anterior to the statements that affect it" (NN 21, original emphasis). That is, the axiom of separation assumes that "it is not possible to move from concept to existence (and thus to number); we can only move to an existence that is somehow carved out of a pre-given existence" (NN 20).

In contrast to Frege, then, Badiou suggests that the existence of zero – or what amounts to the same thing, the empty set or the void – is only secured as the result of an axiomatic decision. To quote Badiou at length on this point:

> The existence of zero, or of the empty set, and therefore the existence of numbers, is in no way deducible from the concept. "Zero exists" is inevitably a *first* assertion; the very one that fixes an existence from which all others will proceed. Far from it being the case that Zermelo's axiom, combined with Frege's logicism, allows us to engender zero and then the chain of numbers, it is on the contrary the absolutely inaugural existence of zero (as empty set) that ensures the possibility of separating any extension of a concept whatsoever. Number comes first here: it is that *point of being* upon which the exercise of the concept depends. Number, as number of nothing, or zero, sutures every text to its latent being. The void is not a production of thought, because it is from its existence that thought proceeds, in as much as "it is the same thing to think and to be". In this sense, it is the concept that comes from number, and not the other way around.
> (NN 23, original emphasis)

The procedure, here, is in keeping with Badiou's insistence that his ontology operate without any explicit definition of what a given multiple is. Zero

– the void, the empty set – does not depend upon the concept, which would reintroduce the one qua definition; rather, it is the posited, fixed point of existence from which the concept proceeds.

Second, in keeping with the previous point, the void, as the suture of a situation to its being, "cannot propose *anything* in particular"; that is, "it can neither be a matter of the one, which is not, nor of the composed multiple, which is never anything but a result of the count, an effect of structure" (BE 66, original emphasis). In order to avoid the reintroduction of the one, Badiou, using the null set axiom, treats the void as a multiple of nothing, that is, a "multiple" to which nothing belongs (BE 67). Recall that, for Badiou, existence is tied to belonging, to being presented in a situation. If all multiples more or less follow this rule, the void, as "multiple" of nothing, serves as the exception that grounds the rule. Otherwise put, the "void is the unpresentable *point of being* of any presentation" (BE 77, original emphasis).

Said differently, if all consistent or presented multiplicities presuppose inconsistency, the void is on the side of inconsistency – the void is the name of inconsistency for a situation, the "latent errancy of the being of presentation" (BE 76). Because the void is on the side of inconsistency and is thus literally nothing according to the situation, it can only be presented as subtracted from the situation. Presented in its subtraction, the void can thus only be made "something" for the situation by assuming a proper name that marks its unpresentability. Following the conventions of axiomatic set theory, Badiou names the void with the mark Ø, a choice which Badiou explains as follows:

> Being thus invests the Ideas of presentation of the pure multiple in the form of unicity signaled by a proper name. To write it, this name of being, this subtractive point of the multiple – of the general form in which presentation presents itself and thus *is* – the mathematicians searched for a sign far from all their customary alphabets; neither a Greek, nor a Latin, nor a Gothic letter, but an old Scandanavian letter, Ø, emblem of the void, zero affected by the barring of sense. As if they were dully aware that in proclaiming that the void alone is – because it alone in-exists from the multiple, and because the Ideas of the multiple only live on the basis of what is subtracted from them – they were touching upon some sacred region, itself liminal to language; as if thus, rivaling the theologians for whom supreme being has been the proper name since long ago, yet opposing to the latter's promise of the One, and of Presence, the irrevocability of un-presentation and the un-being of the one, the mathematicians had to shelter their own audacity behind the character of a forgotten language.
> (BE 69)

The excess of being, of inconsistent multiplicity, then, is not to be located onto-theologically in a presence beyond all thought. This excess is, rather, located in the un-presentation of inconsistent multiplicity, which is only "something" for the situation through the mark of the void. Because "the void alone is" it is thus "the absolutely primary theme of ontology ... because in the last resort, *all* inconsistency is unpresentable" (BE 58). The void is, in this sense, an anti-theological notion, since it replaces the promise of presence with un-presentation, an un-presentation without aura. The positing of the void – and all that follows from this – assures, for Badiou, that "God is dead at the heart of presentation" (TW 37).

Since the void is unpresentable, it cannot, strictly speaking, belong to situations. The void is, however, necessarily included in situations. Badiou writes:

> For if the void is the unpresentable point of being, whose unicity of inexistence is marked by the existent proper name Ø, then no multiple, by means of its existence, can prevent this inexistent from placing itself within it. On the basis of everything which is not presentable it is inferred that the void is presented everywhere in its lack; not, however, as the one-of-its-unicity, as immediate multiple by the one-multiple, but as *inclusion*, because subsets are the very place in which a multiple of nothing can err, just as the nothing itself errs within the all.   (BE 86)

It is here, at the level of inclusion, that the second count of the metastructure or state of the situation comes into play, as a means of warding off the essential errancy of the void. Recall that, according to Badiou, all situations are counted twice, at the level of presentation (the count-as-one) and at the level of re-presentation (the second count, count-of-the-count). The initial count counts the elements of a situation as belonging to the situation, whereas the second count counts the parts or subsets as included in the situation. As mentioned previously, inclusion is always in excess over belonging: counting the parts or subsets of a multiple always produces a multiple larger than the initial multiple. This is what Badiou refers to as "the theorem of the point of excess" (BE 84). The goal of the second count, the state or metastructure of the situation, is to put a measure of control on this excess at the level of inclusion.

However, the degree to which the state or metastructure of a situation can accomplish such control is, according to Badiou, variable. A multiple can be both presented and re-presented, meaning that it both belongs to and is included in the situation. Badiou terms these multiples "normal", and they take the form of a homogeneity or equilibrium between belonging and inclusion, structure and state. In Badiou's words, "Normality consists in the re-securing of the originary one by the state of the situation in which that one is presented" (BE 99). For the most part, Badiou associates normal multiples with nature: "nature is what is rigorously normal in being" (BE 129). However, a multiple can also be "singular", that is, presented but not re-presented; or "excrescent", that is, re-presented but not presented. "An excrescence", according to Badiou, "is a one of the state that is not a one of the native structure, an existent of the state which in-exists in the situation of which the state is the state" (BE 100). Badiou seems to have in mind here something like the bureaucratic or capitalist nation-state, understood along Marxist lines as "a thing or pure representation in the multiples that are present in the situation" (Pluth 2010: 55). Playing with the ontological and political sense of the term "state", Badiou writes, "The State is the necessary metastructure of every historico-social situation, which is to say the law that guarantees that there is Oneness, not in the immediacy of society – that is always provided for by a non-state structure – but amongst the set of its subsets" (BE 105). In contrast, singular multiples, that is, presented but not re-presented multiples, are subject to the initial count of the structure, "but they cannot be grasped as parts because they are composed, as multiples, of elements which are not accepted by the count" (BE 99). That is, singular multiples are "not presented anywhere in the situation in a *separate manner*" (*ibid.*, original emphasis). Singular multiples are the direct result of the metastructure not being able to recount everything in the situation. As Badiou demonstrates in reference to his discussion of the theorem of the point of excess in Meditation 7 of *Being and Event*, "there are always sub-multiples which, despite being included in a situation as compositions of multiplicities, cannot be counted in that situation as terms, and which therefore do not exist" (BE 97). Because these singular multiples refer immediately to the excess of inclusion over belonging, Badiou says that they are "on-the-edge-of-the-void" (BE 175). It is from such multiples that, as we will see in the next chapter, events emerge.

Before moving on, it is worth considering a proposal recently made by Kenneth Reynhout. Reynhout suggests that the void functions as a "hidden God" in Badiou's ontology: "*God is the void*" (Reynhout 2008: 231, original emphasis). Attempting to take seriously Badiou's ontology, Reynhout does not identify this "hidden God" with the metaphysical or onto-theological God of classical Christian theology. Rather, Reynhout attempts to identify God with the void by following Paul Tillich, who re-conceptualizes God as the ground or power of being, as being-itself rather than a being. Reynhout runs with this conception of God as the power of being, mapping it onto Badiou's understanding of the void. Reynhout's thesis is suggestive, and it ultimately rests on the need to posit rather than deduce the existence of the void. Nevertheless, Reynhout's equation of the void with God, understood as the ground or power of being, seems problematic. In order to associate the void with God, Reynhout names God as the suture to being of any situation. But, in doing so, Reynhout goes on to identify God as the "constitutive power of being", the "ground of being" (*ibid*.). It is with this second move that Reynhout goes beyond Badiou's formulation of the void, since for Badiou the void is not a power or ground but merely the point of un-presentation for a situation. If there is any power at all in Badiou's formulation, it would be relegated not so much to the void but to ontology proper, which marks the suture to being that the void is through naming it as such.

Nevertheless, we have said that the positing of the void as the initial point of existence represents the foundational point for any and all situations. There is, however, another point of existence, equally important, that must be posited. This "second existential seal" (BE 151) is nothing other than the infinite. According to Badiou, the set-theoretical notion of the infinite, as Georg Cantor first articulated it, "allows for an immanentization of the infinite, separating it from the One of theology" (TW 18). Badiou's understanding of the immanentization of the infinite should, however, be distinguished from the Romantic articulation of this theme. Romanticism certainly establishes its own form of the immanentization of the infinite. But on Badiou's account, it falls short of disentangling itself from the One, and thus theology, precisely to the extent that it has as its paradigm the Christian doctrine of incarnation and remains an excessive correlate of the finite (TC 152–60). Badiou's problem with the Romantic infinite is, in the final analysis, its ultimate resistance to thought, which for Badiou amounts to a tacit valorization of finitude. Badiou's problem with the Romantic infinite is, in this sense, correlative to his critique of "ontologies of presence", discussed above. Badiou states:

> Mathematics has shown that it has the resources to deploy a perfectly precise conception of the infinite as indifferent multiplicity. This "indifferentiation" of the infinite, its post-Cantorian treatment as mere number, the pluralization of its concept (there are an infinity of different infinities) – all this has rendered the infinite banal; it has terminated the pregnant latency of finitude and allowed us to realize that every situation (ourselves included) is infinite. (TW 27)

Otherwise put, the mathematical conception of the infinite is "subtracted from all jurisdiction by the One, stripped of its horizonal function as the correlate of finitude and released from the metaphor of the Open" (*ibid*.).[12]

In order to understand how this is the case, it is first necessary to discuss how the infinite had generally been understood before Cantor's innovation. The goal in what follows is not to provide a copious overview of the history of the infinite but to isolate and articulate the basic structure that informed pre-Cantorian discussions of the infinite.[13]

The infinite has always been a source of perplexity, consternation and awe for mathematicians, philosophers and theologians. Consider the following example,[14] drawn from the basic laws of addition:

$$a + b > a;$$
$$a + b > b.$$

So long as we stick with finite quantities, this basic law holds: the addition of two positive numbers results in a quantity greater than either number taken individually. However, when an infinite number is introduced into the equation, the basic properties of addition begin to break down:

$$a + \infty = \infty.$$

Using the basic laws of arithmetic, the addition of "∞" to "a" should result in a number greater than "∞". Yet, the addition of any number to "∞" only results in "∞", since an infinite number does not seem to admit quantitative additions. From the perspective of the basic and classical laws of arithmetic, then, infinite numbers are inconsistent – and it is precisely because of this inconsistency that the infinite threatens the "annihilation of number" (Dauben 1979: 122).

The problem, however, extends well beyond mere elementary mathematical exercises to the thinking of space and time. The problem is clearly on display in Zeno's famous paradoxes, which, based on the assumption that spatial and temporal magnitudes are composed of infinite parts, intend to show the impossibility of motion.[15] Aristotle's response to these paradoxes lead him to draw a distinction that until Cantor remained fundamental for thinking the infinite, the distinction between the potential infinite and the actual infinite.

In Book 3 of the *Physics*, Aristotle notes that, when considering the idea of the infinite, it is important to "inquire whether there is such a thing or not, and, if there is, *what* it is" (Aristotle 2001c: 202b, original emphasis). What Aristotle is after is the manner in which the infinite can be said to exist, that is, "*how* it exists" (*ibid.*: 203b, original emphasis). In considering the question concerning what the infinite is and how it exists, Aristotle is led to reject the notion of an actual infinite as applicable to sensible objects, since this notion implies a completed whole, and is thus nonsensical. To give just one example, take any sensible body. Since, by definition, a body is defined as something "bounded by a surface" or, put otherwise, located in a definite space, such a body cannot be said to be actually infinite, since an "infinite body would be extended in all directions *ad infinitum*" (*ibid.*: 204b). An infinite body is no body at all, since the very idea goes against the definition of a body and the normal ways in which we experience and describe bodies as bounded (i.e. as

ALAIN BADIOU

light or heavy, as positioned relative to other bodies, as defined by particular quantities, and so on). Moreover, to admit the existence of an actual infinite leads straight into Zeno's paradoxes. Thus, as Aristotle concludes, "In general, if it is impossible that there should be an infinite place, and if every body is in place there cannot be an infinite body" (*ibid.*: 205b–206a).

Aristotle, however, is not willing to jettison completely the idea of the infinite. As he puts it, to assume "that the infinite does not exist in any way leads obviously to many impossible consequences: there will be a beginning and an end of time, a magnitude will not be divisible into magnitudes, number will not be infinite" (*ibid.*: 206a–b). Although Aristotle rejects the notion of an actual infinite, he is willing to admit the potential existence of the infinite, understood as that which "always has something outside of it" (*ibid.*: 207a). To quote Aristotle more fully:

> *A quantity is infinite if it is such that we can always take a part outside of what has already been taken.* On the one hand, what has nothing outside it is complete and whole. For thus we define the whole – that from which nothing is wanting, as a whole man or a whole box. What is true of each particular is true of the whole as such – the whole is that of which nothing is outside. On the other hand that from which something is absent and outside, however small that may be, is not "all". "Whole" and "complete" are either quite identical or closely akin. Nothing is complete (*teleion*) which has no end (*telos*); and the end is a limit.
> (Aristotle 2001b: 207a, original emphasis)

On the one hand, this notion of the potentiality of the infinite as something that always has something outside of it, as essentially incomplete, results from the quite mundane experience of the world as in a constant state of flux or generation. Hence Aristotle points out that "one thing is always being taken after another, and each thing that is taken is always finite, but always different" (Aristotle 2001c: 206a). On the other hand, such a notion of the infinite is also applicable to spatial magnitudes, as in the case of division: "it will always be possible to take something *ab extra* … [I]n the direction of division every determinate magnitude is surpassed in smallness and there will be a smaller part" (*ibid.*: 206b).

Nevertheless, Aristotle gives two important qualifications concerning this potential understanding of the infinite. First, although it is possible in principle to submit finite magnitudes to an infinite number of divisions, Aristotle argues that such magnitudes are never so divided in actuality. For Aristotle the whole precedes the parts, meaning that the process of division is an abstraction from the existence of the whole. Because of this, "number is not separable from the process of bisection, and its infinity is not a permanent actuality but consists in a process of coming to be" (*ibid.*: 207b). Such abstraction is, of course, necessary for mathematics, but only up to a point. For Aristotle, mathematicians "do not need the infinite and do not use it" (*ibid.*). He goes on to state:

> [The mathematicians] postulate only that the finite straight line may be produced as far as they wish. It is possible to have divided in the same ratio as the largest quantity another magnitude of any size you like. Hence, for the purposes of proof, it will make no difference to them to have such an infinite instead, while its existence will be in the sphere of real magnitudes.   (*Ibid.*)

Second, although Aristotle holds that infinite division is possible in principle, the same does not apply to addition or increase. As he puts it:

> What is continuous is divided *ad infinitum*, but there is no infinite in the direction of increase. For the size which it can potentially be, it can also actually be. Hence since no sensible magnitude is infinite, it is impossible to exceed every assigned magnitude; for if it were possible there would be something bigger than the heavens.   (*Ibid.*)

This last point gets to the heart of the matter, both in reference to Aristotle's understanding of the infinite and, as we will see shortly, Badiou's: Aristotle's notion of the potential infinite both presupposes and lends support to a finitist conception of the universe. If it is impossible to move in the direction of increase *ad infinitum*, this is because the heavens, the outermost sphere in the Aristotelian model of the cosmos, mark the limits of the universe, beyond which nothing is. There is, in Aristotle's words, "no place or void or time outside the heaven" (Aristotle 2001b: 279a), meaning that the universe itself is essentially finite, limited to strict boundaries. Indeed, according to Badiou, this finitist conception of the universe is, in the end, theological, as seen in its need to posit a first cause or an "eternal unmovable substance" to explain motion (Aristotle 2001a: 1071b). Aristotle, of course, associates this first cause with God. Although the function of God in this context is more metaphysical than religious, he can still describe this God as a "living being, eternal, [and] most good" (*ibid.*: 1072b).

We can see clearly the theological import of this notion of the potential infinite in the work of Thomas Aquinas. Although Aquinas employs various and diverse metaphysical conceptions of the infinite throughout his writings (Tomarchio 2002), in essence he adopts and transposes into the realm of theology the Aristotelian distinction between the potential infinite and the actual infinite. Aquinas thus denies the existence of actually infinite magnitudes, by way of either division or addition, based on the assumption that natural and mathematical bodies can only be said to exist by taking on a definite, and hence finite, form (1920: I, Q. 7, Art. 3). For Aquinas we can speak of things as possessing a relative infinity, in the sense that things have the potential to take on an infinite number of accidental forms. But since things do take form, it is impossible to speak of them being "absolutely infinite" (I, Q. 7, Art. 2). The latter designation is reserved for God alone, who is "infinite and perfect" (I, Q. 7, Art. 1).

The distinction between the relative infinite and the absolute infinite is a necessary one, based on Aquinas's doctrine of *creatio ex nihilo*: all created being comes from God, meaning that created being qua created is essentially finite, since it is dependent for its existence on God (I, Q. 45). Not surprisingly, then, Aquinas's notion of the infinite rests on the assumption of two regions of being, the creator and the creature, the infinite and the finite, even if he conceives of these two regions as participating in each other. For Badiou, this splitting of being into two, essentially incommensurate, regions of being is in essence theological. This is the case whether theology is explicitly evoked, as is obviously the case with Aquinas, or not (see TS 190–91).[16]

Moreover, as Badiou stresses, the division between the potential or relative infinite and the actual infinite is based on the assumption that the cosmos is finite, that is, created.[17] For this reason, the theological notion of God's infinity does not "radically rupture with Greek finitism" (BE 144). According to Badiou:

> The speculative possibility of Christianity was an attempt to think infinity as an attribute of the One-being whilst universally guarding ontological finitude, and reserving the ontical sense of finitude for the multiple. It is through a mediation of a supposition concerning the being of the One that these great thinkers were able to simultaneously turn the infinite (God) into a being, turn the finite (Nature) into a being, and maintain a finite ontological structure in both cases. (*Ibid.*)

Indeed, as Badiou makes clear in *Logics of Worlds*, in his view, the correlation of creation with finitude is in essence theological, which is one reason why Badiou seems to reject on speculative grounds the cosmological theory of the Big Bang (LW 111).

John Milbank has recently criticized Badiou's understanding of the infinite in theology. According to Milbank, Badiou's insistence that the medieval theologians primarily understood God qua infinite as the negative exception that grounds and guards the finitude of creation is misleading, in at least two senses:

[F]irst, Badiou reads medieval theology as if it was all Scotist and divided being primarily into finite and infinite. And in fact even Scotist saw the infinite as primary and the finite as exceptional and secondary, whereas Badiou speaks as if, for the Middle Ages, it were the other way around. But more typically, the early to high Middle Ages, as with Aquinas, saw being as such as infinite and finite existence as only participating in this. Aquinas, it is true, did not embrace an infinite cosmos, nor an actual mathematical infinite, but other thinkers of this came near to doing so: Robert Grosseteste saw the Creation as initially constituted by a neoplatonic emanantive series of transfinites which expressed the propagation of light. Finally, Nicholas of Cusa's assertion of the infinity of the cosmos did not for him imply immanence but rather the paradoxical and continuous passing-over of the finite into its constitutively other and yet "not-other" transcendent infinite ground. Essentially the same construal was sustained by Blaise Pascal.   (Milbank 2007: 132)

For Milbank the inaccuracy of Badiou's condensed historical reconstruction of the relationship between the finite and the infinite and his failure to acknowledge the complexity of this relationship in theology shores up the contingency of Badiou's "mere decision" for the "immanence of the infinite" (*ibid.*: 132).

Milbank is certainly correct to point out that Badiou's extremely condensed reconstruction in Meditation 13 of *Being and Event* of classical and medieval understandings of the infinite flattens out many of the apparent differences among individual thinkers. However, Milbank's argument suffers from its own flaws and, in the end, misses Badiou's main point. Milbank seems to assume that the question of the mathematical infinite is a separate concern from infinite being as such, but Thomas, in Question 7 of the First Part of the *Summa*, treats these together, as does Nicholas of Cusa in *On Learned Ignorance* (1997). Likewise, although Milbank is correct to point to the way in which the finite always participates in the infinite for Aquinas, he covers over the fact that such participation presupposes an ultimate distinction between the infinite and the finite, a distinction required by Aquinas's formulation of the doctrine of *creatio ex nihilo* and God's immutability, eternity and unity (Aquinas 1920: I. Q. 9–11, 44–6). As Aquinas states, "The fact that the being of God is self-subsisting, not received in any other, and is thus called infinite, shows Him to be distinguished from all other beings, and all others to be apart from Him" (I, Q. 7, Art. 1). So understood, the infinite for Aquinas functions in the first instance as a negative concept, since "a thing is called infinite because it is not finite" (I, Q. 7, Art. 1). Nevertheless, even if a more nuanced description of the infinite in theology appears to complicate aspects of Badiou's all-too-brief genealogy of it in *Being and Event*, it would still not touch upon what seems to be the primary issue for Badiou: the rationalization and secularization of the infinite and its unbinding from the one. Someone like Nicholas of Cusa, whom Milbank cites to counter Badiou's claims, does make a contribution towards understanding the universe as infinite. But he does not ultimately depart from the theological tradition, to the extent the infinite signifies the breakdown of our knowledge. Nicholas of Cusa still thinks the infinite apophatically in relation to the one, making his theology an ontology of presence, albeit one that is fascinating in its own right.

Milbank's criticisms aside, historically speaking, the move away from a finite conception of the cosmos is a complicated phenomenon, with its roots traceable to the intellectual currents in late medieval and Renaissance science, philosophy and theology. Badiou, however, locates the decisive break with finitism in the early modern period, when nature itself begins to be thought as infinite (cf. Zellini 2005 and Koyré 1957). In Badiou's words, "the audacity of the moderns" lay in "ex-centering the use of [the infinite], in redirecting it from its function of distributing the regions of being in totality towards a characterization of beings-qua-beings: nature, the moderns said, is infinite" (BE 143). But it is not until Georg Cantor's development of the notion of the transfinite that this ex-centring of the infinite became realizable mathematically, in that he provided for the first time "a mathematically precise description of infinite numbers qua numbers" (Hallward 2003: 328).[18]

As we have seen, such a proposition was strictly out of the realm of possibility before Cantor, for the simple reason that the infinite was not really treated as a number at all. Given the distinction between the potential infinite and the actual infinite, the infinite at best was something that one could approach but never actually reach. So much is intuitively expressed in the fact that we can always add one more number to any numerical succession $(1, 2, 3 \ldots n, n + 1 \ldots)$. When and if the infinite did come into play in mathematics, it only did so as a limit concept, as in, for example, infinitesimal calculus (Maor 1987: 17–20). Indeed, taken as anything other than a limit, the infinite represents the breakdown of mathematical knowledge, if not knowledge in general, a sentiment well expressed by Nicholas of Cusa in his treatise *On Learned Ignorance*. To borrow from the title of Nicholas of Cusa's treatise, before Cantor the best that one could do is practise "learned ignorance" in the face of the infinite.

Cantor, however, began from the assumption that the distinction first proposed by Aristotle between the potential infinite and the actual infinite is illegitimate. As Cantor argued, a potentially infinite collection presupposes the existence of actual infinite collections (Dauben 1979: 128). Working from this assumption, Cantor was able to show that the infinite admits a degree of measure, meaning that it is possible in principle to arrive at a fully actual concept of the infinite, so long as one adopts the following definition of a set: "By a set S we are to understand any collection into a whole of definite and separate objects m of our intuition or our thought" (quoted in Hallward 2003: 328). Key here is that, in order to count the elements taken as belonging to a set, it is not actually necessary to enumerate the elements so collected up from zero, as in the case of ordinal numbers. One only needs to put elements in a one-to-one correspondence, which allows one to ascertain the relative size or power of the set in question, its cardinality, irrespective of numeral succession. In finite sets, ordinality and cardinality largely coincide, since they can only be counted in one way, but this is not the case for infinite quantities, whose defining characteristic is the fact that they can be placed into one-to-one correspondences with their subsets or parts. For instance, the set of natural numbers can easily be paired off with its own subset of odd numbers and, as Cantor famously demonstrated, also with the rational numbers. Through such demonstrations, Cantor was able to show that:

> any set (finite or infinite) whose elements might be paired with the natural or counting numbers can thereby be considered denumerable, and all infinite denumerable sets have the same cardinality or size, regardless of how large a part of the "whole" infinitely denumerable set they include. (*Ibid.*: 330)

Counter-intuitive as the claim may seem, the set of rational numbers has the same infinite cardinality as the set of natural numbers, a cardinality that Cantor marked $\aleph_0$.

Cantor was also able to show that, beyond the denumerable infinity of the set of natural numbers, there is at least one other non-denumerable infinity of a different order, whose cardinality exceeds that of $\aleph_0$. Such is the case with the real numbers, which infinitely exceed the denumerable set of rational numbers on the linear continuum. Cantor denoted the cardinality of the continuum c, and was able to show that the power set of the first infinite cardinal number ($2^{\aleph_0}$), that is, all the possible subsets of $\aleph_0$, "could be put in a one-to-one correspondence with the nondenumerable cardinality of the continuum itself, c: $2^{\aleph_0} = c$" (*ibid.*: 332). Given one infinite set of a different order than that of the denumerable infinite set of the natural numbers and using the axiom of the power set, it becomes possible to generate an infinite progression of increasingly larger infinite sets. In an attempt to give some sort of order or consistency to this infinite series of infinities, Cantor formulated the continuum hypothesis (CH), through which he attempted to establish a successive relationship between the first infinite cardinal $\aleph_0$ and its power set, so that $\aleph_1$, the successor infinite cardinal, would correspond to c. Such a relationship would, in principle, extend to the entire sequence of infinite cardinals, so that $\aleph_0$, $\aleph_1$, $\aleph_2$ ... would correspond with $\aleph_0$, $2^{\aleph_0}$, $2^{2^{\aleph_0}}$ ... However, he was unable to prove this thesis, leaving the status of the continuum hypothesis in question until Paul Cohen, who demonstrated its independence of the axiomatic system. Moreover, Cantor's inability to provide a proof of the continuum hypothesis was not the only problem that he confronted. If the existence of any set x necessarily implies the existence of its power set $p(x)$, since it is always possible to create a larger set by taking into account all the subsets of x, then attempting to define the set of all sets leads to an impasse. Defining the set of all sets would entail positing the power set of this set, and so on *ad infinitum*, making it impossible ever to arrive at some ultimate set.

These problems led Cantor to posit a distinction between the transfinite, that is, infinities subject to mathematical operations, and an absolute, inconsistent infinity, which remains inaccessible to all attempts to contain it. On Badiou's account, at this point of impasse in his theory, Cantor falls back on the old idea of divine transcendence that subsists beyond the pale of reason. In Badiou's words, "Cantor, essentially a theologian, therein ties the absoluteness of being *not* to the (consistent) presentation of the multiple, but to the transcendence through which a divine infinity in-consists, as one, gathering together and numbering any multiple whatsoever" (BE 42, original emphasis).[19] Otherwise put, Cantor ultimately falls back on the theological distinction between two realms of being. Nevertheless, Badiou argues that "Cantor, in a brilliant anticipation, saw that the absolute point of being of the multiple is not its consistency – thus its dependence upon a procedure of the count-as-one – but its inconsistency, a multiple deployment that no unity gathers together" (*ibid.*).

Contrary to what we could call Cantor's re-theologization of the infinite, Badiou argues that the set-theoretical notion of the infinite implies an infinity of infinities, that is, "infinite multiples which can be differentiated from each other *to infinity*" (BE 145, original emphasis). Grounded in inconsistency rather than consistency, this infinity of infinities is itself without one, meaning that one cannot speak with any degree of finality of *a* set of all infinities, as the axiom of the power set entails. For this reason, the ontologization of the infinite, its unbinding from the one, is on Badiou's account necessarily "post-Christian, or, if you like, post-Galilean" (BE 143). In Badiou's words, "The ontologization of the infinite, besides abolishing the one-infinite, also abolishes the unicity of infinity; what it proposes is the vertigo of an infinity of infinities distinguishable within their common opposition to the finite" (BE 145–6). Badiou's conception of the infinite qua infinities of infinites, then, does not push the infinite into an inaccessible, theological beyond, a beyond that serves to divide being in two; it rather renders the infinite "thinkable *without the mediation of the one*" (BE 146). Otherwise put – and the anti-theological resonances of the notion are clear:

> [M]athematics localizes a *plurality of infinities* in the indifference
> of the pure multiple. It has processed the actual infinite via the
> banality of cardinal number. It has neutralized and completely
> deconsecrated the infinite, subtracting it from the metaphorical
> register of the tendency, the horizon, becoming. It has torn it
> from the realm of the One in order to disseminate it – whether
> as infinitely small or infinitely large – in the *aura*-free typology
> of multiplicities. By initiating a thinking in which the infinite
> is irrevocably separated from every instance of the One, math-
> ematics has, in its own domain, successfully consummated the
> death of God.   (TW 36, original emphasis)

How is it possible to think this notion of an infinity infinitely disseminated
without one? Badiou shows how it is possible in Meditation 14 of *Being
and Event*, in reference to the generation of ordinal numbers or natural
multiplicities.

   According to Badiou, the thinking of the infinite takes place within the
dialectic of the "already" and "still-more" (BE 146). Three basic elements
are involved: "an initial point of being, a rule which produces some same-
others, and a second existential seal which fixes the place of the Other for
the other" (BE 151). The initial point of being is, as we have seen, the name
of the void, which sutures any situation to being. Once this initial point, the
void, is assumed, a rule is needed to prescribe the immanent construction of
multiples from this point. Using the axiom of replacement, which allows for
the creation of new sets on the basis of replacing the elements of an already
existing set, and the axiom of union, which counts as one each step of the
dissemination of multiples, it is relatively easy to construct a series of successor ordinals whose generation is immanent to itself. To invoke a simple
example:

$$0 = \varnothing$$
$$1 = \{\varnothing\} = \{0\}$$
$$2 = \{\varnothing, \{\varnothing\}\} = \{0, 1\}$$
$$3 = \{\varnothing, \{\varnothing\}, \{\varnothing, \{\varnothing\}\}\} = \{0, 1, 2\} \, \dots$$

(Hallward 2003: 103)

The generation of successor ordinals can, of course, be extended *ad infinitum*, as an intuitive grasp of numerical succession tells us: we can always
repeat the operation to add one more number. The viability of such an
operation has never really been in question, in that the dissemination of
successor ordinals corresponds to a potential notion of infinity. Strictly
speaking, however, the sequence itself does not exist in any actual sense,
it being always incomplete, meaning that we are always dealing with finite
terms. How, though, do we pass from this potential notion of infinity, to

which we can always add one more ordinal, to an actual or existing infinity? Ultimately, we can only make this passage through a decision, a decision on the actual existence of the infinite. Such a decision functions as a "second existential seal" in addition to the void, and is condensed in the statement: "there exists a limit ordinal" (BE 156).

A limit ordinal is simply a non-successor ordinal and, because of this, it fixes the place of the Other with respect to the successor ordinals. Otherwise put, a "limit ordinal is subtracted from that part of the same that is detained within the other under the sign of the 'still-one-more'. The limit ordinal is the non-same of the entire sequence of successors which precedes it. It is not still-one-more, but rather the One-multiple within which the insistence of the rule (of succession) ex-sists" (BE 155). Following Cantor, Badiou designates the first or smallest limit ordinal or, what amounts to the same thing, the first infinite cardinal, $\aleph_0$ or ω_0. This first limit ordinal serves as a border between the finite and the infinite, in that it "marks the threshold of infinity" (BE 158). That is, what belong to ω_0 are the finite successor ordinals or natural multiples. Once this first limit ordinal is marked, however, there is nothing to stop the further and unceasing generation of larger orders of infinity, as implied in the power set axiom and the prohibition against self-belonging (BE 265–80).

What this means for Badiou is, first, that the infinite should no longer be conceived along the lines of an exception to the finite. From the perspective of existence, the finite is indeed primary, since the generation of multiples proceeds from the void on up, so to speak. However, at the level of the concept, "the finite is secondary. It is solely under the retroactive effect of the existence of a limit ordinal ω_0 that we qualify the sets $\varnothing$, $\{\varnothing\}$, etc., as finite: otherwise, the latter would have no other attribute than that of being existent one-multiples" (BE 159). The finite, in the schema of the infinite, is always and only "qualified as a *region* of being, a minor form of the latter's presence" (*ibid*.). Second, since there is not one infinite but an endless plurality of infinities grounded in their own inconsistency, the infinite is unbound from the one. Badiou's notion of infinity, in this sense, is thoroughly antitheological: "Just as the set of all ordinals cannot exist – which is said: Nature does not exist – nor can the set of all cardinals exist, the absolutely infinite Infinity, the infinity of all intrinsically thinkable infinities – which is said, this time: God does not exist" (BE 277).

It is worth pointing out that Frederiek Depoortere has recently argued that Badiou's set-theoretical notion of the infinite does not inevitably lead to the dissolution of the traditional designation of God as infinite. Depoortere attempts to reinstitute Cantor's distinction between the transfinite and the absolute infinite, which latter "is the true infinite" (Depoortere 2009: 125). For Depoortere the transfinite remains closer to the finite, and is thus thinkable; for this reason, however, the transfinite has nothing to say about the absolute infinite, which "can never be crossed" (*ibid.*). "In this way," Depoortere writes, "Aquinas's distinction between finite creation and infinite Creator can simply be kept on the understanding that 'finite' now includes both what has traditionally been understood by it and the transfinite" (*ibid.*).

The problem with Depoortere's suggestion does not so much result from the attempt to posit God as such. The problem, rather, results from Depoortere's attempt to think a more traditional understanding of God, which he derives primarily from Aquinas, from within Badiou's ontology. Depoortere simply assumes that Cantor's distinction between the transfinite and the absolute infinite is adequate, which then allows Depoortere, much like Cantor, to associate the latter with God. However, as should be clear, Badiou in no way reduces set theory to Cantor and, more importantly, Depoortere's move, again like Cantor, amounts to an onto-theological avoidance of the implications of the axiom of the power set and the paradoxes that result from self-belonging. Moreover, as Clayton Crockett has correctly pointed out, "Depoortere relies strongly on the Thomistic and ultimately Aristotelian distinction between actual and potential to decide for God, whereas this traditional opposition may not make as much sense in terms of modern set theory or contemporary philosophy and theology" (Crockett 2010). We can see this specifically in Depoortere's collapsing of the transfinite into the finite. Indeed, it would seem that, in the end, Depoortere falls back on an outdated metaphysics to posit God, despite his claims to the contrary to take the implications of Badiou's ontology and contemporary set theory seriously.[20]

Nevertheless, and by way of conclusion, although the post-Cantorian rationalization of the infinite points to infinities of infinities-without-one, this does not mean that, at present, we have knowledge of these infinities in any determinative sense. Indeed, the power set axiom, coupled with the continuum itself, implies that such knowledge will always remain, to a certain extent, outstanding, at least from the present perspective. Thus Badiou says that the "thorough-going rationalization of the infinite ... in a sense will always be yet to come, since we still do not know how to effect a reasonable 'forcing' of the kind of infinity proper to the continuum" (TW 18). What, however, is to distinguish this notion from the theological notion of the infinite, which, in the end, associates the infinite as such with what cannot be thought? The difference is primarily one of principle. For theological articulations of the infinite, which for Badiou include Romanticism and "ontologies of presence", the infinite remains essentially beyond the grasp of human reason. Hence Badiou's criticism of Cantor's distinction between the transfinite and the absolute infinite, which amounts to a re-theologization of the infinite. From Badiou's perspective, although knowledge of the infinite remains in many respects outstanding or incomplete, this is not an essential feature of the infinite, nor an indication of the absolute limitations of human finitude. Rather, for Badiou our lack of knowledge only means that we have yet to come up with the means to gain such knowledge, since the infinite is in principle fully rationalizable.

Such is the extent of Badiou's anti-theology. The grounding of being in multiplicity rather than the one, the void as the proper name of being, the recognition of the actual existence of a plurality of thinkable infinities – with these fundamental aspects of the mathematically determined ontological situation, Badiou intends to make good on the promise of God's death. Ontology is, however, only one component of Badiou's philosophy, and essentially clears the ground by providing a basic framework from within which to develop a theory of truth and the subject. As we will see in the next chapter, on the surface Badiou continues the basic anti-theological thrust of his thought in the articulation of this theory. I will also begin to suggest, however, that in the theory of truth and the subject some cracks in Badiou's anti-theology begin to appear, cracks that suggest that Badiou does not completely leave theology behind.

2. EVENT, TRUTH AND THE SUBJECT

As we discussed in the previous chapter, Badiou's ontology functions as an anti-theology. The grounding of being in multiplicity rather than the one, the void as the proper name of being, the recognition of the actual existence of a plurality of infinities – these fundamental aspects of the ontological situation entail for Badiou that "God is dead at the heart of presentation" (TW 37). Ontology, however, is only one aspect of Badiou's philosophy, serving in large part as a propaedeutic to philosophy proper, the main concern of which is the construction of a theory of truth and the subject. Badiou's grounding of philosophy in truth and the subject is curious, at least at first glance, especially for one who endeavours to take the death of God to its ultimate conclusion. It is all too common in the wake of God's death to assume the liquidation of truth and the dissolution of the subject, at least in so far as the latter corresponds with a centred locus of consciousness. Badiou's wager, nevertheless, is that philosophy cannot leave truth and the subject behind, even if they will have to be reworked in a direction that is consistent with the anti-theological trajectory outlined in the previous chapter. In order to discuss Badiou's theory of truth and the subject, the first section of this chapter focuses on Badiou's theory of the event, along with the related notions of the evental site, intervention, nomination and evental recurrence. The second section focuses on Badiou's formal theory of truth, with particular attention paid to fidelity and forcing. After having grasped the basic elements of Badiou's theory of truth, the third section discusses Badiou's understanding of the subject as the bearer of truth. Although Badiou's theory of truth and the subject ostensibly continues the anti-theological trajectory of his philosophy, I will also suggest that the question of the role of theology in Badiou's philosophy is more complicated than often assumed.

EVENT AND INTERVENTION

With the introduction of the theme of the event, we pass from the domain of being qua being to "what-is-not-being-qua-being" (BE 173). In order to understand what this means and how it applies to Badiou's doctrine of the event, recall that ontology, understood as the situation that thinks being qua being, prohibits paradoxical multiples, that is, multiples that belong to themselves. As we discussed in the last chapter, the prohibition against self-belonging assures the consistency of the language and operations of ontology in thinking being qua being. The prohibition is formalized in the axiom of foundation, which assures that set theory and ontology only deal with well-founded sets. Given the relationship between belonging and inclusion, allowing only well-founded sets into its purview allows ontology to construct a seemingly seamless hierarchy of sets of increasing size. Such is the sense of the set-theoretical notion of infinity, which, as discussed in the last chapter, relies on a rule of passage and the positing of a limit ordinal for thinking the immanent dissemination of multiples. However, in order to think consistently in this manner, ontology presupposes that the multiples it deals with have a certain amount of stability to them, that is, a maximal bond or equilibrium between belonging and inclusion. The ontological situation is, to recall Badiou's typology of situations discussed in the previous chapter, a normal situation. For this reason, the ontological situation proper, under the effect of its one-count, has as its goal the repetition of itself, the maintenance of its own consistency through the strictures of its axioms.

Ontology's need for consistency is why it "has nothing to say about the event" (BE 190). For Badiou, an event is the source of novelty for a situation; it is that which carries within itself the potential to radically alter a situation from within. An event is the locus of real change for a situation, an immanent break that interrupts the continuity and repetition of the same. If ontology is on the side of consistency, an event is on the side of inconsistency, the breakdown of the count-as-one. Events are "irreducible singularities, the 'beyond-the-law' of situations" (E 44). An event is a "supplement ... committed to chance. It is unpredictable, incalculable. It is beyond what is" (IT 62). To emphasize the equation of the event with the possibility for real change, Badiou often describes the event as a "radical novelty" (SP 33) or something "absolutely new" (SP 43), a "pure beginning" (SP 49) or "absolute beginning" (D 90), "a pure cut in becoming" (LW 384), an "exception" (LW 360) to what there is. Using the technical terminology of Badiou's ontology, an event is a multiple that belongs to itself, meaning that it is prohibited from the ontological situation proper. According to Badiou, "[O]ntology demonstrates that the event is not, in the sense in which it is a theorem of ontology that all self-belonging contradicts a fundamental Idea of the multiple, the Idea which prescribes the foundational finitude of origin for all presentation" (BE 190).

Because the notion of the event has no place within ontology, Badiou associates it with "what-is-not-being-qua-being" (BE 173). The distinction between being qua being and what-is-not-being-qua-being can also be understood as a distinction between the atemporal structure of presentation and time, between the natural and the historical (BE 173, 265). Thus, although associating the event with "what-is-not-being-qua-being" might suggest the contrary, we should be careful not to associate it with non-being; nor should we simply assume that the event has nothing to do with the general themes of Badiou's ontology. The "and" in the title *Being and Event* is important here, and Badiou maintains that there is, in fact, a being of the event, a being that, as we will see, applies to truth and the subject (cf. Clemens 2005: 105–7). Otherwise put, the event, truth and the subject are implied, albeit negatively at first, in the general features of the ontological edifice that Badiou constructs, but they have no place in that ontological edifice as such.

In order to understand the particular being of the event and the emergence of truth and the subject from it, we can begin with Badiou's notion of the evental site. As mentioned above, in so far as the ontological situation relies on a stable relationship between belonging and inclusion, it is, in the end, defined by normality. However, as we discussed in the last chapter, multiples can also be excrescent (re-presented but not presented) or singular (presented but not re-presented). In Meditation 16 of *Being and Event*, in which he first begins to broach the topic of the event in systematic fashion, Badiou marks the distinction between normality and singularity as corresponding to the distinction between being qua being and what-is-not-being-qua-being, between the natural and the historical. In Badiou's words, "the *place* of thought of that-which-is-not-being is the non-natural; that which is presented *other* than natural or stable or normal multiplicities. The place of the other-than-being is the abnormal, the instable, the antinatural. I will term *historical* what is thus determined as the opposite of nature" (BE 173–4, original emphasis). Historical situations are situations defined primarily by singularity, that is, situations in which multiples are presented without being re-presented. Indeed, if natural or normal situations are defined by "an omnipresence of normality", historical situations are defined by "an omnipresence of singularity": "The form-multiple of historicity is what lies entirely within the instability of the singular; it is that upon which the state's metastructure has no hold. It is a point of subtraction from the state's re-securing of the count" (BE 174).

Badiou introduces his notion of the evental site in relation to such singular situations. An evental site is, according to Badiou, "an entirely abnormal multiple; that is, a multiple such that none of its elements are presented in the situation" (BE 175). Now, the site itself is presented in the situation. What is not presented are the elements or parts that compose the site; that is, in line with the definition of singular multiples, the site itself is not re-presented. In Badiou's words, "The site, itself, is presented, but 'beneath' it nothing from which it is composed is presented. As such, the site is not a part of the situation" (*ibid.*). The multiple qua evental site is presented as a multiple but "[n]one of its terms are counted-as-one as such; only the mul-tiple of these terms forms a one" (*ibid.*). Badiou says that such multiples are "*on the edge of the void*" (*ibid.*, original emphasis). Recall that, from the per-spective of the situation, the void is literally nothing, since it is not presented as such. To say that an evental site is "on the edge of the void" is to affirm that, from the perspective of the situation, the multiples that compose the site are nothing for the situation. An evental site thus "in-consists" for the situation, since "*that of which* it is multiple is not" (*ibid.*, original emphasis). Using the axiom of foundation, Badiou also says of evental sites that they are "foundational", in the sense that they are "minimal for the effect of the count" (*ibid.*). That is, such multiples can enter into various combinations, since they can belong to multiples counted-as-one. However, because what belongs to them is not also included in the situation, an evental site "cannot itself result from an internal combination of the situation" (*ibid.*). An evental site is, in this sense, an "undecomposable term", from which it follows that:

> evental sites block the infinite regression of combinations of mul-tiples. Since they are on the edge of the void, one cannot think the underside of their presented-being. It is therefore correct to say that sites *found* the situation because they are the absolutely primary terms therein; they interrupt questioning according to combinatory origin. (*Ibid.*, original emphasis)

Now, it is important to point out that there is nothing absolute about evental sites. Although natural or normal multiples do have a degree of abso-luteness, in that they conserve homogeneity whenever they appear, this is not the case with singular or abnormal multiples. That is, "a multiple could quite easily be singular in one situation (its elements are not presented therein, although it is) yet normal in another situation (its elements happen to be pre-sented in this new situation)" (BE 176). Another way to say this is that there is a dissymmetry between nature and history: "history can be naturalized, but nature cannot be historicized" (*ibid.*). For instance, in a socio-political situ-ation, a singular multiple can always "undergo a state normalization" (*ibid.*). What this means, in effect, is that natural or normal situations are global, whereas evental sites are always local, singular for the situation in which they occur. As local phenomena, we can thus speak of the historicity of evental sites but, in keeping with the ontological mandate on the inexistence of the one or the whole, not a History, understood along "vulgar" Hegelian and/or Marxist lines (*ibid.*).[1] Since the inexistence of History in Badiou's philosophy is important for understanding the latter's relationship to theology, I will return to this point in more detail in Chapter 4.

Nevertheless, the existence of an evental site, an entirely abnormal or singular multiple, is the precondition for an event: there can be no event without an evental site. This is why natural or normal situations, structured as they are on the basis of the equilibrium between belonging and inclusion, structure and metastructure, do not admit events, meaning that the ontological situation itself is devoid of sites. However, similar to the way in which evental sites are not themselves absolute, an event is not a necessary consequence of its site. That is, although there can be no event without an evental site, the existence of an evental site in a situation does not inevitably entail the emergence of an event for that situation. As Badiou puts it, "The site is only ever *a condition of being* for the event ... [T]he existence of a multiple on the edge of the void merely opens up the possibility of an event. It is always possible that no event actually occur" (BE 179).[2] To maintain the contrary – that the event is a necessary outcome of its site – is to fall into the trap of "determinist or globalizing thought" (*ibid.*). The stricture that the site is only a condition for the event is in keeping with Badiou's thesis on the inexistence of History as one or whole, and is meant to preserve the aleatory nature of the event.

Given the existence of an evental site, how, then, do we define an event? Badiou gives the following formal definition of an event: "*I term event of the site X a multiple such that it is composed of, on the one hand, elements of the site, and on the other hand, itself*" (*ibid.*, original emphasis). An event is, according to Badiou, "a one-multiple made up of, on the one hand, all the multiples which belong to the site, and on the other hand, the event itself" (*ibid.*). Recall that for Badiou, the singularity of an evental site consists in its position with regard to its situation: an evental site is a multiple that belongs to its situation but is not included therein. That is, although the evental site of a situation is counted-as-one and is thus presented, the elements of which it is composed are not. The evental site of a situation is presented but not re-presented, meaning that, strictly speaking, "the site is not a part of the situation" (BE 175). To say that the event is composed, on the one hand, of the elements of the evental site is, then, to situate the event on the side of what does not get re-presented by the situation's metastructure or state. If the evental site is situated "on the edge of the void", since its elements are not included in, and count for nothing for, the situation, then an event itself is composed in part of these elements. What this means is that an event, by definition, eludes the re-presentative grasp of the state of the situation.

The event is also, however, composed of itself, meaning that "it is itself a *term* of the event that it is" (BE 180, original emphasis). In addition to presenting the elements of the evental site of which it is composed, the event also "presents itself as an immanent résumé and one-mark of its own multiple" (*ibid.*). The event – or more specifically, as we will see shortly, the name of the event – is thus that which designates its site as evental. In Badiou's words, "The event is ... the multiple which both presents its entire site, and, by means of the pure signifier of itself immanent to its own multiple, manages to present the presentation itself, that is, the one of the infinite multiple that it is" (*ibid.*). Otherwise put, the event "'mobilizes' the elements of its site, but it adds its own presentation to the mix" (BE 182). Take, for instance, the French Revolution, which Badiou uses to illustrate this point in Meditation 17 of *Being and Event*. The evental site is composed of the various features that make up "France between 1789 and, let's say, 1794":

> the electors of the General Estates, the peasants of the Great Fear, the san-culottes of the towns, the members of the convention, the Jacobin clubs, the soldiers of the draft, but also, the price of subsistence, the guillotine, the effects of the tribunal, the massacres, the English spies, the Vendeans, the *assignats* (banknotes), the theatre, the *Marseillaise*, etc. (BE 180)

All of these things certainly constitute, on Badiou's account, elements of an evental site. However, in and of themselves, they do not constitute an event. What qualifies these elements as evental is the effect of the Revolution itself, "the manner in which the conscience of the times ... filters the entire site through the one of its evental qualification" (*ibid.*). For this reason, Badiou says that the event is "supernumerary to the sole numbering of terms of its site, despite it presenting such a numbering" (*ibid.*).

What, however, is the relationship between an event and the situation for which it is an event? At issue in this question is the extent to which we can say that an event belongs to its situation. According to Badiou, the question as to whether an event belongs to its situation or not is, strictly speaking and necessarily, undecidable from the perspective of the situation. In Badiou's words, "If there exists an event, *its belonging to the situation of its site is undecidable from the standpoint of the situation itself*" (BE 181, original emphasis). As mentioned above, the evental site itself, situated as it is on the edge of the void, is presented in the situation but not re-presented; the evental site is not a part of the situation, since its elements are not re-secured or re-counted as one. Based on the distinction mentioned in the previous paragraphs between the evental site and the event, the evental site as such is not enough to determine an event for a situation. In order to determine that an event is presented by or belongs to a situation, it would thus be necessary to show that the event "is presented as an element of itself" (*ibid.*). To return to Badiou's example of the French Revolution, "To know whether the French Revolution is really *an* event in French history, we must first establish that it is definitely a term immanent to itself" (*ibid.*). However, because the event is supernumerary with regard to its site, it is precisely this identi-fication of an event as belonging to itself that cannot be established in the situation, since the axioms of Badiou's set-theoretical ontology prohibit self-belonging. Hence the status of an event is undecidable from the perspective of the situation.

If the belonging of an event to a situation is undecidable, the only way to determine that an event does indeed belong to its situation is to make a decision or "wager" on its belonging, a wager that Badiou understands along the lines of Pascal's wager, Mallarmé's dice-throw and Kierkegaard's either/or (BE 191–8, 212–22; LW 425–35). In Badiou's words, "Since it is of the very essence of the event to be a multiple whose belonging to the situation is undecidable, deciding that it belongs to the situation is a wager: one can only hope that this wager never becomes legitimate, inasmuch as any legiti-macy refers back to the structure of the situation" (BE 201). Badiou refers to this decision as an "intervention", which he defines as "any procedure by which a multiple is recognized as an event" (BE 202). Such recognition has two aspects. On the one hand, an intervention involves designating the mul-tiple concerned as evental, meaning that it is composed of elements of the evental site and the event itself. On the other hand, an intervention must also decide that the designated multiple belongs to the situation. An inter-vention thus consists "in identifying that there has been some undecidability, and in deciding its belonging to the situation" (*ibid.*). However, the problem is that the second aspect of intervention, the decision on the event's belong-ing to the situation, risks annulling the first, the recognition of the evental multiple, by rendering it legitimate from the perspective of the situation.

Badiou's way out of this apparent paradox is to submit the event to an act of nomination, the attachment of a signifier to the event that makes the event available for decision:

> The act of nomination of the event is what constitutes it, not as real – we will always posit that this multiple has occurred – but susceptible to a decision concerning its belonging to a situation. The essence of the intervention consists – within the field opened up by an alternative hypothesis, whose *presented* object is the site (a multiple on the edge of the void), and which concerns the "there is" of an event – in naming this "there is" and in unfolding the consequences of this nomination in the space of the situation to which the site belongs. (BE 203, original emphasis)

Similar to the way in which the evental site is distinct from the event, the event is distinct from its name, but the name of the event is necessary for the event to become effective in and for the situation through an interventional decision. How does this avoid the paradox mentioned above? According to

Badiou, the name of the event must be "drawn from the void at the edge of which stands the intrasituational presentation of its site" (BE 204). To claim that the name of the event emerges from the void, in this instance, simply means that the interventional decision draws from the un-presented elements of the site to name the event. "The initial operation of an intervention", Badiou writes, "is to *make a name out of an unpresented element of the site to qualify the event whose site is the site*" (*ibid.*, original emphasis). This means that the act of nomination is "essentially illegal" from the perspective of the situation, "in that it cannot conform to any *law* of representation" (BE 205, original emphasis).

There is a close relationship, here, between nomination and how Badiou understands the creativity of poetry or poetic language. Indeed, in so far as poetry for Badiou is not primarily descriptive or expressive but creative, Badiou claims that "every name of an event or of the evental presence is in its essence poetic" (HI 26). To quote Badiou at length on this point:

> [W]hen the situation is saturated by its own norm, when the calculation of itself is inscribed there without respite, when there is no longer a void between knowledge and prediction, then one must be *poetically* ready for the outside-of-self. For the nomination of an event – in the sense in which I speak of it, that is, an undecidable supplementation which must be named to occur for a being-faithful, thus for a truth – *this* nomination is *always* poetic. To name a supplement, a chance, an incalculable, one must draw from the void of sense, in default of established significations, to the peril of language. One must therefore poeticize, and the poetic name of the event is what throws us outside of ourselves, through the flaming ring of predictions.
>
> (IT 100, original emphasis)

Now, to be sure, as an act of creation tied to the poetic function of language, there is a certain amount of arbitrariness involved in the act of nomination, an arbitrariness implied in its essential illegality with respect to the situation. Just as the existence of an evental site does not necessarily imply the existence of an event, there is no guarantee that the name of the event will be an adequate index for the event itself, allowing its consequences to be drawn. In the end, the adequacy of the chosen name can only be justified retroactively in light of the consequences drawn from the nomination itself.

We will return to this point below. Nevertheless, at this point it is also important to emphasize that, although the intervention qua naming is certainly an act of creation, the rupture that this act of creation institutes with respect to the situation is limited by what Badiou calls "evental recurrence" (BE 209). As we have seen, there is the event itself, and the name on which the intervention is based; it is this interventional naming that puts the event into circulation for the situation, making the event susceptible to the unfolding of its consequences. To be sure, Badiou stresses, it is "the event alone, aleatory figure of non-being, [that] founds the possibility of intervention" (*ibid.*). But since the event does not properly exist for the situation, in that it is subtracted from the situation, the existence of the event for the situation depends upon intervention. The intervention, in this sense, functions as something like a second event, as the event of the event, so to speak, that puts the initial event into circulation for the situation. There is, as Badiou admits, a great deal of circularity involved here. However, in order to avoid this circularity, Badiou makes the following, crucial point:

> In order to avoid this curious mirroring of the event and the intervention – of the fact and the interpretation – *the possibility of the intervention must be assigned to the consequences of another event.* It is evental recurrence which founds intervention. In other words, there is no interventional capacity, constitutive for the belonging of an evental multiple to a situation, save within the network of a previously decided belonging. An intervention is what presents an event for the occurrence of another.
>
> (*Ibid.*, original emphasis)

This other event is not necessarily the same, as some interpreters hold, as the act of nomination qua second event (Johnston 2009: 33). Rather, the interventional naming of a potentially new event always depends on its being placed in relation to another, already named event in circulation. According to Badiou, "[F]or there to be an event, one must be able to situate oneself within the consequences of another. The intervention is a line drawn from one paradoxical multiple, which is already circulating, to the circulation of another, a line which scratches out. It is a *diagonal* of the situation" (BE 210, original emphasis). Otherwise put, the intervention "evokes the previous situations and uses them precisely to create its own rationality" (Badiou 2006a: 185).

That this other event that Badiou evokes in the passage quoted above is another, previously decided event, and not immediately the act of nomination, is clear in Mediation 21 of *Being and Event*, in which Badiou illustrates intervention and evental recurrence via a discussion of Pascalian Christianity. According to Badiou, Christianity, even if it remains caught up in a metaphysics of presence, bears the formal marks of an event, and is structured through and through by intervention and evental recurrence. To quote Badiou at length:

> The intervention is based upon the circulation, within the Jewish milieu, of another event, Adam's original sin, of which the death

of Christ is the relay. The connection between original sin and redemption definitively founds the time of Christianity as a time of exile and salvation. There is an essential historicity to Christianity which is tied to the intervention of the apostles as the placement-into-circulation of the event of the death of God; itself reinforced by the promise of a Messiah which organized the fidelity to the initial exile. Christianity is structured from beginning to end by evental recurrence; moreover, it prepares itself for the divine hazard of the third event, the Last Judgement, in which the ruin of the terrestrial situation will be accomplished, and a new regime of existence will be established.   (BE 213)

According to Christian doctrine the incarnation of God in Christ and his subsequent death constitute an event, in the sense that it introduces something new into the situation through the intervention of the apostles. However, the possibility of this event depends upon evental recurrence. The eventness of the event of Christ is only possible in light of original sin, the former providing redemption from the latter.[3] Thus the meaning of the Christian event is only "legitimated by exploring the diagonal of fidelity which unites the first event (the fall, origin of our misery) to the second (redemption, as a cruel and humiliating reminder of our greatness)" (BE 216). Fidelity to the second event, moreover, anticipates the third event, the Last Judgement, which will in turn render a full account of the meaning of redemption. As Badiou points out, however, the link between these events is not necessary, at least on the surface; precisely because the event remains undecidable, the diagonal of intervention and fidelity shows the truth of the connection between these events retroactively. That is, although the intervention concerning and fidelity to the incarnation and death of God takes place in light of original sin, the diagonal connecting the latter with the Christian event is only legible after the fact. According to Badiou, "The intervention wagers upon a discontinuity with the previous fidelity solely in order to install an unequivocal continuity" (BE 219).

We should, however, point out that Badiou has seemingly backed away a bit from the event-intervention-evental recurrence scheme found in *Being and Event*, due to criticisms suggesting that the role naming plays in relation to the event implies recourse to some form of transcendence.[4] As Badiou summarizes the criticisms levelled against the importance of nomination for his theory of the event, the act of nomination seems to imply "a mysterious naming" that occurs "from above" (LW 361). In light of such criticisms, Badiou has attempted, in *Logics of Worlds*, to develop things in a different direction, ostensibly without recourse to the act of nomination (cf. E lvi–lvii). Instead of referring the efficacy of an event to the act of nomination, Badiou speaks of the effects of the event as the event's "trace". The "trace" of an event is related to a revised logic of sites, not all of which are necessarily evental as in *Being and Event*: the "trace" of an event is understood in reference to the distribution of various intensities of appearing, in which the site is more directly related to the consequences drawn from it (LW 394, 361).

In *Logics of Worlds*, a site has three main features:

1. A site is a reflexive multiplicity, which belongs to itself and thereby transgresses the laws of being.
2. Because it carries out a transitory cancellation of the gap between being and being-there, a site is the instantaneous revelation of the void that haunts multiplicities.
3. A site is an ontological figure of the instant: it appears only to disappear. (LW 369)

Much like the evental site discussed in *Being and Event*, then, in *Logics of Worlds* a site, understood as a reflexive multiple that reveals the void haunting organized multiplicities, is the locus of real change. Badiou says that a site appears "as the fulminant and entirely unpredictable beginning of a break with the very thing that regulates its appearance" (LW 365); a site is the locus for "an immanent overturning of the law of appearing" (LW 366). In this sense, Badiou associates sites with singularities. But whereas in *Being and Event* an event appears as the possibility of an absolute rupture with a situation, Badiou's theory of change in relation to sites in *Logics of Worlds* is not as unilateral, and takes into account a range of possibilities.

In *Logics of Worlds*, Badiou distinguishes between what he takes to be real change, that is, change that involves the existence of a site, from a notion of change that affirms that the natural and the historical are always constituted through and in a constant state of becoming. Badiou does not deny, of course, that such is the case: among other things, the dissolution of the one entails that the world be understood along the lines of the primacy of flux, process, evolution and differentiation. However, Badiou separates change as becoming from real change, by referring to the former as "modification", which he defines as *"the rule-governed appearing of intensive variations which a transcendental authorizes in the world of which it is the transcendental"* (LW 359, original emphasis). A world or, to use the language of *Being and Event*, a situation, is simply "the set of its modifications" (*ibid.*). What this means, in effect, is that the modification of a world is already included in its own constitution, meaning that modification is "only the transcendental absorption of change, that part of becoming which is constitutive of every being-there" (*ibid.*). Modifications, to be sure, often appear to offer something new but, because they are already authorized in the world in which they occur, from Badiou's perspective no real change can result from them.

Because modification is internal to the transcendental organization of a world, it does not require the existence of a site.

Between mere modification and real, evental change, however, are various intermediate positions that do require the existence of a site. The differences among these positions result for Badiou from the existential value of the site itself and the value of the consequences drawn from the site. The value of a site is said to be non-maximal if it is "ontologically identifiable" but not "within appearing, logically singular" (LW 372). That is, a site is by definition distinct from the transcendental organization of the world in which it appears; it thus differs from the laws of mere modification. However, the force or intensity of its existence is weak, meaning that, in retrospect, it differs little from run of the mill modification, even if it cannot be reduced to the latter. In contrast to modification, a non-maximal site certainly offers the promise of something new; it is just that the site itself lacks the power to make good on this promise. For this reason, a non-maximal site "leads the singularity back to the edges of the pure and simple 'normal' modification of the world" (*ibid.*). Badiou refers to such a site as a "fact" (*ibid.*).

In contrast to a fact, that is, a site whose intensity of existence is non-maximal, singular sites are those that have a maximal degree of intensity. Singular sites, in turn, can be divided into weak and strong, between sites with non-maximal consequences and sites with maximal consequences. The difference between the two, it seems, does not so much rest on the duration of the consequences drawn from the site, or even the initial success that these consequences have in the situation or world in which the site appears. Rather, what differentiates a weak singularity from a strong singularity is the properly evental character of the latter. The difference, in this sense, resides not in the force of the existence of the site but in the force of the consequences drawn, whether these can be said or not to break with or overturn the laws of appearing in that world. In Badiou's words, "For what counts is not only the exceptional intensity of its surging up – the fact that we are dealing with a violent episode that creates appearing – but the glorious and uncertain consequences that this upsurge, despite its vanishing, sets out. Commencements are to be measured by the recommencements they enable" (LW 375).

Although Badiou claims that this new schema gets rid of the problems associated with the act of nomination, in that it associates the potential for change immanently with the site and its consequences, it is not entirely clear that he jettisons the event-intervention-evental recurrence theme completely in *Logics of Worlds*. As Adrian Johnston has pointed out, despite adopting a new terminology in *Logics of Worlds*, Badiou continues to use the same temporal structure that informs *Being and Event*, "that of the future anterior, in which what happens after retroactively determines whether what came before was/is or was/is not an event" (Johnston 2009: 33). Moreover, as Johnston also points out, Badiou explicitly evokes the concept of naming in a 2006 discussion with Simon Critchley, the same year of the publication of *Logics of Worlds* (*ibid.*: 33; cf. Badiou & Critchley 2007). Indeed, as I will suggest in more detail later on, Badiou's concept of "resurrection" in *Logics of Worlds*, which refers to the reactivation of "a subject in another logic of its appearing-in-truth" (LW 65), bears a striking similarity to the notions of intervention and evental recurrence as expressed in *Being and Event*, and seems to require an act of nomination to get off the ground. Even if Badiou claims to have solved the problems associated with nomination in this revised doctrine of change, the latter itself raises its own problems, particularly in regard to the self-reflexivity of the site.[5]

Whatever the case may be, to return to our discussion of intervention and evental recurrence, it is important to point out that evental recurrence, which assumes a relationship between the consequences of prior, already circulating events and new events, entails that the novelty introduced by an event is not absolute but relative. This is an important point, since it attempts to guard against what Badiou refers to as "speculative leftism". In Badiou's words:

> One important consequence of evental recurrence is that no intervention whatsoever can legitimately operate according to the idea of a primal event, or a radical beginning. We can term *speculative leftism* any thought of being which bases itself upon the theme of an absolute commencement. Speculative leftism imagines that intervention alone authorizes itself on the basis of itself alone; that it breaks with the situation without any other support than its own negative will. This imaginary wager upon an absolute novelty – "to break the history of the world in two" – fails to recognize that the real of the conditions of possibility of an intervention is always the circulation of an already decided event. (BE 210, original emphasis)

Speculative leftism so understood wagers on an absolute discontinuity or absolute beginning and, in this sense, represents a "Manichean hypostasis" of the event, a hypostasis whose calling card is "Revolution or Apocalypse" (*ibid.*). Speculative leftism is a type of "fanaticism" of the pure event, and closely corresponds to the Marcionite heresy in Christianity, which posits an absolute disjunction between the old and the new, between what Marcion saw as the malevolent creator God of Judaism and the benevolent, fatherly God of Christianity, the alien God who is known exclusively through the coming of the Son (TS 16–17; SP 25). In its desire for an absolute and unprecedented rupture, speculative leftism in the end substitutes voluntarism, heroism and nostalgia for the sober work of fidelity and, as such, often ends in terror and destruction (C 11–25). In contrast to all forms of specu-lative leftism, Badiou insists that what "the doctrine of the event teaches us is rather that the entire effort lies in following the event's consequences, not in glorifying its occurrence. There is no more an angelic herald of the event than there is a hero. Being does not commence" (BE 211).

Because of this, intervention must avoid all attempts to absolutize the event, to make of it an object of devotion. Absolutizing the event is, as we will discuss below, the origin of evil. Although the event is certainly the rela-tive origin of novelty in and for a situation, the creation of something new, it is more important to follow its consequences. Badiou terms such following faithfulness or fidelity. In the simplest terms possible, fidelity rests on the ethical maxim, "Keep going!" (E 52). Although there are obvious religious connotations to this term, connotations that we will analyse in more detail in Chapter 4, it is important at this point to dissociate Badiou's notion of fidelity from any form of "pious discourse" that would involve waiting for the advent of something Other (E 18–29). Fidelity is, rather, an organized, regu-lated and disciplined procedure. Its "sole foundation", Badiou writes, "lies in a *discipline* of time, which controls from beginning to end the consequences of the introduction into circulation of the paradoxical multiple, and which at any moment knows how to discern its connection to chance" (BE 211, origi-nal emphasis). Fidelity is, strictly speaking:

> the set of procedures which discern, in a situation, those multiples whose existence depends upon the introduction into circulation (under the supernumerary name conferred by an intervention) of an evental multiple. In sum, a fidelity is the apparatus which separates out, within the set of presented multiples, those which depend upon an event. To be faithful is to gather together and distinguish the becoming legal of a chance.   (BE 232)

FIDELITY AND THE FORCING OF TRUTH

We have said that fidelity, or faithfulness, as the set of procedures that dis-cern the terms of and make available an evental multiple for the produc-tion of truth, seems to carry an obvious religious connotation, although Badiou claims that the idea itself is drawn from the amorous relationship, that is, love (BE 232). But unlike some understandings of religious faith, for Badiou there is, first, no general or universal fidelity that would subtend all situations, just as there is no general or universal subject, as we will see in the next section. Fidelity for Badiou is not "a capacity, a subjective qual-ity, or a virtue" but rather "a situated operation which depends upon the examination of situations" (BE 233). Fidelity, as related to an event, is always

particular to that event, meaning that "[t]here is no general faithful disposition" (*ibid.*). "Fidelity is", Badiou emphasizes, "a situated operation which
depends on the examination of situations" (*ibid.*). However, even if fidelity is always particular, situated in relation to an event, it is still possible to
think the general form that fidelity takes across its various instantiations.
Although the content of fidelity necessarily varies according to the event of
which it is an operation – indeed, the same event can and often does produce different fidelities – its form is largely identical whenever and wherever
it appears. More specifically, the form of fidelity always assumes a situation,
the evental multiple introduced into the situation through interventional
naming, and a "*rule of connection* which allows one to evaluate the depend-
ency of any particular existing multiple with respect to the event, given that
the latter's belonging to the situation has been decided by the situation"
(BE 234, original emphasis). The model for this rule of connection is, at least
on the surface, not religious faith but mathematical deduction: fidelity supposes an enquiry of the terms of the situation, to determine whether they
are connected to the event or not (*ibid.*: 327–43).

Second, just as the count-as-one for Badiou is an operation, so too
is fidelity: "fidelity is not a term-multiple of the situation," but "an operation, a structure" (BE 233). Likewise, if the one, because it is an operation,
is not, fidelity is also, strictly speaking, not. If fidelity exists at all, it is in
"the groupings that it constitutes of one-multiples which are *marked*, in one
way or another, by the evental happening" (*ibid.*, original emphasis). Ultimately fidelity can only be grasped or evaluated after the fact, by way of the
results it produces. This means that, on the one hand, "at every moment,
an evental fidelity can be grasped in a provisional result which is composed
of effective enquiries in which it is inscribed whether or not multiples are
connected to the event" (BE 234). To treat fidelity in its provisional result
is, in essence, to treat the sequence that it institutes as finite. But, on the
other hand, it must not be overlooked that fidelity as such is on the side of
the infinite, meaning that all attempts to grasp a faithful procedure in its
provisional results can only ever be approximations "of what the fidelity is
capable of" (BE 235). Otherwise put, if situations are in their being infinite,
so too is fidelity:

> Thought as a non-existent procedure, a fidelity is what opens up
> the *general* distinction of one-multiples presented in the situa-
> tion, according to whether they are connected to the event or
> not. A fidelity is therefore itself, as procedure, commensurate
> with the situation, and so it is infinite if the situation is.
>
> (*Ibid.*, original emphasis)

Fidelity is, in this sense, "the infinity of a virtual presentation" (BE 236).

Third, and related to the second point, if faithful procedures count those parts of the situation connected to the event, then fidelity is, in a certain sense, related to the state of the situation. Fidelity, then, "can appear, according to the nature of its operations, like a counter-state, or a sub-state" (BE 233). The apparently statist character of fidelity is implied in taking a faithful procedure as a provisional result. However, if treated properly as infinite, it is also the case that "fidelity *surpasses* all the results in which its finite-being is set out" (BE 236, original emphasis). Fidelity, then, does not properly take the form of a counter-state; rather, it takes place in subtraction from the state. Indeed, if the task of fidelity is to discern the connection of terms in a situation to the event, which only enters into circulation via the illegality of its name, then strictly speaking it has no necessary relation to either belonging or inclusion. Although fidelity can thus enter into certain relations with the state, at root a "real fidelity establishes dependencies which for the state are without concept, and it splits – via successive finite states – the situation in two, because it also discerns a mass of multiples which are indifferent to the event" (BE 237). Badiou calls such fidelity a "generic fidelity" (*ibid.*), and it is from a generic fidelity that it becomes possible to force the construction of an equally generic truth.

Before going on to explain the formal aspects of how fidelity proceeds in the construction of a truth, we need to discuss in more detail the notions of the generic and forcing, which Badiou borrows from the mathematician Paul Cohen.[6] To begin with some background, recall from the last chapter that Cantor's theory of transfinite numbers ran aground in part on his inability to prove the continuum hypothesis (CH). Cantor was unable to demonstrate a successive relationship between the first or smallest infinite cardinal number and its power set, which ultimately led Cantor to posit an absolute infinity situated beyond the realm of the transfinite. The axiomatization of set theory was, at least in part, an attempt to provide some order to the realm of the transfinite, to secure it from the paradoxes inherent in Cantor's formulation of it. However, the initial axiomatization of the Zermelo-Fraenkel system left untouched the status of CH: axiomatization could not, as Hallward points out, "say why the continuum should be embraced by [the mathematical theory of sets]" (Hallward 2003: 337). Indeed, providing a reason why CH should be embraced is an internal limit to the axiomatization of set theory itself, as suggested by Kurt Gödel's incompleteness theorem. Gödel showed that axiomatic, deductive methods contain an inherent limit, a point at which the consistency of the methods themselves cannot be proven through the resources inherent in the system in which they occur. Applied to CH specifically, this means that it is impossible to provide a proof of its necessity from within the confines of the axiomatic framework in which it operates. However, Gödel was confident that he was able to show the internal coherence of CH, the consistency of it in relation to the other axioms of set theory. In Badiou's words, he established "that accepting the consistency of the continuum hypothesis did not, in any manner, imply breaking with fidelity to the Ideas of the multiple: this decision is coherent with the fundamental axioms of the science of the pure multiple" (BE 296).

However, Gödel was only able to demonstrate the consistency of CH with the other axioms of set theory by limiting the latter to constructible sets, that is, sets that obey the following axiom: "For every multiple γ, there exists a level of the constructible hierarchy to which it belongs" (BE 300). The proof of this axiom and its details need not detain us here, but what it implies is that the excess of the power set, or in more general terms, the excess of inclusion over belonging, is brought under control or restricted by a well-defined language. The axiom of constructability admits only those parts of a multiple that "can be separated out (in the sense of the axiom of separation) by properties which are themselves stated in explicit formulas whose field of application, parameters, and quantifiers are solely referred to [the multiple] itself" (BE 297). It is on this basis that Gödel could claim to show the viability of CH from within the confines of the axiomatic system: the limitation of the excess of inclusion to clearly defined parts assures that one can move from the smallest infinite cardinal number to its successor without remainder. For this reason, Gödel's "constructible universe" proposes a "hierarchy of being, the constructible hierarchy" (BE 296, 298). In Badiou's terms, because it attempts to achieve equilibrium between belonging and inclusion through a well-defined language, the theory of constructible sets corresponds to a normal situation, a situation whose structure is re-secured *in toto* by its state or metastructure: "*the state succeeds the situation*" (BE 308, original emphasis).

However, as Badiou points out, constructability "is *merely* a possible property for a multiple" (BE 299, original emphasis). We have already mentioned that for Badiou there are other situations besides normal situations, namely those that are singular or excrescent. But where Cohen becomes important for Badiou is in Cohen's formulation of a model of set theory in which CH did not hold. Cohen devised set-theoretical models "which contained sets other than constructible sets but which were still denumerable models" (Tiles 1989: 185). As mentioned above, a constructible set is constructible on the basis of well-defined properties; a constructible set requires a well-defined language that sets limits on the parts that are included. But as Tiles points out, intuitively speaking "there is no reason to suppose that every set is definable by a condition which all its members must satisfy" (*ibid.*: 186). In set-theoretical terms, the axiom of extensionality assures that the legitimacy of belonging to a set rests on belonging alone, and has nothing to do with a multiple possessing this or that property, a point that is fundamental to Badiou's ontology, as we discussed in the previous chapter. Because of this, "the powerset of w should include all possible collections of w whether there is a defining condition or not" (*ibid.*). Cohen called these other, nonconstructible, sets generic sets, and for Badiou they designate the point of "the indiscernible, the absolutely indeterminate, which is to say a multiple that in a given situation solely possesses properties which are more or less common to all the multiples in the situation" (BE 356).

We can only give a cursory overview of Cohen's strategy, here. Suffice it to say that what Cohen did was to take a model of set theory, M, that would include all the sets generated by its axioms, or all constructible sets. Since M, however, includes only constructible sets, its selection of possible subsets is limited: it does not include all possible subsets of $\aleph_0$. In order to attain a larger model, a model that would include nonconstructible or generic sets, Cohen held that it was possible to introduce an infinite subset α of M that did not correspond to the defined properties of M, creating an extended model N. How, though, is it possible to speak of α at all if it does not correspond to the defined properties of M? We can speak initially of the elements of α by creating a list of statements that refer to the property of belonging alone. As Sam Gillespie summarizes the matter:

> The simplest way of speaking of such a denumerable subset would be to *list* each element that could belong to α. These terms that will be listed will be made from within M, so the goal is to see if, to each term, there corresponds an element that belongs to α. That is, for each member of the denumerable infinite subset α, there will be a list of successive statements about the elements that belong to α or not.   (Gillespie 2008: 83, original emphasis)

Since the creation of this list refers to belonging alone, it avoids the conditions imposed in M on constructible sets. Nevertheless, if this list can only be made within M, how do we know whether or not these elements exist in α? The problem is, as Gillespie points out, that we can only have knowledge of the elements of α from the perspective of N, the extended model that includes α, but "we can only arrive at N through constructing α from within M" (*ibid.*: 84).

It is at this apparent impasse that Cohen's notion of forcing comes in. If the nonconstructible or generic set is to have validity for the extension of M to N, there has to be a means of deciding whether or not elements belong to α. Because N is infinite, we cannot create an exhaustive list of those elements that belong to α or not. We can, however, posit a minimal condition P that will force an answer to belonging, and thus make N a valid and coherent extension of M from within M:

- P *forces* $\eta \in \alpha_\delta$ ($\eta \notin \alpha_\delta$) to be true if $\eta \in \alpha_\delta$ ($\eta \notin \alpha_\delta$) is one of the conditions in P.

- P *forces* $\chi \notin \alpha_8$ to be true if χ is not in ω. (Tiles 1989: 188)

This procedure can be extended to give further, yet incomplete, information about new infinite sets. Although the technical aspects of this extension are difficult, the point is that "if the statements in M are denumerable, then so too ... is the set of conditions in G [the generic set]" (Gillespie 2008: 84). Cohen's method of forcing, then, does not produce an immediate or direct knowledge of these generic sets; rather, such knowledge always takes place within an anticipatory horizon. In Badiou's words:

> The crucial point, which Paul Cohen settled in the realm of ontology, i.e. of mathematics, is the following: you certainly cannot straightforwardly name the elements of a generic subset, since the latter is at once incomplete in its infinite composition and subtracted from every predicate which would directly identify it in the language. But you can maintain that *if* such and such an element *will have been* in the supposedly complete generic subset, *then* such and such a statement, rationally connectable to the element in question, is, or rather will have been, correct.
> (TW 127, original emphasis)

Now, if it is possible to force an extended model of set theory N, then this also means that it is possible to produce models of set theory in which CH does not hold, since the consistency of CH depends on limiting sets to constructible sets. That is, if we can delineate nonconstructible or generic sets that are in excess of the language of M, then there is nothing in this language to fix the value of the continuum. As Hallward puts it, "The conditions enumerated in G will allow for the distinction of $\aleph_2$, $\aleph_3$, or even $\aleph_{102}$ worth of new subsets α_η. As far as we can tell from the model M, the value of the continuum might be almost anything" (Hallward 2003: 347). What Cohen's demonstration established, then, was not the value of the continuum as such but the independence of CH from the axiom system. Once nonconstructible or generic sets are admitted, then from within this system it becomes impossible to assign an exact measure to the excess of the power set. This rational excess of infinity is, as we discussed in the previous chapter, central to Badiou's ontology. More importantly, however, is Badiou's claim that Cohen's notions of the generic and forcing found the being of truths.

Returning now to the relationship between fidelity and truth, Badiou sets the concept of the generic within a distinction between truth and knowledge, a distinction that largely corresponds, mathematically speaking, to Cohen's generic sets and Gödel's constructible sets. Knowledge, according to Badiou, takes the form of the object. As Badiou puts it, "*Knowledge* is the capacity to discern multiples within the situation which possess this or that property; properties that can be indicated by explicit language or phrases, or sets of phrases. The rule of knowledge is always a criterion of exact nomination" (BE 328, original emphasis). The goal of knowledge is to achieve an encyclopedic summation of the situation, by stabilizing the relationship between belonging and inclusion in a well-defined language for the situation. On the one hand, at the level of belonging, or presentation, knowledge attempts to discern "the connection between language and presented or presentable realities" (ibid.). On the other hand, at the level of inclusion, or representation, knowledge attempts to classify "the connection between the language and the parts of the situation, the multiples of multiples" (ibid.). Knowledge can certainly increase or even change, but because its goal is to achieve an encyclopedic determination of the situation through a well-defined language, Badiou does not associate knowledge with novelty but with repetition (IT 61). The equation of knowledge with repetition is correlative to the idea of modification in *Logics of Worlds*, which we discussed previously in relation to the notion of change. Such is the status of Gödel's constructible sets, but we can also illustrate this point by referring back to the example of the French Revolution. Badiou certainly treats the French Revolution as an event, in the sense mentioned above, but it is also possible to treat it according to the dictates of knowledge, by simply providing a historical catalogue of all the terms of the epoch, without taking into account the manner in which the Revolution belongs to itself. Such knowledge is, to be clear, not necessarily a bad thing – indeed, a truth produces its own knowledge – but "it may well lead to the one of the event being undone to the point of being no more than the forever infinite numbering of the gestures, things, and words that coexisted with it" (BE 180). Because the name of the event is supernumerary with respect to its situation, it is "foreclosed from knowledge ... the event does not fall under any encyclopedic determinant" (BE 329). In contrast to the repetition of knowledge, then, a truth for Badiou is always "something new" (IT 45) with respect to its situation, meaning that it does not fall under the categories of the existing knowledge of the situation. A truth is, properly speaking, subtracted from the knowledge of the situation. As Badiou puts it, "a truth is always that which makes a hole in knowledge" (BE 327).

Given the distinction between truth and knowledge, how does the faithful production of a generic truth proceed? If truth is, strictly speaking, subtracted from the knowledge of the situation, at what point can the faithful procedure take hold in the situation? The problem is to discern the multiples in the situation connected to the event, outside of the knowledge governing the situation. A faithful procedure will thus constitute *another mode of discernment*: one which, outside knowledge but within the effect of an interventional nomination, explores connections to the supernumerary name of the event" (BE 329, original emphasis). In so far as fidelity does its work in relation to the parts of the situation not included in the normal knowledge of the situation – the evental site, the event itself and its name, the intervention, evental recurrence, and so on – it represents a mode of discernment different from that represented by the knowledge of the situation. Fidelity proceeds, then, by making a series of enquiries into the situation, in effect filtering the apparent complexity of the situation through two values: connection or non-connection. A faithful procedure seeks to determine whether "a multiple either is or is not within the field of effects entailed by the introduction into circulation of a supernumerary name" (BE 330). Badiou describes this "minimal gesture of fidelity" as an "encounter" (*ibid.*), an encounter between a multiple and the operator of fidelity that determines whether or not that multiple is connected to the name of the event. What fidelity to an event will produce, at an abstract level, is a string of statements or "minimal reports" that groups together the multiples connected to the event, mobilizing them in the production of a truth. For this reason, a procedure of fidelity resembles knowledge. In Badiou's words:

> [J]ust like knowledge, an enquiry is the conjunction of a discernment – such a multiple of the situation possesses the property of being connected to the event (to its name) – and a classification – this is the class of connected multiples, and that is the class of non-connected multiples … It is the enquiry which lies behind the *resemblance* of the procedure of fidelity *to a knowledge*.
> (BE 330–31, original emphasis)

Although this clarifies, at a formal level, how a procedure of fidelity proceeds in constructing a truth, the question still remains as to how we can distinguish knowledge, the capacity to discern and name multiples with respect to the encyclopedic determinant of the situation, from the procedure of fidelity, the concern of which is to determine and name multiples with respect to the event. To use a different terminology, how do we distinguish "veridical" statements, statements already controlled by an existing knowledge, from "true" statements, statements connected to the name of the event and controlled by a procedure of fidelity? For a finite situation, such a distinction is, as Badiou points out, impossible to make: if every faithful enquiry is a finite part of the situation, and every finite part of the situation is classified by knowledge, then "the results of an enquiry *coincide* with an encyclopedic determinant" (BE 331, original emphasis). If taken in finite terms, "an enquiry *cannot discern the true from the veridical*: its true-result is at the same time already constituted as belonging to the situation" (BE 332, original emphasis).

The initial way out of this apparent bind is to associate the true with the infinite against its finite determination: "*A* truth (if it exists) must be an infinite part of the situation, because for every finite part one can always say that it has *already* been discerned and classified by knowledge" (BE 333, original emphasis). However, although it is necessary to locate truth on the side of the infinite, this in and of itself is not a sufficient condition to distinguish the true from the veridical. Indeed, one of the results of the ontological decision on infinity, its rationalization, is to make the infinite coextensive with knowledge. As Badiou puts it:

> Knowledge ... moves easily amongst the infinite classes of multiples which fall under an encyclopedic determinant. Statements such as "the whole numbers form an infinite set," or "the infinite nuances of the sentiment of love" can be held without difficulty to be veridical in this or that domain of knowledge.   (*Ibid.*)

So how does one proceed? If a faithful procedure exists, it must avoid the encyclopedic determination of the situation. What is then required is a condition that would allow one to discern a set of terms connected to the event that are not also determined by the knowledge of the situation. However, as Badiou points out, this condition cannot be formulated directly, "because this set is always to-come (being infinite) and moreover, it is randomly composed by the trajectories of the enquiry" (BE 336).

It is at this point that Badiou's deployment of Cohen's notions of the generic and forcing come into play, to found the being of the faithful procedure and the production of truth. As we discussed above, Cohen was able to indicate the existence of generic sets, sets that did not correspond to the defined properties of the universe of constructible sets. These generic sets are, in Badiou's words, "subtracted from every predicate which would identify it in the language" (TW 127). In other words, the generic is a "part" of the situation "unnameable by the resources of the language of the situation alone. It is subtracted from any knowledge; it has not been already-counted by any of the domains of knowledge, nor will be, if the language remains in the same state – or remains *that of* the State. This part, in which a truth inscribes its procedure as infinite result, is an *indiscernible of the situation*" (BE 338, original emphasis). Since the generic falls outside the knowledge of the situation, the most one can say about it, at least immediately, is that "its elements *are*", in the sense that it "has no other 'property' than that of referring to *belonging*" (BE 339, original emphasis). However, based on this assumption, it is possible to force or anticipate information or knowledge about generic sets, in effect making them available for the production of truth. Such knowledge, however, exists primarily in the mode of the future anterior, as an anticipation of knowledge: "Forcing is the point at which a truth, although incomplete, authorizes anticipations of knowledge concerning not what is but *what will have been if truth attains completion*" (TW 127, original emphasis).

This admittedly abstract conception should become clearer when we turn to Badiou's notion of the subject in the next section. Nevertheless, a simple example may help to clarify the matter a bit at this point. Within the framework of Newtonian astronomy, it is possible, based on perturbations in the trajectory of certain planets, to make the following claim: "An as yet unobserved planet distorts the trajectories by gravitational attraction" (BE 402). The statement clearly does not immediately correspond to a term represented in the knowledge of the situation, since the planet is not (yet) observable. However, mathematical calculation, which here functions as the operator of faithful connection, can force new knowledge in the situation, even if the planet cannot yet be represented by the existing knowledge. If such a planet is discovered, then the statement will have been veridical for the situation of Newtonian astronomy, and thus retroactively true.

Before moving on to discuss Badiou's understanding of the subject, which he understands in formal terms as the bearer of a particular truth process, we should pause and consider what has been discussed thus far in light of a more theological understanding of faith. It has been suggested by some critics that Badiou's notion of fidelity, as we have discussed it above, seems close to a more religious, specifically Christian, conception of faith. Jean-Jacques Lecercle, for instance, in a review of the main elements of Badiou's ontology in *Being and Event*, asks rhetorically, "Is not faithfulness close to faith, as the French '*fidélité*' is close to '*les fidèles*'?" (Lecercle 1999: 8; see also Critchley 2005b). If we take Badiou at his word and, in turn, isolate the notions of fidelity and forcing, then it should be clear that Badiou's notion of fidelity is, like his ontology, mathematically determined, at least on the surface. Fidelity does not refer to a capacity, quality or virtue; it is rather an operation, a rule-governed procedure always particular to an event. Moreover, Badiou himself claims that he draws the notion of fidelity from love, from the amorous truth procedure:

> The word "fidelity" refers directly to the amorous relationship, but I would rather say that it is the amorous relationship which refers, at the most sensitive point of individual experience, to the dialectic of being and event, the dialectic whose temporal ordination is proposed by fidelity. Indeed, it is evident that love – what is called love – founds itself upon an intervention, and thus on a nomination, near a void summoned by an encounter.[7]
>
> (BE 232)

However, if we understand the notions of fidelity and forcing from within a broader context – a context that takes into account the event, intervention, nomination, evental recurrence and, as we will see in the next section, the role that belief or confidence plays in the constitution of the subject and the notion of resurrection – then it becomes difficult to maintain that Badiou's account of the production of truths has nothing to do with a theological understanding of faith. We could even say that a particular conception of the latter determines to some extent Badiou's understanding of the evental production of truths, even if Badiou often hesitates to admit this directly. We will discuss how and to what extent this is the case in Chapter 4, but for now we can simply note that, when Badiou discusses the notions of intervention and evental recurrence in *Being and Event*, the appeal is not to the amorous relationship but to theology, more specifically Pascalian Christianity (see BE 212–22). It is hard to see how an appeal to the necessity of a "wager" in *Being and Event* – and, as we will see in Chapter 4, the Kierkegaardian leap of faith in *Logics of Worlds* and Paul's notions of faith and grace in *Saint Paul: The Foundation of Universalism* – represents anything but a reliance on a particular theological conception of faith in the matter of truths. If this is the case – and I believe it is – then what I have referred to as Badiou's anti-theology in Chapter 1 is a more complicated affair, particularly when it comes to understanding the production of truths and the role of the subject in the latter, to which we now turn.

THE SUBJECT

Having discussed the main elements of his formal theory of truth, we can now move on to an explication of Badiou's understanding of the subject. Badiou's notion of the subject is inextricably linked to the process of the construction of truth. To begin with, however, it is worth separating Badiou's notion of the subject from other, commonly held notions to which it is opposed. At the most basic level, it is important to note that Badiou's subject does not immediately correspond to the human individual. Subjects certainly presuppose the activity of individuals, but there is in Badiou's theory no one-to-one relationship between them. This gap between individuals and subjects rules out thinking of the subject in finite terms, as a category of morality, a locus or register of experience, or an ideological fiction. We can take each of these in turn.

First, concerning the subject as a category of morality, it does not matter for Badiou if it is the (neo-)Kantian subject of human rights or the Levinasian subject that underpins the "ethics of difference": both tend to flatten the subject "onto the empirical manifestness of the living body. What deserves respect is the animal body as such" (LW 48; cf. E 4–29). Conceiving the subject primarily in moral terms ultimately reduces the human being to "the status of victim, of suffering beast, of emaciated, dying body, [it] equates man with his animal substructure, it reduces him to the level of a living organism, pure and simple" (E 11). These claims are, perhaps, a bit overdrawn, but Badiou's main point is that understanding the subject as a category of morality confines the subject to finitude, to the limitations constitutive of individual human beings. The reduction of the subject to finitude is part and parcel of what Badiou pejoratively refers to in *Logics of Worlds* as "democratic materialism", whose axiom is: "There are only bodies and languages" (LW 1). Democratic materialism, and the subject that corresponds to it, takes as its horizon "the dogma of our finitude, of our carnal exposition to enjoyment, suffering and death" (*ibid.*). The claim that "there are only bodies and languages" amounts to little more than a "bio-materialism" that reduces "humanity to an overstretched vision of animality" (LW 2).

Second, if the subject is not a category of morality, it is also not "a register of experience, a schema for the conscious distribution of the reflexive and the non-reflexive; this thesis conjoins subject and consciousness and is deployed today as phenomenology" (LW 48). The phenomenological or existential subject is, as Badiou points out, irrevocably bound to meaning, to the circulation of sense. It does, to be sure, exercise a transcendental function in relation to experience, but this subject can only conceive of the infinite as a horizon, as a negative correlate of the immediacy of its own essential finitude (BE 391). Moreover, if we accept Badiou's conflation of "religion" with "everything that presupposes continuity between truths and the circulation of sense" (MP 143), then the phenomenological or existential subject is at bottom a religious subject. It is little surprise, then, that the so-called "turn to religion" in philosophy is bound up with the continental phenemonological tradition (see Janicaud *et al.* 2001). Badiou, however, has little time for such things: philosophy's task is not to resurrect religion and its dispositions; rather, as we have discussed, it must proclaim God's death more forcefully than ever, even if this proclamation goes against the current fascination with religion's apparent return.

Third, although Badiou rejects conceiving the subject in either moral or existential terms, this does not lead him to reduce the subject to a mere ideological fiction, an "interpellation" of the state and its apparatuses, as Louis Althusser thought (Althusser 2001). At both the political and the ontological level, the state certainly reproduces itself through various ideologies and their mechanisms. But strictly speaking the state exerts this pressure through the re-presentation of individuals, which latter, we have said, do not correspond to subjects for Badiou.

In contrast to these three broad understandings of the subject, Badiou's subject is a formal category. Badiou's subject is "any local configuration of a generic procedure from which a truth is supported" (BE 391); the subject is for Badiou the "*local* status of a procedure, a configuration in excess of the situation" (BE 392, original emphasis). Recall that, in *Being and Event*, the institution of a generic procedure requires, on the one hand, the introduction of the event into the situation through interventional naming and, on the other hand, the operator of faithful connection that situates multiples with respect to the name of the event. It is the operator of connection that "rules the procedure and institutes the truth" (*ibid.*). Badiou refers to the emergence of the operator of connection attendant upon interventional nomination "subjectivization", and, in this sense, it is subjectivization that makes possible the construction of a truth. The subject is, then, "neither the intervention nor the operator of fidelity, but the advent of their Two, that is, the incorporation of the event into the situation in the mode of a generic procedure" (BE 393). Otherwise put, the subject for Badiou is "the process of liaison between the event (thus the intervention) and the procedure of fidelity (thus its operator of connection)" (BE 239). Badiou often uses the language of "encounter" to describe the relationship of the subject to the generic procedure. Thus Badiou says, "If we consider the local status of a generic procedure, we notice that it depends on a simple encounter. Once the name of the event is fixed, e_x, both the minimal gestures of the faithful procedure, positive ... or negative ... and the enquiries, finite sets of such gestures, depend on the terms of the situation encountered by the procedure" (BE 395). To give one more example, "And if it is true that a truth is an exception to what there is, if we consider that, when given the 'occasion' to encounter it, we immediately recognize it as such" (LW 6).

I will return to Badiou's use of the language of "encounter" in Chapter 4. For now we can simply note that there is no direct or immediate correspondence between the subject and the generic procedure itself. The subject, to be sure, is the local status of the generic procedure; the subject, in this sense, is what makes truth possible in a situation. However, because the generic procedure is, by definition, infinite, the subject can in no way exhaust the possibilities of the generic procedure itself. The generic procedure, because it is infinite, is in excess over its local, subjective configuration, meaning that the subject can only ever approximate truths in situations. "Every truth is transcendent to the subject," Badiou writes, "precisely because the latter's entire being resides in supporting the realization of truth" (BE 397).

How can the subject, which is local and finite, even begin to approximate truths, if these are both generic, not discernible in the language of the situation, and infinite? Badiou expresses the difficulty implied in this question as follows:

> [A] subject, which realizes a truth, is nevertheless incommensurable with the latter, because the subject is finite and the truth is infinite. Moreover, the subject, being internal to the situation, can only know, or rather encounter, terms or multiples presented (counted as one) in that situation. Yet a truth is an un-presented part of the situation. Finally, the subject cannot *make a language* out of anything except combinations of the supernumerary name

of the event and the language of the situation. It is in no way guaranteed that this language will suffice for the discernment of a truth, which, in any case, is indiscernible for the resources of the language of the situation alone.   (BE 396, original emphasis)

Badiou attempts to solve this apparent difficulty by resting the relationship between the subject and the generic trajectory of an infinite truth that it supports on belief or confidence: "the subject believes that there is a truth, and this belief occurs in the form of knowledge. I term this knowing belief *confidence*" (BE 397, original emphasis).

Because a truth is infinite, its status is always, to a certain degree, to come, suspended into the future. A truth only exists in the mode of the "future anterior": a truth "will have been presented" (BE 400). Since a generic procedure takes place under the mode of the future anterior, then, conversely and strictly speaking, knowledge of a truth is always retroactive, meaning that it can be partially grasped only through the positing of provisional results. The same goes, as we have seen, for the event itself: an event, as undecidable, "is only recognized in the situation by its consequences", meaning that "there will have been some chance in the situation" (BE 207). For Badiou confidence on the part of the subject, it seems, is just to adopt the mode of the future anterior as constitutive of fidelity, understood as the set of procedures that discern multiples or terms connected to the name of the event. Thus, speaking of confidence, Badiou states, "This 'to come' is the distinctive feature of the subject who judges. Here, belief is what-is-to-come, or the future, under the *name* of truth" (BE 397, original emphasis). Confidence or belief "represents the genericity of the true as detained in the local finitude of the stages of its journey" (*ibid.*). If, in the end, the truth of a generic procedure is only legible retroactively, the subject, under the mode of the future anterior, is the anticipation of this retroaction. The subject "does not coincide with the retroactive discernibility of its results", but is, rather, "confidence in itself", which assures that "the operator of faithful connection does not gather together the chance of the encounters in vain" (*ibid.*).

For this reason, the subject of a generic procedure is simultaneously situated "inside" and "outside" the situation. On the one hand, confidence or belief takes the form of the knowledge of the situation, since the subject must necessarily use the language of the situation to produce terms that connect multiples to the name of the event. Badiou uses the examples of "faith", "charity", "sacrifice" and "salvation" for Saint Paul; "party", "revolution" and "politics" for Lenin; and "sets", "ordinals" and "cardinals" for Cantor (*ibid.*). These terms are, of course, presented in the established language governing the respective situations of Saint Paul, Lenin and Cantor. Paul, for instance, uses the language of "faith", "charity", "sacrifice" and "salvation", precisely because these terms are available to him in the milieu of first-century

Judaism. However, the use of these terms does not merely reduplicate the knowledge of the situation, because the terms *"do not, in general, have a referent in the situation"* (BE 398, original emphasis). That is, the terms themselves circulate in the knowledge of the situation, but since these terms refer to the name of the event and the generic procedure, their sense undergoes an anticipatory shift: the meaning of these terms "'will have been' presented in a *new* situation" (*ibid.*, original emphasis). As Badiou puts it:

> With the resources of the situation, with its multiples, its language, the subject generates names whose referent is in the future anterior: this is what supports belief. Such names "will have been" assigned a referent, or a signification, when the situation will have appeared in which the indiscernible – which is only represented (or included) – is finally presented as a truth of the first situation. (*Ibid.*)

Of course, from the perspective of the situation, the use of these terms will either appear redundant or, since the terms lack a referent in the situation, "empty", imaginary parts of "an arbitrary and content-free language" (*ibid.*). But for those "caught up" in a generic procedure of truth, the lack of an exact referent in the situation is precisely what sustains belief or confidence. Because of this, "Every subject can thus be recognized by the emergence of a language which is internal to the situation, but whose referent-multiples are *subject to the condition* of an as yet incomplete generic part" (*ibid.*, original emphasis).

The language that the subject uses to indicate the parts of the emerging generic procedure, then, is always and necessarily conditional, "suspended from the unfinishable condition of a truth" (BE 399). The names that the subject uses are thus not primarily representative in function, since truth, as something that is always to come, is strictly speaking incalculable. Rather, they take the form of hypotheses concerning the future of a truth, hypotheses that are only ruled by the faithful encounter of terms indexed to the name of the event. Again, the structure here is that of the future anterior:

> *if* this or that term, when it will have been encountered, turns out to be positively connected to the event, *then* this or that name will probably have such a referent, because the generic part, which remains indiscernible in the situation, will have this or that configuration, or partial property. (*Ibid.*, original emphasis)

Otherwise put, the names that the subject uses to effect a finite configuration of a generic procedure "*displace* established significations and leave the referent void: this void will have been filled if truth comes to pass in a new situation (the kingdom of God, an emancipated society, absolute mathematics, a new order of music comparable to the tonal order, an entirely amorous life, etc.)" (*ibid.*, original emphasis). For this reason, Badiou says that the subject of a generic procedure is:

> by the grace of names, both the *real* of the procedure (the enquiring of the enquiries) and the *hypothesis* that its unfinishable result will introduce some newness in the situation. A subject emptily names a universe to come which is obtained by the supplementation of the situation with an indiscernible truth.
>
> (*Ibid.*, original emphasis)

If the names that correspond to the generic procedure are empty in the situation, suspended in the mode of the future anterior, what criteria are available to the subject to judge whether or not these names actually designate something new? What assures that the operations of the subject hit their mark, so to speak, in the generic procedure? Of course, there can be no ultimate guarantee, since the generic procedure is lawless, aleatory in its trajectory. This is why confidence or belief is required as a means of assuring "that the operator of faithful connection does not gather together the chance of the encounters in vain" (BE 397). Key to assuring that belief does not lapse into sheer fideism is Badiou's philosophical deployment of Cohen's notion of forcing, which allows the subject to gain a limited amount of knowledge from within the current situation about the new situation to come. Forcing, in this sense, is "the law of the subject", or, what amounts to the same thing, "the law of the future anterior" (BE 401).

Forcing, as the law of the subject, allows the subject to gain a limited amount of knowledge from within the current situation about the situation to come. As indicated above, the referents of the language that the subject uses to demarcate the process of the generic procedure are under the law of the future anterior. This law, which is also the law of the subject, amounts to the following: "if a statement of the subject-language is such that it will have been veridical for a situation in which a truth has occurred, this is because *a* term of the situation exists which both belongs to that truth (belongs to the generic part which *is* the truth) and maintains a particular relation with the names at stake in the statement" (*ibid.*). Since these names do occur in the situation, the subject-language of the generic procedure is, to a certain extent, determined by the knowledge of the situation: the ultimate sense of these names in a new, generic situation is suspended in the mode of the future anterior. Nevertheless, because of this dual referentiality of the subject-language, Badiou argues that it is possible to know in a post-evental situation "whether a statement of the subject-language has a chance of being veridical in the situation which adds to the initial situation a truth of the latter" (*ibid.*). What is required for such knowledge is the existence of at least "*one* term linked to the statement in question by a relation that is itself discernible in the situation" (*ibid.*, original emphasis). If the existence of such a term can be verified, then this term will be said to force the veracity of the initial statement for the situation to come, with the new situation configured along the lines of the generic procedure of truth.

Now, Badiou's conception of the subject so outlined rests on a distinction between subjects and non-subjects: there are those who are faithful to the event, working in confidence to force a generic truth, and those who fall outside the trajectory of the generic procedure. So much is implied, when Badiou says that the terms of the generic procedure can and often do appear "empty" from the perspective of the situation. To be sure, Badiou does seem to recognize in *Being and Event* that the issue is far more complex. As he points out in Meditation 23, which is concerned with fidelity, there can be different fidelities to the same event in the same situation. For instance, "At the empirical level, we know that there are many manners of being faithful to an event: Stalinists and Trotskyists both proclaimed their fidelity to the event of October 1917, but they massacred each other" (BE 234). However, Badiou does not work this claim out in any detail, opting instead for a more formal analysis that focuses only on the operator of connection involved in all faithful procedures. However, in *Logics of Worlds*, Badiou modifies his theory of the subject to include three formal, subjective types (faithful, reactive and obscure) that organize a relation to a post-eventual truth in the present in four destinations (production, denial, occultation, resurrection).

The faithful subject, whose destination is the production of truth in the present, corresponds to the subject as outlined in *Being and Event*, which we have been discussing. The other two subjective types – the reactive subject and the obscure subject – add a new complexity to Badiou's theory of the subject, to explain how a truth procedure gets abandoned, rejected or opposed.[8] The reactive subject, according to Badiou, consists in a negation of the event and the drawing of its consequences. Importantly, however, this negation does not rest on a simple opposition between the old and the new; it is not merely the case that the reactive subject says no to the possible novelty opened up by the event, so as to maintain the old – the way things were – against the new. Although Badiou tends to think along these lines in his earlier work and, to a certain extent, in *Being and Event*, in *Logics of Worlds* Badiou stresses that the reactive subject "is the contemporary of the present to which it reacts" (LW 54). That is, in order to counteract the potential novelty of the event, the reactive subject must "create arguments of resistance appropriate to the novelty itself" (*ibid.*). Like the faithful subject, then, the reactive subject does claim to produce something new in the present. But this novelty is not "the affirmative and glorious present of the faithful subject" but rather an "extinguished present", "a measured present, a negative present, a present 'a little less worse' than the past, if only because it resisted the catastrophic temptation which the reactive subject declares is contained in the event" (LW 55). To illustrate the reactive subject, Badiou uses the example of the *nouveaux philosophes*, who in the early 1970s traded in their leftist credentials "in the name of democracy and human rights, a counter-revolutionary restoration, an unbridled capitalism and, finally, the brutal hegemony of the USA" (*ibid.*). Indeed, it seems that in so far as the reactive subject has as its destination the denial of truth, it just is the subject of democratic materialism, which rests on the axiom: "There are only bodies and languages" (LW 1). Nevertheless, because the reactive subject takes its place vis-à-vis the faithful subject, the latter remains as the former's repressed content: the faithful subject "remains the unconscious of the reactive subject" (LW 55).

Whereas the destination of the reactive subject is to deny the present of the faithful subject through its own, attenuated version of the present, the destination of the obscure subject is rather "the abolition of the new present, considered in its entirety as malevolent and *de jure* inexistent" (LW 59). Like the reactive subject, at first glance it seems that the obscure subject rests on the simple opposition between the old and the new. The obscure subject would, from this perspective, consist merely in the conservation of the previous situation. But the apparent conservation of the previous situation always takes place in light of the potential novelty of post-evental fidelity, as the occultation of the present. There is thus an important distinction to be made between the reactive subject and the obscure subject. The reactive subject, to be sure, denies the event, but not the present itself: it opts for an attenuated or moderate present that considers the event and its consequences useless, even dangerous. The obscure subject, in contrast, aims at the destruction of the present itself through the occultation of the truth of the event. Hence, in order to raze the present, the reactive subject often calls upon "an atemporal fetish: the incorruptible and invisible over-body, be it City, God, or Race. Similarly, Fate for love, the True without admissible image for art and Revelation for science correspond to the three types of obscure subject which are possessive fusion, iconoclasm and obscurantism" (LW 60). As an example of the obscure subject, Badiou points to "political Islamism":

> This political Islamism represents a new instrumentalization of religion – from which it does not derive by a natural (or "rational") lineage – with the purpose of occulting the post-socialist present and countering the fragmentary attempts through which emancipation is being reinvented by means of a full Tradition or Law. From this point of view, political Islamism is absolutely contemporary, both to the faithful subjects that produce the present of political experimentation and to the reactive subjects that busy

> themselves with denying that ruptures are necessary in order to invent a humanity worthy of the name – reactive subjects that parade the established order as the miraculous bearer of uninterrupted emancipation. Political Islamism is simply one of the subjectivated names of today's obscurantism. (LW 59)

Similar claims could be made regarding other forms of fundamentalism as well (see TO 26–7). Nevertheless, the appeal of the obscure subject, it seems, can be found in its attempt to invoke some sort of transcendent principle (e.g., City, God, Race, Law, Tradition) to give meaning in, but against, the present. Thus "to the hodgepodge of ordinary existence the obscure subject offers the chance of a new destiny, under the incomprehensible and salvific sign of an absolute body, whose only demand is that one serves it by nurturing everywhere and at all times the hatred of every living thought, every transparent language and every uncertain becoming" (LW 61).

As this typology of the three subjective forms – faithful, reactive, obscure – suggests, the faithful subject is primary: "the contemporaneousness of a figure of the reactive or obscure type depends on the minimal production of the present by a faithful figure" (LW 62). There is thus "a certain order" implied in the articulation of subjective types, in that "the denial of the present supposes its production, and its occultation supposes a formula of denial" (*ibid.*). What Badiou wants to emphasize by grounding the faithful subject as the presupposition for both the reactive and obscure subjective types is the affirmative character of truth, the novelty of its production. To make the faithful subject secondary to either the reactive subject or the obscure subject, it seems, would confine the production of the truth of the present to pre-established forms, as merely the negation or subversion of these. To use the language of *Being and Event*, this would confine the operations of the faithful subject to the state of the situation.

Nevertheless, this schema remains incomplete. There is in *Logics of Worlds* another type of faithful subject that has as its destination the "resurrection" of a truth. The theological overtones of the name of this subjective type should be obvious, and it is something that we will analyse in more detail in Chapter 4. For now we only need to point out that the denial and/or occultation of a truth is never a done deal: "of no truth can it be said, under the pretext that its historical world has disintegrated, that it is lost forever" (LW 66). According to Badiou, it is always possible to resurrect a truth that has been lost in a different context, making this truth available for the generation of a new truth procedure. Badiou describes the destination of resurrection in the following terms:

> We will call this destination, which reactivates a subject in another logic of its appearing-in-truth *resurrection*. Of course, a

resurrection presupposes a new world, which generates the context for a new event, a new trace, a new body – in short, a truth-
procedure under whose rule the occulted fragment places itself
after having been extracted from its occultation.

(LW 65, original emphasis)

Now, although the name "resurrection" is new, the idea itself, it seems, is
implied in Badiou's understanding of the relationship between intervention
and evental recurrence, discussed above.[9] Moreover, although he does not
refer explicitly to the notion of resurrection in his discussion of Pascal in
Meditation 22 of *Being and Event*, the idea is present, when Badiou states:

Pascal's particular genius lies in his attempt to renovate and
maintain the evental kernel of Christian conviction under the
absolutely modern and unheard of conditions created by the
advent of the subject of science. Pascal saw quite clearly that
these conditions would end up ruining the demonstrative or
rational edifice that the medieval fathers had elaborated as the
architecture of belief. He illuminated the paradox that at the very
moment in which science finally legislated upon nature via demonstration, the Christian God could only remain at the centre of
subjective experience if it belonged to an entirely different logic,
if the 'proofs of the existence of God' were abandoned, and if the
pure evental force of faith were restituted.   (BE 214)

Indeed, as we will see in Chapter 4, this notion of resurrection is important
for considering Badiou's own reading of *Saint Paul* and the relationship of
Badiou's philosophy to theology in general.

Before concluding this chapter, it is worth dwelling for a moment on the
formal ethical limits that Badiou imposes on subjects and the production
of truths. What is it that keeps Badiou's militant theory of truth, resting as
it does on the mode of the future anterior, from going astray, from devolv-
ing into disaster and terror? Indeed, it is the risk of disaster and terror that
forms, at least in part, the reactive subject against the faithful subject. In
light of this concern, it is important to distinguish between truth and what
Badiou refers to as a "simulacrum of truth" (E 73), which is formally similar
to truth. Specifically, a simulacrum of truth rests on a break with the situation, perceived as an event, nomination of that "event", the construction
of a fidelity, the advent of a subject, and so on. Indeed, like the process of
truth, a simulacrum of truth proceeds on a "more or less militant, combat-
ive" trajectory (E 75). The key difference between truth and a simulacrum
of truth lies in the place of the void. Whereas a procedure of truth relates
to its situation from the void of its being, a relationship sustained by the

evental nomination, a simulacrum of truth conceives of the event in terms of plenitude and substance. Practically speaking, the difference amounts to the difference between the real universality of truth versus conceiving of that universality along the lines of a closed particularity. As Badiou puts it in reference to Nazism:

> Fidelity to a simulacrum, unlike fidelity to an event, regulates its break with the situation not by the universality of the void, but by the closed particularity of an abstract set [*ensemble*] (the "Germans" or the "Aryans"). Its invariable operation is the unending construction of this set, and it has no other means of doing this than that of "voiding" what surrounds it. The void, "avoided" [*chasse*] by the simulacrous promotion of an "event-substance", here returns, with its universality, as what must be accomplished in order that this substance can be. This is to say that what is addressed to "everyone" (and "everyone", here, is necessarily that which does not belong to the German communitarian substance – for this substance is not an "everyone" but, rather, some "few" who dominate "everyone") is death, or that deferred form of death which is slavery in the service of the German substance.   (E 74)

Thus a simulacrum of a truth has as its content "war and massacre", which "make up the very real of such a fidelity" (*ibid.*).

Although, technically speaking, all that a simulacrum of truth shares with a real truth is the latter's form, meaning that it falls outside truth as such, a truth procedure itself can go wrong if it assumes that its power is total. As we discussed above, a truth proceeds through the invention of a new subject language, based on the terms of the situation. The "power" of a truth, in this sense, "forces the pragmatic namings (the language of the objective situation) to bend and change shape upon contact with the subject-language" (E 82–3). In contrast, to assume that truth exercises a total power implies "the ability to name and evaluate *all* the elements of the objective situation from the perspective of a truth-process. Rigid and dogmatic (or 'blinded'), the subject-language would claim the power, based on its own axioms, to name the whole of the real, and thus to change the world" (E 83, original emphasis). Otherwise put, the process of truth can go wrong, can lead to "disaster", when its power is absolutized; such absolutization, in Badiou's words, is "to force the naming of the unnameable" (E 86).

In conclusion, where does all this leave us with regard to the question of theology? We have said and shown that Badiou's theory of truth and the subject and its underpinning concepts ostensibly continue the anti-theological trajectory of Badiou's philosophy set out originally at the level of ontology. We have also suggested, however, that understanding the notions of fidelity and forcing from within a broader context, a context that takes into account the event, intervention, nomination, evental recurrence and the role that belief or confidence plays in the constitution of the subject and the notion of resurrection, suggests a more complicated relationship to theology. Indeed, that the relationship is more complicated is further supported by the fact that Badiou often appeals to theology to construct his theory, despite his anti-theological pretensions. Before moving head on into a discussion of the extent of this relationship, in Chapter 4, the next chapter discusses in more detail Badiou's theory of truth and the subject as it relates to the truth procedures of art, science, politics and love as conditions for philosophy and how philosophy relates to sophism and anti-philosophy. The discussion of anti-philosophy and its relationship to religion and theology will provide the groundwork for arguing, in Chapter 4, that Badiou's philosophy contains an anti-philosophical core that coincides with theology.

3. PHILOSOPHY AND ITS CONDITIONS

Having discussed in the previous chapter the formal elements of Badiou's theory of truth and the subject, this chapter focuses specifically on the four domains of truth Badiou recognizes: science, art, love and politics. Since the publication of *Being and Event*, Badiou has insisted on the irreducible singularity of each of these domains, meaning that each produces truth in its own right. Because the domains of science, art, politics and love are productive of truths, they also function as conditions for philosophy, meaning that philosophy is only such in light of its conditions. The first section of this chapter focuses on what it means to take science, art, love and politics as conditions for philosophy, and includes a lengthy discussion of the particularity of each of these domains. Noting Badiou's lack of any clear articulation of the relationship among the truth procedures, the second section of this chapter attempts to articulate a way to interrelate the four truth procedures, based largely on Badiou's notion of intervention as found in Meditation 20 of *Being and Event*. The third and final section of this chapter, concerned with the roles that sophism and anti-philosophy play in the construction of philosophy, is in many ways the most important for the argument that follows in Chapter 4. Specifically, the discussion of anti-philosophy serves as the foundation for the claim made explicit in Chapter 4 that Badiou's philosophy contains an anti-philosophical core that coincides with theology.

PHILOSOPHY AND ITS CONDITIONS

Philosophy for Badiou has as its primary concern truths and their subjects, but philosophy does not actually construct the truths and subjects with which it is concerned. Badiou repeatedly stresses that philosophy "does not itself produce truths" (MP 35). Truths, rather, always occur external to philosophy proper, in one of four material domains or generic procedures: science, art, politics and love. The choice of science, art, politics and love as the loci for the production of truths, as the domains in which truths occur, is by no means arbitrary. With varying degrees of emphasis, science, art, politics and love have made up the subject matter of philosophy since Plato, even in philosophies that downplay the importance of or ostensibly deny the existence of truths.[1] Although Badiou allows for the possibility that there might be types of truths other than those produced in the generic procedures of science, art, politics and love, human knowledge has been and continues to be, at least at present, limited to these four (LW 74). Since the actual production of truths is always internal to the generic procedures themselves, it is the subject of a generic procedure – not philosophy – that evaluates what it means to be faithful to an event and determines the trajectory that a truth takes, in light of the situation and the type of truth in question. In the matter of truths, then, Badiou gives priority to the generic procedures.

If philosophy in no way produces the truths with which it is concerned, what, then, is the relationship between philosophy and science, art, politics and love? On the one hand, Badiou emphasizes that the generic procedures serve as "conditions" for philosophy, which means, quite literally, that science, art, politics and love serve as the foundation for philosophical reflection. "Philosophy is prescribed by conditions that are the types of truth procedures or generic procedures", Badiou says (MP 101). Indeed, without these conditions, philosophy as Badiou understands it is simply not possible. On the other hand, although philosophy takes its cue from its conditions, it is not strictly confined to them, as if philosophy could simply be reduced to science, art, politics, love, or any combination of these. The relationship between philosophy and its conditions is not hermeneutic, in the sense that it would fall to philosophy to merely interpret its conditions. In Badiou's words:

> If philosophy had only to *interpret* its conditions, if its destiny was hermeneutic, it would be pleased to turn back towards these conditions, and to interminably say: such is the sense of what happens in the poetic work, the mathematical theorem, the amorous encounter, the political revolution. Philosophy would be the tranquil aggregate of an aesthetics, an epistemology, an erotology and a political sociology.   (IT 101, original emphasis)[2]

For Badiou, to confine philosophy to an interpretation of its conditions is, in the end, to limit truths to the circulation of sense, to the vagaries of language and experience. Such limitation from Badiou's perspective can only amount to a devaluation of truth, hence Badiou's overt distaste for much contemporary hermeneutic, analytic and postmodern philosophy (IT 39–57). The task of philosophy is, rather, to compose the compossibility of disparate truths, to construct a generic category of Truth from the generic procedures of art, science, politics and love. To quote Badiou at length on this point:

The specific role of philosophy is to propose a unified conceptual space in which naming *takes place* of events that serve as the point of departure for truth procedures. Philosophy seeks to *gather together all the additional-names*. It deals within thought with the compossible nature of the procedures that condition it. It does not establish any truth but it sets a locus of truths. It configurates the generic procedures, through a welcoming, a sheltering built up with reference to their disparate simultaneity. Philosophy sets out to think its time by putting the state of procedures conditioning it into a common place. Its operations, whatever they may be, always aim to think "together", to configurate within an unique exercise of thought the epochal disposition of the matheme, poem, political invention, and love (or the event status of the Two). In this sense, philosophy's sole question is indeed that of truth. Not that it produces any, but because it offers a mode of access to the unity of a moment of truths, a conceptual site in which the generic procedures are thought as compossible.   (MP 37, original emphasis)

Understood primarily as a conceptual site that configures the compossibility of truths, philosophy occupies the space between the irreducible plurality of truths and the composition of their unity, that is, their Truth. However, we should not confuse the Truth subtracted from truths with anything substantial. As Badiou emphasizes, the category of Truth constructed from truths "is by itself *void*. It operates but presents nothing" (MP 124, original emphasis). Although labelling the category of Truth "void" bears the marks of the main elements of his ontology, the void in question here is not ontological but logical: "it is an operational void, and not a presented one" (*ibid.*). To borrow the words of Justin Clemens, "philosophy has no *object*; it is simply a particular torsion of active thought – an *act* of philosophy – which involves the grasping of new possibilities of existence in the course of their production" (Clemens 2001: 206, original emphasis).

Before discussing each of the four truth procedures individually in relation to philosophy, it is important to mention two consequences of Badiou's understanding of philosophy as conditioned by science, art, politics and love. First, since it is conditioned by the truths that constitute its concern, philosophy is only possible, according to Badiou, in so far as each of the generic procedures is in play, so to speak. If philosophy is concerned with creating a conceptual space for the organization of truths, a topos for the construction of the category Truth, then all of its conditions must be present for philosophy to do its work. Badiou emphasizes that, since there are four conditions for philosophy, "the lack of a single one gives rise to its dissipation, just as the emergence of all four condition[s] its apparition" (MP 35).[3] Second, and related to the first point, if philosophy is only possible on the condition that all its conditions be present, then it is also necessary to avoid giving primacy to one generic procedure over the others. Borrowing a term from Jacques Lacan, Badiou refers to elevating one condition above others as a "suture" of philosophy to one of its conditions; a "suture" occurs when "philosophy *delegates* its functions to one or other of its conditions, handing over the whole of thought to *one* generic procedure" (MP 61, original emphasis). According to Badiou, the history of modern philosophical thought is largely defined by a series of such sutures: to generalize, positivism sutured philosophy to its scientific condition, Marxism sutured philosophy to its political condition, psychoanalysis sutured philosophy to its amorous condition, and Heidegger and his progeny sutured philosophy to its poetic condition (MP 61–7). Since the suturing of philosophy to one of its conditions inevitably entails the devaluation of the others, on Badiou's account it leads to the impoverishment of philosophy itself, an impoverishment of the category of Truth with which it is concerned. So much is clearly seen today, Badiou argues, in the lingering effects of the poetic suture, which Badiou's grounding of ontology in mathematics attempts to redress, as we discussed in Chapter 1.[4] It is important to emphasize this point, since it is common among interpreters of Badiou to focus on one of the four conditions at the expense of the others.[5] Overemphasizing the importance of one condition at the expense of others is understandable, perhaps even inevitable, since individual interpreters tend to gravitate towards those aspects of Badiou's thought considered most salient to their own particular interests, respective projects, and areas of expertise.[6] Nevertheless, focusing on one condition over the others risks grounding Badiou's philosophy itself in one of its four conditions, taking one condition – science, art, politics or love – as determinative of the whole. In Badiou's terminology, this would be to "suture" his thought to one condition, which would, in effect, present a distorted picture of Badiou's own philosophy.

To sum up, we have said that for Badiou philosophy itself does not produce truths; truths occur in positions external to philosophy, positions that Badiou identifies with science, art, politics and love. These four domains of truth serve as conditions for philosophy, all of which must be present for philosophy to do its work. Philosophy, in this sense, comes "after" the material production of truths; truths are, in turn, initially independent of philosophy proper. As Badiou puts it, "*Prior* to philosophy, a 'prior to' that is not temporal, there are *truths*. These truths are heterogeneous, and proceed within the real independently of philosophy" (MP 123, original emphasis). To put the matter in other terms, truths "are the factual, historic, or pre-reflexive conditions of philosophy" (*ibid.*). It is precisely the task of philosophy to wrest truths from the factual and historical conditions in which they occur, to turn the pre-reflexive into the reflexive. So understood, Badiou also speaks of the task of philosophy with respect to science, art, politics and love as an "act of seizing" truths from sense. Philosophy "roots out truths from the gangue of sense. It *separates* them from the law of the world" (MP 142, original emphasis). In this sense, philosophy for Badiou serves a desacralizing or secularizing function. Although explicitly concerned with the relationship between philosophy and poetry, the following quotation serves as an apt description of the task of philosophy in general: "[P]hilosophy can only begin by desacralization: it institutes a regime of discourse which is its own earthly legitimation. Philosophy requires that the *profound* utterance's authority be interrupted by argumentative secularization" (IT 93, original emphasis).

We can see how philosophy operates with respect to its conditions by focusing specifically on science, art, love and politics. In what follows, we are not so much concerned with the actual truths produced in the domains of science, art, love and politics. Badiou litters his writings with examples of truths from each, and we will mention some of these below when necessary. What we are primarily interested in, rather, are the domains themselves, the formal elements that make up each of the conditions and which, in turn, condition philosophy in its construction of the category of Truth.

In Badiou's philosophy, the domain of science largely corresponds to mathematics. So much is evident, textually speaking, in the fact that Badiou often culls his examples of scientific truth from mathematics and in his tendency, at times, to substitute the name "mathematics" for the name "science" when referring to it as a generic procedure (cf. LW 10ff). More to the point, what constitutes science as a generic procedure of truth is mathematical formalization and deduction, the ability to make general and universal statements about objects in complete abstraction from particular properties and to draw out a rational set of consequences from a well-defined starting point. As Ray Brassier notes, "[T]he 'scientificity' of a given science is directly proportional to its mathematization: science is 'scientific' precisely to the extent that it is mathematical. By the same token, the less a science depends upon mathematical formalization, the less scientific it is" (2005: 136). For this reason, to the extent that it provides a mathematical description of material reality, Badiou can include the investigations of physics within the general purview of scientific truth procedures. However, on the one hand, he tends to exclude from the realm of truth those sciences that resist explicit formalization. Badiou refers to biology, for instance, as "that wild empiricism disguised as science" (quoted in *ibid.*). On the other hand, he also excludes from science qua generic procedure what we commonly refer to as the "human sciences", such as statistics, economics, sociology and so on. The human sciences do often attempt to apply mathematization to human affairs, producing a body of supposedly verifiable facts and numerical correlations, but on Badiou's account they do so largely in the service of opinion, for the maintenance of the state. Echoing Michel Foucault's work on governmentality, Badiou writes, "[W]hat is called 'science' here is a technical apparatus whose pragmatic basis is governmental" (NN 2).

Since science or, more specifically, mathematics, serves as a condition for philosophy, meaning that it is initially external to philosophy, the various truths that it produces can be taken on their own terms, as applicable primarily to mathematics itself and its purview. Thus, for instance, Cantor's discovery of the transfinite is, in a real sense, an intra-mathematical affair, concerned largely with number and the comparison of infinite quantities. However, since all science has as its concern "the intelligibility of the world and the invariance of its equations" (LW 75), its significance for philosophy is, in the end, primarily ontological. What science qua generic procedure is concerned with at root is the thinking of being qua being and, consequently, the logical exposition of being-there. Science or mathematics, read philosophically, just is "the truth of multiple-being" (IT 102). As Justin Clemens puts it, "Mathematics *is* the place of the inscription of Being; the letters of mathematics *are* directly ontological" (2005: 100, original emphasis). We discussed the sense of these claims in detail in Chapter 1, so there is no need to repeat it here. Nevertheless, Badiou's explicitly ontological texts (*Being and Event, Number and Numbers, Briefings on Existence* and, to a certain extent, Book II of *Logics of Worlds*) serve as so many attempts to give a philosophical articulation of science or mathematics, to take the truth produced in the latter as a condition for constructing the category of Truth.

In contrast to science or mathematics, whose concern is the truth of multiple being in all its abstract generality, art has as its concern the sensible as such; art qua truth procedure is concerned with "the transformation of the sensible into the event of the Idea" (P 144). To quote Badiou at length:

> What distinguishes art from other truth-processes is that the subject of truth is extracted from the sensible … Art makes an event of what lies at the edge of what is given to perceptual experience, that is, at the edge of the indistinctly sensory, and it is in this respect that it is an Idea, that is, in so far as it turns what there is into what must come to pass within the finitude of the work. In art, the Idea is imposed through the transformation of what can be perceived into an improbable imperative. To force to see something, as if it were practically impossible, something that is anyhow clearly visible, is precisely what painting does, for example. Art affirms that at the same point of an impossible-to-be-felt, the Idea holds on, as sensed in the sensible effects of the work. (*Ibid.*)

In contrast to an aesthetic that would take art as an object for philosophical scrutiny, Badou offers an "inaesthetics", which is concerned with "the intraphilosophical effects produced by the independent existence of some works of art" (quoted in During 2010: 85).

Badiou contrasts his "inaesthetic" articulation of the relationship between art and philosophy with three historically dominant ways of configuring the relationship: the didactic, the Romantic and the classical. According to Badiou, didacticism holds that "art is incapable of truth, or that all truth is external to art" (HI 2). Such an understanding of the truth of art, more precisely its lack of truth, is at the root of the Platonic injunction against art as mimesis, as mere imitation or semblance of truth. When understood as mimesis, art has the potential to lead astray, in that it appeals to the immediacy of the senses, over against the labour required for dialectical thinking, that is, *dianoia* or discursive thought. For Plato, of course, this means that art, and poetry in particular, must be brought under control, even almost entirely banished from ideal *politeia*: "we can admit no poetry into our city save only hymns to the gods and the praises of good men" (2005: 607b). More generally, Badiou argues that didacticism emerges when art is either "condemned or treated in a purely instrumental fashion" (HI 3). Understanding the relationship between philosophy and art in purely didactic terms, it thus seems, is correlative to the way in which philosophies of mathematics tend to understand the relationship between philosophy and mathematics, as we discussed in Chapter 1. Similar to the way in which philosophies of mathematics limit mathematics to predefined philosophical categories, a didactic view of the relationship between philosophy and art limits "art to the philosophical surveillance of truths … The norm of art must be education; the norm of education is philosophy" (*ibid.*).

In direct opposition to didacticism's penchant for eliding the truth of art, the Romantic articulation of the relationship between philosophy and art holds that "art *alone* is capable of truth" (*ibid.*, original emphasis). In holding that the provenance of truth is uniquely and exclusively related to art, the Romantic understanding of the relationship between art and philosophy represents, in effect, a suture of philosophy to one of its conditions. Hence Badiou's criticism of the Heideggerian emphasis on the poem as uniquely situated to think being, which we discussed in Chapter 1. Moreover, the Romantic articulation of the relationship between philosophy and art is, on Badiou's account, implicitly or explicitly religious, more specifically Christian, in nature. As Badiou puts it:

> Its thesis is that art *alone* is capable of truth. What's more, it is in this sense that art accomplishes what philosophy itself can only point toward. In the romantic schema, art is the real body of truth, or what Lacoue-Labarthe and Nancy have named "the literary absolute". It is patent that this real body is a glorious body. Philosophy might very well be the withdrawn and impenetrable

Father – art is the suffering Son who saves and redeems. Genius is crucifixion and resurrection. In this respect, it is art itself that educates, because it teaches of the power of infinity held within the tormented cohesion of a form. Art delivers us from the subjective barrenness of the concept. Art is the absolute as subject – it is *incarnation*.   (HI 3, original emphasis)

Badiou's rejection of this Romantic, incarnational conception of art, as we will see in Chapter 4, is important for understanding his reading of the incarnation in *Saint Paul*.

Nevertheless, Badiou also rejects what he refers to as the classical schema of the articulation of the relationship between art and philosophy. The classical schema represents a type of middle position between "didactic banishment" and "romantic glorification", insisting on a "relative peace between art and philosophy" (*ibid.*). Badiou traces the classical schema back to Aristotle. Like didacticism, classicism holds that art as mimesis is incapable of truth. However, unlike didacticism, which considers the incapability of art to grasp truth a problem that must be brought under control, classicism does not consider art's non-relation to truth a problem, for the simple reason that "the *purpose* of art is not in the least truth" (HI 4, original emphasis). As Badiou puts it:

Of course, art is not truth, but it also does not claim to be and is therefore innocent. Aristotle's prescription places art under the sign of something entirely other than knowledge and thereby frees it from the Platonic suspicion. This other thing, which he sometimes names "catharsis", involves the deposition of the passions in a transference onto semblance. Art has a therapeutic function, and not at all a cognitive or revelatory one. Art does not pertain to the theoretical but to the ethical (in the widest possible sense of the term). It follows that the norm of art is to be found in its utility for the treatment of the affections of the soul.
(*Ibid.*)

Although, as Badiou points out, this position has the advantage of settling the putative quarrel between philosophy and art, it does so only by denying that art has any purchase on truth. In Badiou's words again, "Without doubt, art is innocent, but this is because it is innocent of all truth. In other words, it is inscribed in the imaginary. Strictly speaking, within the classical schema, art is not a form of thought. It is entirely exhausted by its act or by its public operation" (HI 4–5).

In *Handbook of Inaesthetics*, Badiou proposes a fourth way to understand the relationship between art and philosophy, which involves taking seriously the relationship of art to truth. Doing so requires treating art as both singular and immanent. Each of the three previously mentioned articulations of the relationship between art and philosophy fails, according to Badiou, to take seriously this requirement: didacticism treats art as singular but not immanent, since it conceives of art as the mere semblance of an external truth; Romanticism treats art as immanent but not singular, since it conceives of all truth in relation to art as the incarnation of the idea; and classicism, since it understands art in its non-relation to truth, dissolves the conditions of immanence and singularity entirely. In contrast to each of these positions, to understand art as both singular and immanent with respect to truth involves considering art as a truth procedure in its own right. Badiou writes:

> Art *itself* is a truth procedure. Or again: The philosophical identification of art falls under the category of truth. Art is a thought in which artworks are the Real (and not the effect). And this thought, or rather the truths that it activates, are irreducible to other truths – be they scientific, political, or amorous. This also means that art, as a singular regime of thought, is irreducible to philosophy. (HI 9, original emphasis)

To take art as a truth procedure, to understand it as its own, irreducible regime of thought, satisfies the conditions of immanence and singularity: the relationship between art and truth is immanent, to the extent that art is "rigorously coextensive with the truths that it generates", and singular, in so far as the "truths [of art] are given nowhere else than in art" (*ibid.*). Otherwise put, to claim that the relationship between art and truth is immanent simply means that truth is internal to art, that art, contra didacticism and classicism, actually produces truths. Likewise, to claim that the truth of art is singular is to claim that, contra the Romantic disposition, the truths produced in art are in some sense unique, different from those produced in science, love and politics. At a general level, this singularity is located in art's particular relationship to the sensible, its transformation of the sensible into the Idea.

It is important to emphasize, however, that the truth associated with art does not directly correspond to various works of art. Claiming that artistic works are truths would be to reinstate the Romantic schema outlined above. Badiou thus says that "if one wishes to argue that the work is a truth, by the same token, one will also have to maintain that it is the descent of the infinite-true into finitude. But this figure of the descent of the infinite into the finite is precisely the kernel of the romantic schema that thinks art as incarnation" (HI 11). The work of art is, rather, a subjective response to an event, a response that takes the form of a finite, artistic enquiry into the local status of a generic and infinite truth. In this sense, various post-eventual works of art constitute the being of artistic truth, the subject of artistic truth.

What this means, in effect, is that the proper unit of analysis for thinking the truth of art, understood as both singular and immanent, is:

> neither the work nor the author, but rather the artistic configu-
> ration initiated by an evental rupture … A configuration is not
> an art form, a genre, or an "objective" period in the history of
> art, nor is it a "technical" *dispotif*. Rather, it is an identifiable
> sequence, initiated by an event, comprising a virtually infinite
> complex of works, when speaking of which it makes sense to say
> that it produces – in a rigorous immanence to the art in question
> – a truth *of this art*, an art-truth.   (HI 13, original emphasis)

The task of philosophy, in this respect, is not to think the truth found in art. As a generic procedure originally external to philosophy, art is the thinking of its own truth. The task of philosophy is, rather, to make manifest the truth that art is, to extract the idea that the sensible works of art compose. More generally, philosophy "seizes truths, shows them, exposes them, announces that they exist. In so doing, it turns time toward eternity – since every truth, as a generic infinity, is eternal" (HI 14).

Artistic truths can, of course, take on a variety of forms, and Badiou discusses throughout his writings various artistic practices, such as cinema, theatre and dance. However, in considering the truth of art, he tends to give preference to poetry. Indeed, similar to the way in which mathematics serves as the paradigm of scientific truth, Badiou treats poetry as the exemplar of art qua truth procedure. The privilege that Badiou accords to poetry may, of course, be the result of personal preference. Nevertheless, there are at least two good philosophical reasons for Badiou's apparent emphasis on poetry in relation to artistic truths. First, as we discussed in Chapter 1, Badiou's equation of mathematics with ontology is at least in part an attempt to subvert the Heideggerian suture of philosophy to the poem, a suture that Badiou takes as a defining feature of much contemporary philosophy. Focusing on the poem, or poetic speech in general, as representative of artistic truth can be understood, then, as part of a de-suturing effort, an effort to put the truth of the poem in what Badiou considers its proper place: as a condition for philosophy but not its sole condition, as productive of truth in its own right but not exhaustively so. Second, and as we will discuss in more detail below, unlike the other forms of artistic truth, the poem, and poetic utterance in general, is more fundamental to Badiou's theory of generic truth, in so far as each of the four truth procedures must rely on the resources of language, more specifically, naming, to become effective. As Badiou puts it:

> [W]hen the situation is saturated by its own norm, when the cal-
> culation of itself is inscribed there without respite, when there is

no longer a void between knowledge and prediction, then one must be *poetically* ready for the outside-of-self. For the nomination of an event – in the sense in which I speak of it, that is, an undecidable supplementation which must be named to occur for a being-faithful, thus for a truth – *this* nomination is *always* poetic. To name a supplement, a chance, and incalculable, one must draw from the void of sense, in default of established significations, to the peril of language. One must therefore poeticize, and the poetic name of the event is what throws us outside of ourselves, through the flaming ring of predictions.

(IT 100, original emphasis)

It is precisely poetic nomination that allows an event to be susceptible to an interventional decision, making the production of truth possible.

What, then, constitutes the truth of the poem, and poetic speech in general? The poem itself is, of course, a differential point in the construction of a truth procedure. The poem is thus the local exhibition of an artistic truth procedure. From the perspective of philosophy, however, what is it that constitutes "the poem's genuinely intelligible vocation" (HI 20)? Badiou stresses that the poem is not primarily descriptive or expressive in nature, as if the world functioned as an object for the poem's interpretative gaze. Indeed, Badiou credits the modern poets such as Hölderlin, Mallarmé, Rimbaud, Trakl, Pessoa, Mandelstam and Celan with "the destitution of the category of the object, and of objectivity, as necessary forms of presentation" (MP 72). The poem, in this sense, is not primarily concerned with meaning, and should be dissociated from any hermeneutic enterprise. Like all truth procedures, "[t]he poem is an operation" (HI 29). More specifically, "The poem teaches us that the world does not present itself as a collection of objects. The world is not what 'objects' to thought. For the operations of the poem, the world is that thing whose presence is more essential than objectivity" (*ibid.*). The poem, rather than representing anything, "offers us a taking place in language" (*ibid.*). What characterizes the poem, then, and all truly poetic speech, "is its capacity to manifest the powers of language itself" (*ibid.*).

Contrasting the operation of the poem with that of mathematics is helpful here. As we know, both mathematics and poetry are truth procedures. Indeed, Badiou even indicates that both have a common reference point: the pure multiple, out of which both mathematics and poetry make truth. However, whereas mathematics qua ontology makes truth out of the presentation of inconsistent multiplicity, the poem "makes truth out of the multiple, conceived as a presence that has come to the limits of language. Put otherwise, poetry is the song of language qua capacity to make the pure notion of the 'there is' present in the very effacement of empirical objectivity" (HI 22). As the making-present of the "there is", the poem situates the power of language at the threshold between absence and presence, disappearance and appearance. The poem, as the manifest power of language, is, in this sense, fundamentally concerned with naming, even if it cannot name its own power to name itself, which latter falls to philosophy. The poem pushes the limits of language so as to effect "a powerful anticipation, a forcing of language enacted by the advent of an 'other' language that is at once immanent and created" (HI 23). The poem addresses itself to the infinite "in order to direct the power of language toward the retention of a disappearance" (HI 25).

We will return to this point below, when we discuss the relationship among the four truth procedures. For now, we can move on to love, which taken as a generic procedure is concerned with the truth of the disjunction of sexual difference, as thought in and through sexual difference. Similar to the way in which he distinguishes his understanding of art from other dominant conceptions of it, Badiou is careful to distinguish his understanding of love qua truth from three other common conceptions of love. In his essay "What is Love?", Badiou notes that, first, love should not be understood as Romantic fusion, the ecstatic identification of lovers – the Two – in the One. Subsuming the Two under the One is, in the end, "a *suppression of the multiple*", the "remembrance of a philosopheme, the philosopheme of the One" (WL 38–9, original emphasis). Reinstating the one through the subsumption of the two would, of course, violate the fundamental principles of Badiou's ontology. Second, love has nothing to do with a relation to or experience of the Other, it "is not the prostration of the Same at the altar of the Other" (WL 39). Love, instead of being subject to the dialectic of the Same and Other, is, rather, a post-evental experience of a situation or world through the disjunction of the Two. Third and finally, love is not simply an illusory notion, a semblance that covers over the real of sex, desire or jealousy, as assumed in some forms of psychoanalysis. Love is rather a supplement, "a production of truth" (*ibid.*). Love is, according to Badiou, "the guardian of the universality of the true. It elucidates possibility, *because it makes truth of the disjunction*" (WL 46, original emphasis).

What does it mean to say that love is a production of truth, that it makes truth out of the disjunction of sexual difference, of the Two? First, it means that there are two, sexuated positions of experience in love, "woman" and "man". As Badiou makes clear, these positions do not immediately correspond to their empirical, biological or social counterparts. Chaining the sexuated positions of love to any of these is, in the end, to adopt the existing knowledge of the situation as determinative for each position and the truth of love in general; otherwise put, to do so would assume that the sexuated positions, defined either biologically, empirically or socially, pre-exist love qua truth procedure. For Badiou, in contrast, the sexuated positions are axiomatic or structural, and in no way pre-exist love as a generic procedure. Indeed, in keeping with the anticipatory character of truth, the two positions can, strictly speaking, only be established retroactively, in light of the truth of love. In Badiou's words, "That there have been *two* positions can only be established retroactively. It is effectively love alone that authorizes us to formally pronounce the existence of two positions" (WL 40, original emphasis). The retroactive establishment of the two positions is entailed, second, by Badiou's claim that "*nothing* in experience is the same for the positions of man and woman" (*ibid.*, original emphasis). The masculine and feminine positions do not respectively carve out distinct regions of a more general and overarching experience, nor do the two positions intersect or coincide with each other. Rather, the "relationship" between "man" and "woman" is one of "disjunction", which Badiou defines as follows: "*Everything* is presented in such a way that no coincidence can be attested to between what affects one position and what affects the other" (*ibid.*, original emphasis). Third, one can only grasp this disjunction immanently, meaning that there is no third position available "to *pronounce on the disjunction*" (*ibid.*). As Badiou puts it:

> The sexuated positions are disjointed with regard to experience in general. The disjunction is not observable, and cannot itself be made the object of an experience or of a direct knowledge [*savoir*]. All such experiences or knowledges are themselves positioned within the disjunction and will never encounter anything that attests to any other position. (*Ibid.*)

Rather than being subject to some third position that would pronounce upon love, the truth of the disjunction is related to an event or an "encounter", which "initiates the amorous procedure" (WL 41).

If each position in love is distinct, then the experience of "man" and "woman" in love is, simply put, different. This difference, although marked materially, rests primarily on the different functions that each position performs in the amorous procedure itself. Badiou defines these functions as follows:

- a *wandering* function, of *alea*, of a perilous voyage through the situation, that supports the articulation of the Two and infinity. A function that exposes the supposition of the Two to the infinite presentation of the world;
- an *immobility* function, that protects, that withholds the primary nomination, that ensures that this nomination of the event-encounter is not engulfed by the event itself;
- an *imperative* function: continuing always, even in separation, and which holds that absence is itself a mode of continuation;
- a *story* function which, as the work proceeds inscribes by a sort of archivage the becoming truth of the wandering.

(WL 48, original emphasis)

"Woman", according to Badiou, takes up the first and fourth functions, the wandering function and the story function. In his essay "The Writing of the Generic", whose subject is, among other things, love as disjunction in the works of Samuel Beckett, Badiou notes that the wandering function is "a journey in the dark, which presents the infinite chance of the faithful journey of love, the endless crossing of a world henceforth *exposed* to the effects of the encounter" (OB 31–2, original emphasis). This wandering function, which translates into the opening of love to and an enquiry into its pure contingency is, in turn, coupled with the story function, which works to form the contingency of the procedure into a narrative. In Badiou's words, the story function, "from the standpoint of the Two, offers up the latent infinity of the world and recounts its unlikely unfolding, inscribing, step by step – like an archive that accompanies wandering – everything that one may discover in what Beckett calls 'the blessed days of blue'" (OB 32). Although Badiou does not directly say as much, it seems that the feminine functions of wandering and story primarily concern the interplay of anticipation and retroaction in the production of truth, which we discussed in Chapter 1 in reference to forcing and the subject. "Man", in contrast, exercises the two middle functions, that is, the immobility and imperative functions. Contrary to the wandering of "woman", "man" is immobile, in that "he" "watches over, guards or maintains the fixed point of the first naming, the naming of the event-encounter" (*ibid.*). Coupled with this is the imperative function: "always to go on, even in separation; to decree that separation itself is a mode of continuity" (*ibid.*). In light of these claims, it seems that the primary content of the two masculine functions is ethical, which, for Badiou, condenses fidelity to an event into the maxim "Keep going!" (E 52). Thus Badiou says, "In the case of love, a 'man' is the name's silent custodian. And because the function of wandering is missing, to be a man within love is also to do nothing that bears witness to this love, but only to retain, motionless in the dark, love's powerful abstract conviction" (OB 32).

Badiou also marks the difference between "woman" and "man" by noting that the feminine position presents love's relation to humanity. Now, humanity for Badiou is not a substantial notion, concerned with a putative essence, but a formal concept or function that supports the four truth procedures, in effect knotting them together. "Humanity is the historical body of truths", Badiou writes (WL 41). However, the masculine position, according to Badiou, gives value to humanity through "each type of procedure itself ... without taking account of the existence of the others" (WL 51). For "man" each of the four truth procedures, each aspect of humanity, is taken as valuable in and of itself, without regard to the possible relations among them. That this is the position of "man" is, perhaps, not surprising, considering that "he" exercises the immobility and imperative functions. In contrast, according to Badiou, "woman" bases the value of the three other truth procedures on the inclusion of love among them, meaning that "for the female position, the type 'love' *knots the four*, and that it is only on its condition that H, humanity, *exists* as a general configuration" (WL 52, original emphasis). It is in this sense that "woman" can be said to be "the bearer of love's relation to humanity" (WL 51).

What is it, however, that makes the truth of love universal, available to all, if it is immanent to the encounter, the absolute disjunction between "man" and "woman"? As Badiou frames the question, "[H]ow is it possible that a truth is transpositional, or a truth for all, if there exists at least two positions, man and woman, that are radically disjunct in regard to experience in general?" (WL 42). Badiou is aware of an apparent paradox, here, and his way to treat it is to claim that love is precisely the working through of this paradox. That is, love "makes truth of the paradox itself" (WL 43). Although we will attempt to flesh out this admittedly abstract characterization in more detail shortly, Badiou notes that the universality of love ultimately rests on its "numerical schema":

> This schema states that the Two fractures the One and tests the infinity of the situation. One, Two, infinity: such is the numericity of the amorous procedure. It structures the becoming of a generic truth. What truth? The truth of the situation *insofar as there exist two disjunct positions*. Love is nothing other than a trying sequence of investigations on the disjunction and the Two, such that in the retroactivity of the encounter it verifies that it has always been one of the laws of the situation.
>
> (WL 45, original emphasis)

Indeed, because love makes truth of the disjunction, out of the seeming paradox of the Two, Badiou says that it "is the guardian of the universality of the true" (WL 46).

Although Badiou makes it clear that the two sexuated positions do not immediately correspond to their biological, empirical and social counterparts, meaning that the structural places of "woman" and "man" can both be occupied by either women or men, he also acknowledges that his articulation of these positions relies to some extent on common, sexist stereotypes.[7] In his words, the functions "do not hesitate to blend both coarse and refined commonplaces" (WL 49). To be sure, the dislocation of "woman" and "man" from biological, empirical and social specificity is meant, at least in part, to counteract an all too easy association of the functions of love with fixed and determinate gender roles. The problem, however, is that the roles themselves still remain. That is, the relativization of the positions "woman" and "man" with regard to "actually existing" women and men does nothing to challenge the necessity of assigning particular functions to *a* sexed position, functions that are, at least in part, drawn from a more traditional and already determined understanding of the roles of women and men, respectively. This would, perhaps, not be much of a problem if Badiou's analysis were meant to be primarily descriptive. But Badiou endows his analysis with normative status, as is self-evident in taking love as a truth procedure. In so far as Badiou grants normative status to the masculine and feminine functions, it is difficult to see how he avoids buttressing more traditional conceptions of gender, even if these are formalized into structural positions. As we will see below, Badiou needs the functions that he assigns to the roles of "man" and "woman". But if it is of the essence of a truth procedure to subtract itself from the state of the situation, then, in so far as the functions assigned to "man" and "woman" are at least partially drawn from the existing knowledge of the situation, it would seem that Badiou's analysis falls short of the type of subtraction that the production of truth needs.

Nevertheless, we can now turn to the fourth truth procedure, politics. Not surprisingly, Badiou's understanding of politics as a truth procedure owes much to his own commitment to militant political engagement. The political sequences that Badiou commonly identifies as examples of politics as a truth procedure – the French Revolution, the Paris Commune, the Chinese Cultural Revolution, May 1968 – all share a militant trajectory. Although Badiou's commitment to radical leftist politics has taken various forms in its development – from his early Marxism, to his explicit Maoism from 1968 up to the early 1980s, to his more recent involvement with *L'Organisation politique* – there is no question that that commitment itself has remained a "great constant" (Hallward 2003: 29) in his life and work.[8] Indeed, before his explicit articulation of the compossibility of the four truth procedures as conditions for philosophy, one could say that Badiou's philosophy was primarily determined by or "sutured" to politics (cf. TS 28).

Politics for Badiou is concerned with collective action against the dominance of the state. Understood in this sense, politics, taken as a truth procedure, has at least three formal conditions. First, the event that gives impetus to a political sequence of truth has as its material the collective as such, meaning that it is "immediately universalizing" in its effects (M 141). Indeed, it is the irreducibly collective aspect of politics that distinguishes it qua truth procedure from science, art and love. To quote Badiou at length on this point:

> Only politics is intrinsically required to declare that the thought that it is is the thought of all. This declaration is its constitutive prerequisite. All that the mathematician requires, for instance, is at least one other mathematician to recognize the validity of its proof. In order to assure itself of the thought that it is, love need only assume the two. The artist ultimately needs no one. Science,

art, and love are aristocratic truth procedures. Of course, they are addressed to all and universalize their own singularity. But their regime is not that of the collective. Politics is impossible without the statement that people, taken indistinctly, are capable of the thought that constitutes the post-evental political subject. The statement claims that a political thought is topologically collective, meaning that it cannot exist otherwise than as the thought of all. (M 142)

Simply put, politics is "the truth of the collective as such" (IT 70).

Second, because of its inherently collective character, the immediacy of its universality, politics "presents as such the infinite character of situations" (M 142). Badiou's ontology, as we discussed in Chapter 1, assumes that most situations are ontologically infinite. However, because the truth of politics coincides with the collective, Badiou says that only politics presents the infinite immediately, "as subjective universality" (M 143). It is worth quoting Badiou at length again on this point:

Science, for example, is the capture of the void and the infinite by the letter. It has no concern for the subjective infinity of situations. Art presents the sensible in the finitude of a work, and the infinite only intervenes in it to the extent that the artist destines the infinite to the finite. But politics treats the infinite as such according to the principle of the same, the egalitarian principle. This is its point of departure: the situation is open, never closed and the possible affects its immanent subjective infinity. We will say that the numericality of the political procedure has the infinite as its first term; whereas for love this first term is one; for science the void; and for art a finite number. The infinite comes into play in every truth procedure, but only in politics does it take first place. This is because only in politics is deliberation about the possible (and hence about the infinity of the situation) constitutive of the process itself. (*Ibid.*)

The collective and universal character of politics means that politics is first and foremost "organized collective action, following certain principles, and aiming to develop in reality the consequences of a new possibility repressed by the dominant state of affairs" (MS 11).

Third, as this last quotation hints at, Badiou maintains that politics qua truth procedure does not coincide with the state and its workings, in both an ontological and political sense. Recall that in Badiou's ontology, the state of the situation exercises a re-presentative function; it is a second count at the level of inclusion, assuring that what "is *included* in a situation *belongs* to its state" (BE 95, original emphasis). Otherwise put, the state or metastructure of the situation has as its goal stability and consistency, against the latent excess of the void in the situation. The state of the situation, understood in ontological terms, also has, according to Badiou, "a metaphorical affinity with politics" (*ibid.*), since the state as a political entity is likewise concerned with the parts of its situation. The state, understood in political terms, has as its purview the inclusion or re-presentation of its parts. Because of this, Badiou rejects the common liberal notion that the state is originally and positively founded on some social bond. The foundation of the state is, rather, negative, focused in the end on inconsistency. As Badiou puts it, "*[T]he State is not founded upon the social bond, which it would express, but rather upon un-binding, which it prohibits. Or, to be more precise, the separation of the State is less a result of the consistency of presentation than of the danger of inconsistency*" (BE 109, original emphasis). The purpose of the state, then, is to keep this inconsistency at bay, since it is inconsistency, as excess, that threatens to disrupt its re-presentative count, its control over the parts of the situation.

As we discussed in Chapter 2, an event eludes the re-presentative grasp of the state of the situation, since it is a multiple that belongs to the situation without being included therein. Indeed, it is precisely this singularity of an evental multiple that allows for the construction of a new truth, over against the knowledge of the situation governed by its state. However, keeping in mind the ontological and political meanings of the term state, what this means for politics is that politics must be radically anti-statist in character. That is, if politics is a truth procedure, and all truth procedures proceed in opposition to the state of the situation, then politics must proceed at a distance from the state. In Badiou's words, politics must be "subtracted from the pure prescription of the State, because the State itself does not think" (M 88). Politics, according to Badiou, "stakes its existence on its capacity to establish a relation to both the void and excess which is essentially different from that of the State; it is this difference alone that subtracts politics from the one of statist re-insurance" (BE 110).

If politics is subtracted from the operations of the state, then political truth sequences do not immediately correspond to identifiable forms of political organization, such as particular forms of government or existing political parties. Such forms of political organization, according to Badiou, largely coincide with state power, with the governance and maintenance of that power. The limitation of politics to what the state legitimates as political is a limitation on politics qua truth, which amounts to a denial of the subjective infinity proper to it. The distinction between politics as Badiou understands it and existing forms of political organization also applies to democracy, which today "is the principle organizer of consensus" (M 78). On the whole, Badiou has little positive to say about democracy, at least as currently practised among countries that more or less identify themselves as democratic. Badiou's distaste for democracy, which he often refers to pejoratively as "capitalist-parliamentarianism", is perhaps not all that surprising, considering his Maoist credentials and basic adherence to the Marxist, revolutionary political tradition, along with Plato.[9] For Badiou, democracy, at least as currently articulated and practised in existing state formations, refers to little more than a vehicle for opinion, a vehicle that uses opinion to support and solidify the collusion between monetary abstraction and the power of states (MS 90–92). Democracy in this sense is little more than a sophistical political formation, meaning that it is devoid of both thought and truth (M 10–25).

Badiou's disdain for contemporary democracy, so understood, also serves as the stepping-off point for *Logics of Worlds*, where in the Preface he contrasts what he refers to as "democratic materialism" with his own "materialist dialectic". According to Badiou, our "spontaneous belief" today is some version of "democratic materialism", which is based on the axiom: "There are only bodies and languages" (LW 1). Such belief can be said to be a materialism, in so far as it equates humanity with its animality, with the finitude of its existence. In Badiou's words, the materialism of "democratic materialism" assumes that "the body is the only concrete instance for productive individuals aspiring to enjoyment. Man, under the sway of the 'power of life', is an animal convinced that the body harbors the secret of its hope" (LW 2). This materialism is democratic, to the extent that it is based, in turn, on consensus and the juridical equality of particularities and differences. To quote Badiou on this point:

> Hence, the assimilation of humanity to animality culminates in the identification of the human animal with the diversity of its sub-species and the democratic rights that inhere in this diversity. This time, the progressive reverse borrows its name from Deleuze: "minoritarianism". Communities and cultures, colours and pigments, religions and clergies, uses and customs, disparate sexualities, public intimacies and the publicity of the intimate: everything and everyone deserves to be protected by the law.
>
> (LW 3)

Now, to be clear, Badiou is not against differences *per se*, as if his goal were to dissolve linguistic, cultural, sexual, religious and other particularities into homogeneity. So much is evident when, discussing the notion of difference in his *Ethics*, Badiou claims, "Infinite alterity is quite simply *what there is*. Any experience at all is the infinite deployment of infinite difference" (E 25).[10] Badiou's problem is, rather, the reduction of humanity to these particularities and differences, a reduction that takes finitude as its foundation and telos and fits all too easily with the logic of the market, which demands the constant proliferation of new identities "to homogenize its space of action" (SP 10–11). In contrast to "democratic materialism", Badiou, borrowing from his teacher Louis Althusser, argues for a "materialist dialectic", based on the axiom: "There are only bodies and languages, except that there are truths" (LW 4). It is precisely this "except that" that Badiou takes as missing from existing, state-based democratic political formations. Since truths only exist as exceptions to what there is, democracy for Badiou can be said to be without truth.

Badiou has recently argued for a politics based on what he calls "the communist hypothesis" (C; see also MS 97–117). Badiou distinguishes between his own communist hypothesis, that is, communism as an idea, and its various adjectival uses (communist parties, communist states, and so on). Although Badiou maintains that the idea of communism can be found in its historical forms (the Soviet Union, the PCF) and in identifiable political sequences (the Paris Commune, the Cultural Revolution, May 1968), it should not and cannot be reduced to these. More specifically, the communist hypothesis refers not so much to forms and sequences deemed "communist" but the following "general set of intellectual representations":

> The communist hypothesis is that a different collective organization is practicable, one that will eliminate the inequality of wealth and even the division of labour: every individual will be a "multipurpose worker", and in particular people will circulate between manual and intellectual work, as well as between town and country. The private appropriation of monstrous fortunes and their transmission by inheritance will disappear. The existence of a coercive state separate from civil society, with its military and police, will no longer be a self-evident necessity. There will be, Marx tells us – and he saw this point as his major contribution – after a brief sequence of "proletarian dictatorship" charged with destroying the remains of the old world, a long sequence of reorganization on the basis of "free association" of producers and creators, which will make possible a "withering away of the state". (C 99)

If his description of the communist hypothesis, the assertion of which he takes as fundamental to the upholding of the truth of politics, seems to have a ring of the utopian to it, Badiou claims that the opposite is the case. It is precisely the assertion that things cannot change, that things must stay the same, that is utopian, as implied in Francis Fukuyama's thesis on liberal democracy as the "end of history" (1992).

In contrast to this utopianism of the status quo, Badiou's politics is fundamentally concerned with justice. Indeed, for Badiou, "justice" is "the name by which a philosophy designates the possible truth of a political orientation" (IT 70). Justice, the concern of politics as truth, is a combination of freedom and equality, not so much as the goal of politics but as its foundation. That is, freedom, which Badiou understands as putting the state at a distance, and equality, which refers to the generic representation of the collective, are axiomatic for politics (IT 72). Freedom and equality, then, are not objectives of action but axioms for action (*ibid.*). Otherwise put, politics for Badiou means living with "an idea, and that what deserves to be called a real politics begins with that vision" (C 67).

Before concluding this section, we should pause for a moment and consider the relationship of Badiou's understanding of political truth procedures to violence. We have mentioned above that Badiou's conception of politics is resolutely leftist in orientation, drawn mainly from a quite orthodox list of nineteenth- and twentieth-century revolutionary political sequences (the French Revolution, the Paris Commune, the Russian Revolution, the Chinese Cultural Revolution, May 1968). So much is not surprising, given Badiou's political commitments. Indeed, Badiou tends to emphasize these and similar sequences as foundational for understanding politics as such, meaning that anything that does not measure up, so to speak, is considered a deviation from the norm. Hence Badiou's delineation of the reactive subject, in *Logics of Worlds*, and his contempt for parliamentary democracy as it expresses itself in the current capitalist configuration of the world.

One of the major difficulties with his understanding of politics is that the sequences he takes as exemplary are also related, in one way or another, to violence, oppression and totalitarianism. Such a concern cannot merely be dismissed as reactive, as Badiou tends to do at times (see LW 54–8). Indeed, Badiou himself is keenly aware of the difficulty, as is clear in *The Century*, in which he discusses the various political sequences of the twentieth century as manifesting a "passion for the real" that corresponds with destruction. Badiou writes, for instance:

> The real, as all key players of the century recognize, is the source of both horror and enthusiasm, simultaneously lethal and creative. What is certain is that it is – as Nietzsche splendidly put it – "Beyond Good and Evil". Any conviction about the real advent of a new man is characterized by a steadfast indifference to its cost; this indifference legitimates the most violent means. If what is at stake is the new man, the man of the past may very well turn out to be nothing but disposable material. (TC 33)

However, rather than simply dismissing this "passion for the real" because of its all too evident violent features, as would the reactive subject, Badiou provides an immanent critique of it, in essence dividing this destructive "passion for the real" from a "subtractive" understanding of that passion. If, on Badiou's account, the "passion for the real" that leads to destruction depends for its operation on conceiving of the real itself in the form of identity, subtractive passion rests on the construction of a minimal difference, taking the gap between the real and its semblance as real. The model for this gap in *The Century*, which interestingly enough comes not from politics but from art, is Kazimir Malevich's painting *White on White*, although the notion of subtraction functions at a more abstract level in *Being and Event*. If the passion for the real in the mode of destruction has as its concern identity, the purification of the false for the sake of authenticity, the subtractive passion for the real constitutes itself as "a differential and differentiating passion devoted to the construction of a minimal difference, to the delineation of its axiomatic. *White on White* is a proposition in thought that opposes minimal difference to maximal destruction" (TC 56). One could say, then, that Badiou's identification of politics with the revolutionary sequences mentioned above, his constant reading of and return to these, is an attempt to draw out this subtractive element, apart from the destructive "passion for the real". As Badiou says, "I am undertaking the exegesis of a singularity and of the greatness that belongs to it, even if the other side of this greatness, when grasped in terms of its conception of the real, encompasses acts of extraordinary violence" (C 53).

However, what this shift from destruction to subtraction looks like concretely, with regard to actual political sequences and practices, is not at all clear (see Toscano 2010: 30). Moreover, even if we were to grant Badiou the efficacy of the shift from destruction to subtraction, it is not entirely evident that Badiou has completely made it himself. To take just one pertinent example, in the final sub-section of Book 5, Section 1 of *Logics of Worlds*, Badiou explicitly relates "the creation of a new subject of truth" with destruction. Concluding this section, Badiou writes:

> When the world is violently enchanted by the absolute consequences of a paradox of being, all of appearing, threatened by the local destruction of a customary evaluation, must reconstitute a different distribution of what exists and what does not. Under the pressure that being exerts on its own appearing, the world may be accorded the chance – mixing existence and destruction – of an other world. It is of this other world that the subject, once grafted onto the trace of what has happened, is eternally the prince. (LW 380)

At the very least, such a claim complicates the relationship between destruction and subtraction in Badiou's thought.

INTERRELATING THE TRUTH PROCEDURES

As we have discussed, each of Badiou's four truth procedures is both immanent and singular, meaning that the production of truths is internal to the
procedure in question and irreducible to the others. However, because of
Badiou's emphasis on the immanent and singular character of truths, he
has paid little explicit attention to how science, art, politics and love might
be mutually implicated. Although Badiou has provided extended analyses
of the four truth procedures on their own terms, he has not, to date, provided any explicit and systematic treatment of the connection among the
four truth procedures, of the ways in which they potentially cross each other
in the production of truths.[11] This would not necessarily be a problem, if
Badiou were to maintain that there was no relation among the four procedures, although such a claim would, perhaps, raise its own issues. However,
if philosophy is only possible on the basis of the circulation of all four truth
procedures, if the task of philosophy is to compose their compossibility in
the present, then it would seem that there is, indeed, some relation among
the four truth procedures.

This seeming blind spot on Badiou's part to develop a coherent account
of the ways in which the four truths procedures interact and intersect has
not gone unnoticed among interpreters of Badiou. For instance, at the end of
an interview with Badiou, Justin Clemens asked him the following question:

> For you it seems absolutely crucial that love, mathematics, poli-
> tics, they're absolutely separate, absolutely heterogeneous, they
> don't intermingle with each other in any way, yet in "What is love?"
> there are two sexuated positions, there's man who metaphorizes,
> and woman who knots the four truth-processes together. Insofar
> as these are a knotting – that is, in fidelity to an event of love a
> woman knots all of these – is one not in love when one is faithful
> to a political event? (IT 191–2)

Badiou responded with the following answer, which acknowledges the problem but fails to give any adequate solution:

> The problem is the problem of the connection between the differ-
> ent procedures. It is a problem which is very interesting and com-
> plex. For instance, there are some similarities between politics and
> love, and I demonstrate this with technical concepts, numericity
> and the unnameable and so on; a singular connection between
> artistic creation and political thought also, and also a connec-
> tion between love and science because love and science are the
> two procedures which don't know that they are procedures, in

fact. It is not the same with artistic creation. We know perfectly that it is a procedure of truth in rivalry with science. It is not the same, naturally, for other conditions. It is necessary to elaborate a general theory of the connections of the knots between different procedures but the difficult point is to have criteria for such an evaluation: however, it is possible once you have categories for the different steps of the procedures. I am working on this point.

(IT 192)

The interview took place in 1999, and if, at that time, Badiou mentioned that he was "working on this point", any adequate discussion of it has failed to materialize. Indeed, in *Logics of Worlds*, the four truth procedures are still, on the whole, treated as distinct from each other.

Nevertheless, I want to suggest in what follows a possible way to articulate the relationship among the four truth procedures, at least at a formal level. The relationship is, I suggest, already present in Badiou's thought, particularly in *Being and Event*, although he does not explicitly draw it out. Specifically, we can begin to elaborate how the formal substance of each of the four truth procedures contributes to the production of any one of them, whether that truth be mathematical-scientific, artistic-poetic, amorous, or political, if we revisit Meditation 20 of *Being and Event*, which is concerned with intervention.

Although the event qua event, along with its associated ideas, falls on the side of what-is-not-being-qua-being, this does not mean that it lacks any ontological characteristics whatsoever, as we discussed in Chapter 2. Recall that the event is "a one-multiple made up of, on the one hand, all the multiples which belong to its site, and on the other hand, the event itself" (BE 179). As an ontological definition of the event, it is applicable to any event whatsoever, whether it occurs in the domain of mathematics-science, art-poetry, love or politics. What this means, however, is that all events contain a formal element of mathematical-scientific truth, that is, ontological truth. Otherwise put, the emergence of any event presupposes an ontological foundation, a foundation whose truth falls to the domain of mathematics-science. The mathematical-scientific domain of truth, then, crosses itself and art-poetry, love and politics, providing the ontological base from which any truth procedure must initially proceed.

The grounding of all events in the mathematical-scientific domain does give a certain priority to that domain itself, since it is foundational. Such priority is, of course, a direct consequence of Badiou's identification of ontology and mathematics, and it goes to the heart of his anti-theology. Nevertheless, although the mathematical domain has a certain degree of priority, it does not work on its own, at least as regards the production of truths. To assume as much would amount to a hypostasization of the event at the expense of the actual process of the production of truths, in which the other procedures come into play.

Take the role of art-poetry to begin with. Recall that, for Badiou, since the belonging of an event to a situation is, strictly speaking, undecidable from the perspective of the situation, a decision must be made concerning its belonging to the latter. This decision takes the form of what Badiou refers to as an intervention, which involves an act of nomination that makes the event available for the production of truth. However, this act of nomination is, as we discussed in the previous section, irreducibly poetic. Badiou thus says that "in summoning the retention of what disappears, every name of an event or of the evental presence is in its essence poetic" (IT 26). Moreover, this irreducible poetic element applies not just to the initial act of nomination, but also to the formation of truth itself through the faithful activity of the subject, in so far as the subject must force the construction of a new language adequate to the truth of the event in question. All this is to say, just as mathematical-scientific truth crosses itself and each truth procedure at the ontological level, so too does artistic-poetic truth, as that which names an event and its consequences, making them susceptible to thought.

Although the naming of the event and its consequences is, in essence, poetic, the structure of naming itself also relates to love, understood as the truth of the disjunction or the two. Recall that, for Badiou, the "initial operation of intervention is to *make a name out of an unpresented element of the site to qualify the event whose site is the site*" (BE 204, original emphasis). Intervention qua naming makes the event available for the production of truth but, importantly, the event itself remains "sutured to the unpresentable" (BE 206). There is thus a gap between the event itself, as unpresented, and the event as named, as governed by the interventional signifier. The two are not the same, which is why it is possible to treat the name of the event as a second event, the event of the event, so to speak, that makes the original event legible for decision. Both the event itself and its name, however, are necessary:

> It is certain that the event alone, aleatory figure of non-being, founds the possibility of intervention. It is just as certain that if no intervention puts it into circulation within the situation on the basis of an extraction of elements from the site, then, lacking any being, radically subtracted from the count-as-one, the event does not exist. (BE 209)

Now, as Badiou points out, the form of intervention, as based on the disjunction between the event and its name, is the two. Badiou writes, "The event, pinned to multiple-being by the interventional capacity, remains sutured to the unpresentable. This is because the essence of the ultra-one is the Two" (BE 206). Indeed, Badiou even says that the disjunction between the event and its name founds the maxim, "there is Twoness" (*ibid.*). We know from our discussion of Badiou's truth procedures above that the investigation of the two, the two itself, falls primarily to the domain of love, which makes truth out of the paradox of the two, out of the disjunct relation between "man" and "woman". In Badiou's words, love concerns the:

> truth of the situation *insofar as there exist two disjunct positions.*
> Love is nothing other than a trying sequence of investigations on
> the disjunction and the Two, such that in the retroactivity of the
> encounter it verifies that it has always been one of the laws of the
> situation.   (WL 45, original emphasis)

It would seem, then, that at a formal level love crosses the truth procedures themselves in the two, in the disjunction between the event and its name.

Where, then, does politics fit in? Recall from our discussion of the political truth procedure that politics, as Badiou understands it, subtracts itself from the state. Based on Badiou's own claim that the term "state" functions both ontologically and politically, I would suggest that subtraction itself is the political element in all truth procedures. Otherwise put, it is the actual break with the situation that depends upon the political truth procedure, the decision to intervene with respect to the event. Consider, for instance, Badiou's discussion of the conflict at the beginning of the twentieth century among mathematicians over the axiom of choice, which in the realm of ontology formalizes intervention. Badiou writes:

> The conflict between mathematicians at the beginning of the
> century was clearly – in the wider sense – a political conflict,
> because its stakes were those of admitting a being of interven-
> tion; something that no known procedure or intuition justified.
> Mathematicians – it was Zermelo on the occasion – had to inter-
> vene for intervention to be added to the Ideas of being.   (BE 228)

What is interesting here is the way Badiou characterizes an intra-mathematical intervention, an intervention on the being of intervention, in political terms: it is, as he puts it, "a political conflict". Or consider the following remark, in regard to the expansion of the meaning of the term "politics" among the twentieth-century avant-garde:

> The word "politics" names the desire of beginning, the desire that
> some fragment of the real will finally be exhibited without either
> fear or law, through the sole effect of human invention – artistic
> or erotic invention, for example, or the inventions of the sciences.

> The art/politics connection is incomprehensible if the word "pol-
> itics" is not accorded this expanded, subjective meaning.
>
> (TC 150)

In so far as this "expanded, subjective meaning" tends to fuse the other truth procedures to politics, it is a thesis that Badiou rejects. However, in so far as politics names the break with the situation as such, as is clear from the previous quotation and the example given above, it is applicable at a formal level to any truth procedure.

This sketch of the interrelation of Badiou's four truth procedures is, admittedly, all too brief, and more work needs to be done in this regard. Nevertheless, it is a fruitful exercise in its own right, and one that seems nec-essary if, as Badiou maintains, philosophy is only possible so long as all four of its conditions – science, art, politics, love – are in play. Indeed, the inter-relation of the four truth procedures, both at the level of the construction of philosophy itself and formally in each individual procedure, cautions against reducing Badiou's philosophy to any one of its conditions. We could say that Badiou's philosophy is in excess over any one of its conditions, which is an important point to keep in mind as we consider the relationship that his philosophy maintains with theology.

PHILOSOPHY, SOPHISTRY, ANTI-PHILOSOPHY

So far we have been concerned primarily with how Badiou understands phi-losophy in relation to its conditions and these conditions themselves, under-stood as sites for the production of truths. We also attempted to interrelate science, art, love and politics, showing how each one at a formal level is present in the production of any one truth. However, our discussion of phi-losophy and its conditions should not lead to the conclusion that philosophy has a monopoly on its conditions, that philosophy exhausts the thinking of its conditions, without remainder. The actual production of truths, as we have discussed, falls to the conditions themselves, but philosophy is not the sole discourse concerned with these conditions. Specifically, we need to understand the role that sophistry and anti-philosophy play with respect to truths, philosophy in general, and Badiou's own philosophy in particular.

We can begin with sophistry. Given Badiou's general allegiance to Plato, it is, perhaps, not all that surprising that Badiou finds in sophistry an enemy of philosophy as such.[12] Sophistry is, however, only an enemy of philosophy to the extent that it resembles philosophy itself. Hence Badiou notes that sophistry is "from the outset the enemy-brother, philosophy's implacable twin" (MP 116). What, then, constitutes sophistry for Badiou, that "enemy-brother" of philosophy? Peter Hallward gives a concise summation of it, when he says that sophistry "privileges rhetoric over proof, the seductive manipulation of appearance over the rigorous demonstration of a reality, and the local contingency of rules over the deduction of a universal principle" (Hallward 2003: 16). The classic exemplar of the sophistic position is, of course, Gorgias, although there is for Badiou little difference in the end between Gorgias and more contemporary forms of sophistry. Badiou defines the latter in the following terms:

> The modern sophists are those that, in the footsteps of the great Wittgenstein, maintain that thought is held to the following alternative: either effects of discourse, language games, or the silent indication, the pure "showing" of something subtracted from the clutches of language. Those for whom the fundamental opposition is not between truth and error or wandering, but between speech and silence, between what can be said and what is impossible to say. Or between statements endowed with meaning and others devoid of it. (MP 116–17)

Given Badiou's definition, on his account much of what passes for contemporary philosophy is really a form of sophism, whether the designation is accepted or not. Thus Badiou writes:

> Language games, deconstruction, feeble thinking, irremediable heterogeneity, differends and differences, the ruin of Reason, the promotion of the fragment and discourse in shreds: all of these argue in favor of a sophistic line of thinking and place philosophy at an impasse. (MP 135)

However, it is somewhat ironic that in this last quotation, and in general, Badiou's dismissal of sophism relies on one of sophism's key strategies: the privileging of rhetoric over proof. Badiou has a tendency to flatten out the complexities and differences in contemporary philosophy, summing these up and dismissing them all too easily under the label "sophism". Nevertheless, this strategy is also in keeping with Badiou's polemical conception of philosophy, which in relation to sophism maintains "the sophist as its adversary", through "dialectical strife" (MP 134). This is an important point, since it makes the relation between philosophy and sophism more complicated, a recognition that can easily be overlooked by focusing too much on Badiou's militant and dismissive rhetoric. We can get a handle on the relation between philosophy and sophism by discussing what Badiou sees as the three key differences that set the philosopher against the sophist.

In his essay "The (Re)turn of Philosophy *Itself*", Badiou notes first that the "sophist says there are no truths, that there are only technics of statements and loci of enunciation" (*ibid.*). The philosopher, in contrast, throws in with the existence of truths, the compossibility of which is made possible by the philosophical construction of the operational category Truth. Although the philosopher holds fast to the existence of truths against their sophistic reduction to the effects of language, Badiou also notes that the philosopher cannot fall back on a "dogmatic" conception of Truth, a conception of an overriding Truth, in the singular, thought along the lines of presence. "Philosophy may raise the objection to the sophist of the local existence of truths", Badiou states, but "it goes astray when it proposes the ecstasy of a place of truth" (*ibid.*).

Second, according to Badiou, the sophist "says there is a multiplicity of language games, that there is plurality and heterogeneity of names" (*ibid.*). Now, at one level, this claim is something with which the philosopher, and Badiou himself, can agree. As Badiou puts it in his *Ethics* in reference to the ethics of the other, "Infinite alterity is quite simply what there is ... and such is the way of the world" (E 27). Indeed, as we have seen, Badiou's ontology is an ontology of the multiple. However, for Badiou difference as such – the multiplicity of language games, the sheer diversity of morals, customs and beliefs, the differences in and among cultures – holds no interest for philosophical thought. Philosophy, for Badiou, is not concerned with what is but with what is not, with truths and the construction of the category of Truth. Thus, against the sophistic reduction of thought to the plurality of language games and the infinite dissemination of names, Badiou says, "It is philosophically legitimate to reply by constructing, by means of the category of Truth, a locus wherein thought indicates its unity of time. To show, by means of their seizing, that truths are compossible" (MP 133). This does not mean, however, that truths can be located under one name, that a single, substantial name can subsume the individual names of truths; doing so would be "dogmatic" and "ruinous" for philosophy (MP 134).

Third, according to Badiou, the sophist "says that being *qua* being is inaccessible to the concept and to thought" (*ibid.*). Such a statement, of course, contrasts with Badiou's mathematical ontology and falls under what Badiou would call a metaphysics of presence, in so far as it locates being as such outside the thinkable. Concerning the question of truth, Badiou writes, "It is philosophically legitimate to designate, and to think, the empty locus on the seizing of truths by means of the pincers of Truth" (*ibid.*). However, and again, this is not a substantial notion. Badiou writes:

> It is no longer legitimate to claim that, under the category of Truth, the void of being befalls to the unique thought of its act, or its destiny. To the sophists, philosophy must oppose the real of the truths whose seizing it carries out. It goes astray when it proposes the terroristic imperative of being-True as such.   (*Ibid.*)

115

In the end, it seems that what Badiou calls "sophism" keeps philosophy in check, reminding philosophy that its central category – Truth – can easily become dogmatic. As Badiou puts it:

> The sophist is required at all times for philosophy to maintain its ethics. For the sophist is the one who reminds us that the category of Truth is void. Indeed, he only does it to negate truths, whereby he must be combated. But combated within the ethical norms of this combat. Philosophical extremism, a figure of disaster within thinking, strives for the annihilation of the sophist. But it is in fact to his triumph that it contributes and abets. For, if philosophy renounces its operation and its void, the category of Truth has only dogmatic terror left to establish itself. Against which, the sophists will have an easy time showing the compromises of philosophical desire with tyrannies.   (MP 135)

It is for this reason that philosophy must maintain a relation to the sophist through "dialectical strife", as mentioned above. The sophist, to be sure, must be countered and argued against, but never dismissed or destroyed. As Badiou puts it, "The disastrous moment is the one when philosophy declares the sophist *must* not be, the moment when it decrees the annihilation of its Other" (MP 134, original emphasis).

Turning now to anti-philosophy, there is a degree of overlap between it and sophism. Indeed, some of the figures whom Badiou identifies with sophism, such as Nietzsche and Wittgenstein, also serve as prominent proponents of anti-philosophical discourse. What, then, is anti-philosophy? Badiou borrows the term "anti-philosophy" from Jacques Lacan, who used it to describe what he took to be his own particular relation, or non-relation, to philosophy (WA 16).[13] Now, as Bruno Bosteels (2008) points out, Lacan's own use of the term is sparse, enigmatic, and by no means systematic, making it virtually impossible to reconstruct the precise sense of his usage of the term.[14] Nevertheless, Lacan seems to have used the term to pit the discourse of the analyst against the university discourse or the discourse of the master (see C 228). Whatever the case may be, although Badiou borrows the term from Lacan, Badiou's use of the term is by no means confined to Lacan's own use of it. Summing up Badiou's use of the term, Bosteels notes that the category of anti-philosophy for Badiou:

> emerges as the name for a longstanding tradition of thinkers who, with regard to the dominant philosophical trends of the time, situate themselves in the strange topological position of an "outside with", or of an "internal exteriority" ... in an attitude that typically oscillates between distance and proximity, admiration and blame, seduction and scorn.   (Bosteels 2008: 158)

That is, anti-philosophy takes its place within philosophy itself, passing through it in order to denounce it.

It is thus important to emphasize from the outset that, generally speaking, for Badiou anti-philosophy is not an entirely negative practice, something that can be either ignored or easily swept aside. Indeed, it seems that if anti-philosophy must pass through philosophy in order to make its anti-philosophical claims, then philosophy must also pass through anti-philosophy in order to make philosophical claims. For instance, in reference to Lacan, that "great detractor" of philosophy, Badiou states, "In my view, only those who have had the courage to work through Lacan's anti-philosophy without faltering deserve to be called 'contemporary philosophers'" (TW 119). Likewise with reference to Lacan, Badiou states that "he is an anti-philosopher, and no one is entitled to take this designation lightly" (2006c: 7). This perhaps explains why Badiou devotes so much attention to the work of the great anti-philosophers: Saint Paul, Pascal, Kierkegaard, Nietzsche, Wittgenstein, Lacan, to name a few of the most prominent.

Although individual anti-philosophers differ, of course, in their emphases, anti-philosophy in general has three formal elements in common, all of which give body to a "philosophical contempt of philosophy" (WA 16). First, anti-philosophy has as its target truth or, more specifically, all philosophical attempts to construct a systematic account of truth. Through linguistic, logical and/or or genealogical critiques of philosophical statements – critiques that, for Badiou, border on the sophistical – anti-philosophy attempts to demolish the theoretical pretentions of philosophy. For this reason, Badiou states that anti-philosophy represents "[a] destitution of the category of truth" (WA 16).

A key move for anti-philosophers, in this respect, is to label the philosopher's search for truth not merely as false, but at best misguided, at worst a sickness or absurdity. Thus in light of the resurrection, both Saint Paul and Pascal see no need for philosophy; Kierkegaard chastises the systematic pretentions of Hegelianism for depleting the singularity of existence; Nietzsche takes philosophy as a sickness, a disease of *ressentiment* caught from Plato; Wittgenstein understands most philosophical questions and propositions as senseless or absurd; and Lacan associates philosophy with the discourse of the master, whose desire for a completed knowledge propagates the illusions of the imaginary (see SP 58; LW 425; WA 17; C 228–47). The various denials of philosophy's systematic pretentions also shed light on the form that anti-philosophy often takes. On the one hand, it is a common practice among anti-philosophers to insert themselves into their texts, to vest their own, individual experience with a general authority fit to overturn philosophical pretensions. For instance, Saint Paul rests his authority and the truth of his gospel on his Damascus road experience of the risen Christ. Or, as Badiou notes in reference to Kierkegaard, "the most garrulous among the anti-philosophers", "To get the better of Hegel, Kierkegaard must turn the pitiful episode of his own betrothal to Regine into an existential feuilleton" (LW 557). On the other hand, in keeping with the singularity of their own experience, the writings of the anti-philosophers are more often than not unsystematic, occasional and fragmentary, showing little concern for the deductive rigour and consistency that Badiou favours. Otherwise put, the writings of the anti-philosophers take the form of militant interventions against philosophy. Badiou writes:

> This format, in which the opportunity for action takes precedent over the preoccupation with making a name for oneself through publications ("poubellications," as Lacan used to say), evinces one of the antiphilosopher's characteristic traits: he writes neither system nor treatise, nor even really a book. He propounds a speech of rupture, and writing ensues when necessary.   (SP 31)

Second, in its critique of philosophy, anti-philosophy does not merely focus its attention on the discursive appearance or articulation of philosophy, the statements and propositions it constructs. Indeed, in so far as anti-philosophy comes out against truth, the careful and patient refutation of the statements and propositions designed to construct a systematic account of truth seems, from the perspective of anti-philosophy, a pointless exercise. Statements and propositions, the form of philosophy itself, are, in the end, only secondary to what philosophy essentially is: an act. As Badiou explains in reference to what the anti-philosopher thinks, "Philosophy is an act, of which the fabulations around the 'truth' are the clothing, the propaganda, the lie" (WA 17). The anti-philosophical identification of philosophy with act, then, dovetails with the anti-philosophical suspicion of the philosopher's search for truth: what the philosopher calls "truth" only serves to conceal what is really going on in his or her discourse, whether this be understood along the lines of Nietzsche's will to power, the effacement of the division between the decidable and undecidable for Wittgenstein, or in reference to the master's discourse for Lacan (see WA 23; C 228).

Third, and significantly, against the philosophical act, the anti-philosopher appeals to another act, an act of radical novelty that breaks through the limits of thought, speech and experience, an act that serves as a substitute for the philosophical pretention towards truth (WA 17). As Bruno Bosteels has observed, this appeal to another act beyond the pretensions of philosophy "is without a doubt the most important element in the formal characterization of any anti-philosophy, namely, the reliance on a radical gesture that alone has the force of destituting, and occasionally overtaking, the philosophical category of truth" (2008: 167). Another way to put this is to say that anti-philosophy "proclaims an ineffable, transcendent Meaning, grasped in the active refutation of philosophical pretentions to truth" (Hallward 2003: 20). The anti-philosophical gesture, combined with and authorized by an appeal to the ineffable, however understood, brings anti-philosophy close to religion. Indeed, Hallward has suggested that, differences aside, anti-philosophy is little more than religion through another means: "Antiphilosophy is religion in philosophical guise, argued on philosophical terrain" (*ibid*.). The close relationship between religion and anti-philosophy can be seen further in the role that Christianity often plays in those thinkers that Badiou commonly identifies and treats as anti-philosophers. As Badiou puts it:

> The connection of Christianity to modern antiphilosophy has a long history. We can easily draw up the list of antiphilosophers of strong caliber: Pascal, Rousseau, Kierkegaard, Nietzsche, Wittgenstein, Lacan. What jumps to the eye is that four of these stand in an essential relation to Christianity: Pascal, Rousseau, Kierkegaard, and Wittgenstein; that the enraged hatred of Nietzsche is itself at least as strong a bond as love, which alone explains that the Nietzsche of the "Letters from madness" can sign indifferently as "Dionysos" or "the Crucified"; that Lacan, the only true rationalist of the group – but also the one who *completes* the cycle of modern antiphilosophy – nonetheless holds Christianity to be decisive for the constitution of the subject of science, and that it is in vain that we hope to untie ourselves from the religious theme, which is structural. (WA 24–5; quoted in Bosteels 2008: 171–2)

The close relationship between anti-philosophy and religion, in particular Christianity, raises important questions about the role of anti-philosophy and religion in Badiou's own philosophy. As I will argue in the next chapter, Badiou's philosophy, although explicitly designed against anti-philosophy, contains an irreducible anti-philosophical element, an element that coincides with a theological element at work in Badiou's thought.

Nevertheless and in conclusion, we could say that the distinction between philosophy and anti-philosophy rests on the role that rationality plays in each. For Badiou, philosophy is primarily a rationalizing enterprise. This is the case, as we have seen, with Badiou's ontology and his philosophy proper, including his theory of truth and the subject and the manner in which he treats the four conditions of philosophy. Anti-philosophy, in contrast, puts its trust in what cannot be rationalized, in something other than rationality. Otherwise put, anti-philosophy rests on the idea of the "remainder":

> This idea of the "remainder" can be found in every antiphilosophy, which builds very subtle networks of relations only so as to track down the incompleteness in them, and to expose the remainder

to its seizing in the act. This is precisely where antiphilosophy destitutes philosophy: by *showing* that which its poor theoretical pretension has missed, and which is nothing less, in the end, than the real. Thus for Nietzsche, life is that which appears as a remainder of every protocol of evaluation. Just as for Pascal Grace is entirely subtracted from the order of reasons, for Rousseau, the voice of conscience from the preachings of the Enlightenment, for Kierkegaard existence from the Hegelian synthesis. And for Lacan, we know that the philosopher neither can nor wants to know anything of enjoyment and the Thing to which it is yoked.

(WA 34, original emphasis; quoted in Bosteels 2008: 165)

We will see in the next chapter to what extent this notion of the remainder, whose theological name is grace, informs Badiou's philosophy

4. BADIOU'S THEOLOGY

The goal of this chapter is to show the manner in which Badiou continues to rely on theological concepts to construct some of the basic aspects of his own philosophy, despite the overt anti-theological thrust of the latter. As we will see, a theological element remains at work at the core of Badiou's philosophy, an element that coincides with anti-philosophy and takes on an eschatological form. As a point of departure for discussing Badiou's reliance on theology, the first section of this chapter discusses the various attempts that Badiou's critics have made to identify a theological core in Badiou's philosophy. The second section of this chapter focuses on Badiou's seeming identification of Christianity with the formal element of truths and analyses his use of theological language, and is followed in the third section with a critical reading of Badiou's *Saint Paul: The Foundation of Universalism*. These discussions serve to indicate how Badiou's philosophy is determined by an anti-philosophical element that coincides with theology, which is the subject of the fourth and final section of this chapter. Although, as we will see, Badiou attempts to limit this theological element, his way of doing so leads him straight into theology again, particularly into the structure of eschatology.

READING BADIOU THEOLOGICALLY

The question of Badiou's relationship to theology has generated conflicting views among his interpreters. On one end of the spectrum are those interpreters who either ignore or present an entirely negative picture of Badiou's relationship to theology. Take Peter Hallward, for example, author of *Badiou: A Subject to Truth*, which is widely regarded as the most comprehensive introduction to and assessment of Badiou's philosophy to date.[1] Hallward's presentation of Badiou's philosophy is, on the whole, remarkably thorough. Nevertheless, when it comes to *Saint Paul: The Foundation of Universalism*,

Badiou's most sustained engagement with theology, Hallward only devotes roughly two and a half pages to it, treating it mainly as an illustration or "example" of the evental constitution of the subject (see Hallward 2003: 108–10). When Hallward does discuss Badiou's relationship to religion and theology at a more general level, he largely presents it in a negative light, sticking to the explicit text of Badiou's own philosophy. For instance, in the first chapter of *Badiou: A Subject to Truth*, entitled "Taking Sides", Hallward stresses the manner in which Badiou's philosophy comes out against religion and theology at every turn. Thus Hallward states:

> No one, perhaps, has taken the death of God as seriously as Badiou. He aims to take Nietzsche's familiar idea to its absolute conclusion, to eliminate any notion of an originally divine or creative presence (however "inaccessible" this presence might remain to the creatures it creates), and with it, to abolish any orig-inal intuition of Life or Power. (*Ibid.*: 7)

Likewise, Hallward emphasizes the religious aspects of anti-philosophy, and grounds Badiou's philosophy as "anti-antiphilosophy". Quoting Hallward again, "The difference between religion and antiphilosophy is slight. Anti-philosophy is a rigorous and quasi-systematic extrapolation from an essen-tially religious *parti pris*. Antiphilosophy is religion in philosophical guise, argued on philosophical terrain" (*ibid.*: 20).

Hallward's negative portrayal of Badiou's relationship to religion and theology is, perhaps, most clearly on display in his argument with Simon Critchley. In an article entitled "On the Ethics of Alain Badiou", Critchley argues that there is no reason to exclude religion as a condition for ethical action in Badiou's philosophy, even if religion is considered by Badiou to be anti-philosophical.[2] In Critchley's words, "If it is granted that religion, at least for Saint Paul but perhaps also for Levinas, is antiphilosophical, then I do not see why it cannot be a condition for ethical action. Obviously for Paul, Pascal, and others, such as Luther and Kierkegaard, religion plays *pre-cisely* this role and it is privileged *because* it is anti-philosophical" (Critchley 2005b: 224, original emphasis). Based on this assumption, Critchley suggests that religion be included among Badiou's four truth procedures, as a condi-tion for ethical action on a par with science, art, politics and love. However, Critchley goes on to claim that, in light of Badiou's emphasis on the impor-tance of Paul for understanding the relationship between a subject and an event, we should ground religion as the paradigm for ethical action itself, above and beyond the four truth procedures. In Critchley's words, "Yet, one might want to go further and claim that precisely because of the exemplary way in which the logic of the event plays itself out in relation to Paul, namely, that Paul's notion of grace shows most clearly the subjectivity of the event, religion is perhaps the paradigm of ethical action, a paradigm upon which the other four conditions should be modeled" (*ibid*.: 224).

Hallward's response to Critchley focuses on Badiou's putatively absolute opposition to anti-philosophy. Noting with disdain Critchley's attempt to treat religion as "the paradigm of ethical action" in Badiou's philosophy, Hallward argues that, although Badiou thinks it necessary to think in proximity to anti-philosophy, Badiou's position leaves no room for ambiguity: Badiou is at all turns against anti-philosophy (Hallward 2000: 27).

Hallward goes on to argue against Critchley that "the real model of Badiou's four conditions [is] not religion but that most anti-hermeneutic of disciplines, mathematics" (*ibid*.: 27). Hallward makes a similar point in an article entitled "Depending on Inconsistency", where he notes that, although Badiou's notion of subjectivization "invites pertinent comparisons with Saint Paul or Pascal ... the paradigm of Badiou's notion of a subject has always been the subject not of religious fervor but of a mathematical proposition" (Hallward 2005: 23). Emphasizing the mathematical pole of Badiou's philosophy, Hallward thus ultimately understands Badiou's philosophy as disjunct from anti-philosophy, meaning that there is no real place for concepts drawn from the realms of religious experience and theology in Badiou's thought. If and when such concepts do make an appearance in Badiou's work, they only do so as examples, examples that Badiou finds useful for illustrating his own position but that, in the end, remain dispensable, in the sense that they do not directly inform the shape of his philosophy, as does mathematics.[3]

If Critchley were alone in detecting an apparent theological element at work in Badiou's philosophy, we could, perhaps, chalk up his interpretation to misunderstanding. The problem, however, is that Critchley's interpretation of Badiou is by no means anomalous. On the other end of the spectrum are those who tend to see Badiou's philosophy as heavily influenced by theology to its core, informing the substance of its key concepts, even if he fails to acknowledge as much. Attempts to identify Badiou's philosophy with religion and theology are not all that surprising, considering his mainly positive reading of Saint Paul in *Saint Paul: The Foundation of Universalism*, a text that we will discuss in detail later on in this chapter. Take for instance Slavoj Žižek's influential reading of the basic aspects of Badiou's philosophy in *The Ticklish Subject*. Žižek, to be sure, does provide an overview of the more strictly ontological aspects of Badiou's philosophy as articulated in *Being and Event*, but he tends to privilege Badiou's reading of Paul, taking the latter as the ultimate example of Badiou's truth-event. So much is evident even in the title of Žižek's chapter on Badiou: "The Politics of Truth, or, Alain Badiou as a Reader of Saint Paul" (Žižek 1999: 127–70). Žižek's privileging of Badiou's reading of Paul as a way into Badiou's philosophy as a whole allows Žižek to claim that religion – more specifically,

ALAIN BADIOU

Christianity – functions as the unacknowledged condition that grounds or knots together Badiou's four generic procedures of truth. Thus Žižek states, "So, perhaps, if we take Badiou's thought itself as a 'situation' of Being, subdivided into four *génériques*, (Christian) religion itself is his 'symptomal torsion', the element that belongs to the domain of Truth without being one of its acknowledged parts or subspecies" (Žižek 1999: 141). Because Christianity is excluded from the material truth procedures of art, science, politics and love, Žižek suggests that it occupies the place of the generic as such in Badiou's philosophy. In Žižek's words, "[W]ith regard to Badiou's own classification of generic procedures in four species (politics, art, science, love), does not religious ideology occupy precisely this generic place? It is none of them, yet precisely as such it gives body to the generic as such" (*ibid.*: 144).

Jean-Jacques Lecercle has also suggested that Badiou's philosophy maintains a close relationship with theology. In his overview of the main elements of Badiou's philosophy, Lecercle points out that Badiou's theory of evental truth seems to be at least partially based on "a kind of negative theology" (Lecercle 1999: 8). Lecercle makes this claim in light of the fact that the concepts associated with Badiou's theory of evental truth – the undecidable, the indiscernible, the generic, the unnameable – assume and assure that truth occur "outside meaning" or knowledge (*ibid.*). Lecercle goes on to suggest that, in addition to the explicit truth procedures of art, science, politics and love, one should consider adding a fifth: religion. Lecercle writes:

> There is not only an ontology, there appears to be a theology in Badiou. For what is more "eventual" in his sense than the Resurrection? Does it not puncture the old situation, and change it for the good? Is it not undatable in terms of its encyclopaedia? Does it not engineer encounters, provoke conversion? Is not faithfulness close to faith, as the French "fidélité" is close to "les fidèles"? (Badiou claims the word is borrowed from the category of love, but this smacks of Freudian denial.) Cannot every single term of his system of concepts be translated into religious terms, so that we shall have no difficulty in finding equivalents in Badiouese for terms like "conversion", "grace", "the elect", and so on? Does not he himself recognize this by hailing St Paul as the archetypal figure of the subject of a process of truth? (*Ibid.*: 11)

Oliver Marchart makes a similar claim in light of Badiou's reading of Paul. Noting that many of Badiou's key concepts give Badiou's philosophy "a somewhat Christian ring", Marchart asks, "Is there a secret, or not so secret, Christian model upon which Badiou's atheistic philosophy relies to some extent?" (Marchart 2007: 124). As the framing of the question implies,

Marchart's answer is in the affirmative: fidelity, truth, infinity, universality, Badiou's call for a "materialism of grace" based on his reading of Paul – all this suggests that "Badiou's philosophy secretly relies on the Christian paradigm as its model (or one of its models)" (*ibid.*: 126).

Not surprisingly, Badiou's supposedly unacknowledged reliance on Christianity has not escaped the notice of biblical scholars, theologians and philosophers of religion, although to date the focus from such quarters has largely been on Badiou's reading of Paul (see Caputo & Alcoff 2009; Harink 2010; Miller 2008).[4] We will return to aspects of some of these readings below. Suffice it at this point to mention Paul J. Griffiths' reading of Badiou, in his article "Christ and Critical Theory". Griffiths argues that the recent interest in Christianity, particularly Paul, among certain critical theorists and philosophers is best understood as "a pagan yearning for Christian intellectual gold" (Griffiths 2004: 55). On Griffiths' account, the lack of any viable resources for the construction of a critical discourse among contemporary cultural theorists makes Christianity increasingly attractive, since "our intellectual tradition is long-lived, rich, and subtle, and any attempt by European thinkers to do without it is not likely to last" (*ibid.*: 46). Hence Badiou's search for a new militant figure in Saint Paul, a search that for Griffiths "shows the depth of the yearning nostalgia to which post-Marxist cultural theorists are now almost inevitably subject" (*ibid.*: 52). Graham Ward has reached a similar conclusion, even suggesting that Badiou's reading of Saint Paul ironically makes Badiou "one of our best defenders of the Christian faith" (Ward & Daniels: 2008).

How are we to understand these two, seemingly opposed, readings of Badiou's philosophy as it relates to Christian theology? Is there a way to take into account the strengths in both readings, to determine the role that theology plays in Badiou's philosophy? As a preliminary way into these and related questions, consider for a moment Oliver Feltham's reading of Badiou in *Alain Badiou: Live Theory*. Feltham suggests that there are three "voices" present in Badiou's philosophy: (i) "the old mole" stresses that change is a slow, gradual process, the unceasing supplementation of the new in the situation through the generic procedure of fidelity; (ii) "the owl" represents a more conservative voice that identifies change primarily with genesis, that is, with the structural reorganization of already existing elements of the situation; and (iii) "the eagle" speaks in a more voluntarist and idealist voice, associating change with a radical break in the situation, an excessive rupture that converts the impossible into the possible (2008: 53–67; 110–23). For now we can leave aside the voice of the owl, a voice that originates in Badiou's early work on Althusser but remains present in *Being and Event*, where it "advances a genetic interpretation of the count-for-one and claims that all situations are generated through generic truth procedures" (*ibid.*: 118). What is most important for the argument of this chapter is the relationship between the voice of the old mole and the voice of the eagle. As Feltham points out, the voice of the old mole corresponds to the role that forcing plays in the production of truths, a concept that we discussed in Chapter 2. The voice of the eagle, in contrast, corresponds to the event, understood as a combination of the elements of the evental site and its name. The two voices relate to each other, according to Feltham, in the sense that the old mole is "the dialectization of the eagle" through forcing (*ibid.*: 122).

Feltham's identification of competing voices in Badiou's philosophy is helpful, since, as I will suggest below, it allows us to draw out differing and perhaps even conflicting aspects of Badiou's philosophy, without falling into the trap of emphasizing one aspect at the expense of the others. From this perspective, it is not a matter of taking sides on the question of religion and theology in Badiou's philosophy, but of showing how both sides are related. As I will ultimately suggest, Badiou's philosophy itself wavers somewhere between philosophy and anti-philosophy, which also means that we can read his thought as situated between anti-theology and theology.

THE TRUTH OF CHRISTIANITY

We know that in Badiou's philosophy religion is excluded from being associated with the production of actual truths. So much is evident, of course, in Badiou's identification of science, art, politics and love as the four domains in which effective truths can occur, but it is also clearly on display throughout the whole of Badiou's philosophy, in so far as it takes its cue from the death of God. The death of God declares "the fact of religion dead" (TO 24). Nevertheless, a close reading of certain elements of Badiou's philosophy suggests that the relationship between it and religion, specifically as represented in the Christian theological tradition, is far more complex than a simple exclusion of the latter on the grounds that it has nothing to do with truths. Indeed, as we discussed above, in one way or another Critchley, Lecercle, Žižek, not to mention numerous others, all point to Christianity as an important condition for Badiou's own philosophy, in the sense that it functions as a resource for philosophical reflection. Even Bruno Bosteels, who on the whole tends to follow in Badiou's footsteps more closely than others, refers to Christianity as an "eternal shadow condition" of Badiou's philosophy (TS x). How, then, are we to understand the role that Christianity and its theological concepts play in Badiou's philosophy?

A good place to start is with Meditation 21 of *Being and Event*, which deals with Pascal. Badiou begins his discussion by noting that "Lacan used to say that if no religion were true, Christianity, nevertheless, was the religion which came closest to the question of truth" (BE 212). Badiou goes on to gloss this statement as follows:

This remark can be understood in many different ways. I take it to mean the following: in Christianity and in it alone it is said that the essence of truth supposes the eventual ultra-one, and that relating to truth is not a matter of contemplation – or immobile knowledge – but of intervention. For at the heart of Christianity there is that event – situated, exemplary – that is the death of the son of God on the cross. By the same token, belief does not relate centrally to the being-one of God, to his infinite power; its interventional kernel is rather the constitution of the meaning of that death, and the organization of a fidelity to that meaning. (*Ibid.*)

Although Badiou is clear that, on his reading, classical Christian theology remains captive to "an ontology of presence" that "diminishes the concept of infinity", he affirms nevertheless that "[a]ll the parameters of the event are thus disposed within Christianity" (*ibid.*).

We will return to a more detailed discussion of this claim later on in this chapter. For now, suffice it to note that, throughout the rest of *Being and Event*, an interesting slippage occurs at the textual level: Christianity takes its place alongside the other truth procedures, without qualification. For instance, when discussing the way in which the subject forces a truth through the generation of a particular language, a concept we discussed in detail in Chapter 2, Badiou states:

What is most explicitly attached to the proper names which designate a subjectivization is an arsenal of words which make up the deployed matrix of faithful marking-out. Think of "faith," "charity," "sacrifice," "salvation" (Saint Paul); or of "party," "revolution," "politics," (Lenin); or of "sets," "ordinals," "cardinals" (Cantor), and of everything which then articulates, stratifies and ramifies these terms. (BE 397)

A few pages later, when discussing how names of this type support the future anterior of a generic procedure, Badiou notes:

That such is the status of names of the type "faith," "salvation," "communism," "transfinite," "serialism," or those names used in the declaration of love can easily be verified. These names are evidently capable of supporting the future anterior of a truth (religious, political, mathematical, musical, existential) in that they combine local enquiries (predications, statements, works, addresses) with redirected or reworked names available in the situation. They *displace* established significations and leave the referent void: this void will have been filled if truth comes to pass in a new situation

> (the kingdom of God, emancipated society, absolute mathematics,
> a new order of music comparable to the tonal order, an entirely
> amorous life, etc.). (BE 399, original emphasis)

We could give numerous other examples (see BE 232–9, 393, 397, for instance), but note in these quotations that at the formal level there is no distinction between the terms that constitute Christianity and the terms that constitute the other, material truth procedures that Badiou recognizes. Indeed, if these passages were read on their own, one could easily assume that Christianity is a truth procedure in its own right.

But we know that is not the case, so we should, perhaps, not give too much weight to such formal textual similarities. The problem, however, is that Badiou often uses terms drawn from the "arsenal of words" that make up the specificity of the Christian "truth" procedure in order to construct his own philosophical position, as critics have often pointed out. This is, of course, obviously the case in *Saint Paul*, which we will discuss shortly, where the analysis of the subject matter demands the use of theological language, even if Badiou works to secularize the latter. But it is also on display throughout his other writings, where he freely and often seamlessly uses terms drawn from the theological tradition to construct his philosophy. For instance, when describing the subject of a generic procedure in Meditation 35 of *Being and Event*, Badiou notes that a "subject is thus, by the *grace* [my emphasis] of names, both the *real* of the procedure (the enquiring of the enquiries) and the *hypothesis* that its unfinishable result will introduce some newness into presentation" (BE 399). Likewise, when Badiou discusses the relationship of fidelity between event and subject, he often uses the term "encounter". To cite just a few pertinent examples:

> And it is true that a truth is an exception to what there is, if
> we consider that, when given the "occasion" to *encounter* [my
> emphasis] it, we immediately recognize it as such. (LW 6)

> This minimal gesture of a fidelity, tied to the *encounter* [my
> emphasis] between a multiple of the situation and a vector of the
> operator of fidelity ... (BE 330)

> As we've already said, the Christian paradox (which for us is one
> of the possible names for the paradox of truths) is that eternity
> must be *encountered* [my emphasis] *in* time. (LW 65)

As Badiou notes in *Saint Paul*, he considers the terms "grace" and "encounter" as originally belonging to the Christian lexicon (SP 66). So much is evident, when, discussing Paul's anti-dialectical understanding of the resurrection,

Badiou writes, "Grace, consequently, is not a 'moment' of the Absolute. It is affirmation without preliminary negation; it is what comes upon us in caesura of the law. It is pure and simple *encounter*" (SP 66, original emphasis). Concerning the term "encounter", it is also interesting to point out that in his essay "God is Dead", which we discussed in detail in the Introduction, it is the notion of "encounter" that seems to define religion: "Let it be said then that the God of metaphysics makes sense of existing according to a proof, while the God of religion makes sense of living according to an encounter" (TO 26). Badiou's use of the vocabulary of theology is perhaps most transparently on display in his designation of the subject of a truth procedure as "faithful", and his recent use of the term "resurrection" to label the reactivation of "a subject in another logic of its appearing-in-truth" in *Logics of Worlds* (LW 65).

When pressed on his use of such terminology to construct and describe elements of his own philosophical system, Badiou insists that these terms "are only metaphors" (Badiou 2006a: 181). Nevertheless, such an explanation seems unconvincing, based on the terms of Badiou's own philosophy. Recall that naming, in reference to both the event and the subsequent terms that construct any faithful procedure, is in essence poetic, dependent upon the artistic-poetic truth procedure. The essence of poetic language in general is, however, not for Badiou metaphorical, at least when thought qua truth procedure. Poetic language for Badiou is non-objective, in the sense that it "is neither a description nor an expression" but "an operation" (HI 29). To claim the contrary would be to lapse back into a hermeneutical stance, which Badiou otherwise consistently seeks to avoid. Otherwise put, language, when understood in poetic terms as related to truth, is not so much metaphorical or hermeneutical as it is directly inscriptive of the being of the process with which it is concerned. As Badiou puts it, "Language is the very being of truth via the combination of current finite inquiries and the future anterior of a generic infinity" (BE 399). Such an understanding is not limited to the poetic truth procedure alone but, based on what we said in Chapter 3 concerning the poetic element present in all naming, applies to truth procedures across the board. Take Badiou's claims regarding mathematics, which we discussed at length in Chapter 1. The claim that "mathematics is ontology" is not in any way metaphorical for Badiou, as if mathematics functioned merely as a useful analogue for expressing something more fundamental about being. The claim "mathematics is ontology" is a literal claim, in the sense that it is directly inscriptive of being itself. The language of mathematics is inseparable from both what mathematics thinks and how it thinks. The same could be said about the subject language of any other truth procedure, including that which comes close to a truth procedure, Christianity.

The upshot of this understanding of the language of truth procedures is that, since the language of truths is intimately linked to the ideas expressed in the truths themselves, it would seem that the use of such language, even outside its original context and for other purposes, implicates the truth of that language in its very use. One could, of course, say something similar about metaphor, but the difference lies in the fact that metaphor is easily dispensable, whereas the language of truth is not. The indispensability of the language of truth procedures does not mean that there is anything substantial about the language itself. As we discussed in Chapter 2, the names that constitute truth procedures are ultimately drawn from the void. Nevertheless, once a language of truth is in place, it acquires significance beyond the mere contingency of its appearance. This is why, for instance, Badiou insists on retaining the word "communist" as a political signifier: it, more than any other term according to Badiou, points to the truth of the idea of "collective emancipation" (see C 229–60; MS 97–103).

What I am getting at, here, is that Badiou's use of the language of theology, the language of the Christian "truth" procedure, implicates Badiou's philosophy in that "truth" procedure, at least at the linguistic level. Before going on to show how this implication is also at work conceptually in Badiou's thought, it is worth noting the following in further support of this claim. As we have discussed, Badiou's philosophy, taken as a whole to include ontology and the theory of truth and the subject, endeavours to be anti-theological. So much is consistent with Badiou's claim that God is dead, the God of religion, the God of metaphysics, and the God of the poem. It would seem, however, that one of the best ways to avoid any lingering hint of theology would be to avoid the language of theology altogether, except by way of critique or dismissal. This is something that Badiou simply does not do. We have given numerous examples above, but take for instance Badiou's use of the term "resurrection" in *Logics of Worlds* to describe the re-appearance of an occulted truth in a different logic or world. If one wanted to avoid theology at all costs, would it not be better to simply avoid this obvious theological term? Indeed, more than any other term, "resurrection" names the "truth" of Christianity. The term "reactivation", which Badiou uses to describe the operation of "resurrection", would seem to imply the same idea, unless of course there is something in the term "resurrection" itself that remains indispensible. To claim the latter is, however, to suggest that Badiou's philosophy remains captive to theology, conditioned by certain theological concepts, even if Badiou fails to explicitly acknowledge as much. Showing the extent to which this is the case is the burden of what follows, and we can begin with an analysis of Badiou's reading of Paul in *Saint Paul: The Foundation of Universalism*.

SAINT PAUL

The basic thrust of Badiou's reading of Paul's letters in *Saint Paul: The Foundation of Universalism* is by now well known, especially among theologians, biblical scholars, philosophers of religion and critics of Badiou. Badiou reads Paul as a "a poet-thinker of the event, as well as one who practises and states the invariant traits of what can be called the militant figure. He brings forth the entirely human connection, whose destiny fascinates me, between the general idea of a rupture, an overturning, and that of a thought-practice that is this rupture's subjective materiality" (SP 2). What interests Badiou in Paul is how the "paradoxical connection" that Paul institutes and investigates "between a subject without identity and a law without support provides the foundation for the possibility of a universal teaching within history itself" (SP 5). Paul is for this reason "a subjective figure of primary importance" (SP 1), even if Badiou will ostensibly have nothing to do with the explicit theological elements that populate Paul's discourse.

How, then, should we understand the relationship between Badiou and Paul, the relationship between Badiou's philosophy and the resolutely theological themes that make up the substance of Paul's letters? As we have mentioned above, Peter Hallward understands Badiou's reading of Paul's letters as an example of the relationship between truth and subjectivization. For Hallward, Paul's brand of Christianity serves as a "pertinent illustration" of Badiou's understanding of a generic procedure of truth, but it is only an illustration; in the end, it is dispensable, in that it does not directly inform Badiou's philosophy (Hallward 2003: 108). That Hallward takes Badiou's reading of Paul primarily as an illustration or example is evident, when he writes that although Badiou's understanding of the subjective process of truth "invites pertinent comparisons with Saint Paul or Pascal ... the paradigm of Badiou's notion of a subject has always been the subject not of religious fervor but of a mathematical proposition" (Hallward 2005: 23).

However, Badiou himself describes his reading of Paul in *Saint Paul: The Foundation of Universalism* somewhat differently, as a "reactivation": "When a step forward is the order of the day, one may, among other things, find assistance in the greatest step back. Whence this reactivation (*réactivation*) of Paul. I am not the first to risk the comparison that makes of him a Lenin for whom Christ will have been the equivocal Marx" (SP 2). Lest we think that this is a mere quibbling over words, it is important to note that the language of "reactivation" dovetails with Badiou's description in *Logics of Worlds* of the subjective destination of resurrection. Recall that, for Badiou, it is always possible to reconstitute or resurrect in a different context a prior sequence of truth. In Badiou's words, the resurrection of a truth "reactivates (*réactive*) a subject in another logic of its appearing-in-truth" (LW 65). Understood in this light, Badiou's reading of Paul is not so much an example that he finds useful for illustrating his own philosophical position; rather, and more substantively, it is a "resurrection" of Paul and his discourse in a different logic.

We will see for what purpose Badiou "reactivates" or "resurrects" Paul in a moment, but for now we should point out that it is a strange move on

Badiou's part. To begin with, in *Logics of Worlds*, the subjective destination of resurrection is clearly reserved for Badiou's four truth procedures: art, science, politics and love. This seems like an obvious point. One can only resurrect *a* truth if it is, in fact, a *truth*, and we are ostensibly limited to just four general options. Paul's discourse clearly does not encompass a real truth procedure for Badiou, and not just because it falls under some general notion of religion. Rather, its externality to truth lies in its mythological core, the resurrection of the crucified. As Badiou puts it, "Thus, unlike effective truth procedures (science, art, politics, love), the Pauline break does not base itself upon the production of a universal. Its bearing, in a mythological context implacably reduced to a single point, a single statement (Christ is resurrected), pertains rather to the laws of universality in general" (SP 108).

Moreover, Badiou explicitly and repeatedly identifies Paul and his discourse with anti-philosophy and its operations. Thus, in reference to Paul's failed attempt at the Areopagus to convince the Athenians of the truth of the resurrection from the dead, Badiou notes that what gets Paul in trouble is "antiphilosophy", "the contempt in which he holds philosophical wisdom" (SP 27). In reference to the importance of the resurrection for Paul, Badiou states, "Let us emphasize once more that, since the event that he takes to identify the real *is not* real (because the Resurrection is a fable), he is able to do so only by abolishing philosophy" (SP 58, original emphasis). Unlike the philosopher, Paul "writes neither system nor treatise, nor even really a book. He propounds a speech of rupture, and writing ensues when necessary" (SP 31). Likewise, if the anti-philosopher relies on the enunciative position to lend authority to his or her claims, Paul certainly does the same: "Whenever Paul addresses his writings, he always draws attention to the fact that he has been entitled to speak as a subject" (SP 17). Paul is an anti-philosopher "precisely because he assigns his thought to a singular event, rather than a set of conceptual generalities" (SP 108). Badiou goes on:

> That this singular event is of the order of fable prohibits Paul from being an artist, a scientist, or a revolutionary of the State, but also prohibits all access to philosophical subjectivity, which either subordinates itself to conceptual foundation or auto-foundation, or places itself under the condition of *real* truth procedures. For Paul, the truth event repudiates philosophical Truth, while for us the fictitious dimension of this event repudiates its pretension to real truth. (SP 108, original emphasis)

Otherwise put, for Badiou "*Paul is an antiphilosophical theoretician of universality*" (*ibid.*, original emphasis).

Why, then, turn to this anti-philosopher? Why resurrect him and his thought? Lest there be any confusion, Badiou makes it clear from the outset that he wants nothing to do with the specific, ultimately theological content of Paul's discourse. In Badiou's words, "Paul is not an apostle or a saint. I care nothing for the Good News he declares, or the cult dedicated to him" (SP 1). Paul's gospel, centred as it is on the resurrection, is, we have said, nothing more than a "fable" that "fails to touch on any Real", since for Badiou "it is rigorously impossible to believe in the resurrection of the crucified" (SP 5).[5] Nevertheless, according to Badiou, it is possible to subtract from the theological content of Paul's discourse a kernel of truth, a formal element concerning the relationship between subject and law that has general applicability. In Badiou's words:

> For our own part, what we shall focus on in Paul's work is a sin-
> gular connection, which it is formally possible to disjoin from
> the fable and of which Paul is, strictly speaking, the inventor: the
> connection that establishes a passage between a proposition con-
> cerning the subject and an interrogation concerning the law. Let
> us say that, for Paul, it is a matter of investigating which law is
> capable of structuring a subject devoid of all identity and sus-
> pended to an event whose only "proof" lies precisely in its having
> been declared by a subject. (*Ibid.*)

Badiou goes on to say:

> What is essential for us is that this paradoxical connection
> between a subject without identity and a law without support
> provides the foundation for the possibility of a universal teach-
> ing within history itself. Paul's unprecedented gesture consists
> in subtracting truth from communitarian grasp, be it that of a
> people, a city, an empire, a territory, or a social class. What is
> true (or just; they are the same in this case) cannot be reduced to
> any objective aggregate, either by its cause or by its destination. (*Ibid.*)

What Paul provides, according to Badiou, is a discourse that allows for a re-founding of the connection between truth and the subject – and it is this refounding that makes Paul, in a sense, our contemporary, despite his histor-ical and cultural distance. Paul's "interrogation" of the relationship between law and subject is "precisely our own" (SP 7).

Specifically, Badiou's reading of Paul grounds the latter's thought as a thinking of truth as "universal singularity", a thinking that allows us to think beyond the parameters of our current situation, governed as it is by the "false universality" of monetary abstraction and the "democratic" prolifera-tion of various "communitarian particularisms" (SP 6). Although these two parameters may, at first glance, seem opposed, they function together to form a seamless whole:

> Capital demands a permanent creation of subjective and territorial identities in order for its principle of movement to homogenize its space of action; identities, moreover, that never demand anything but the right to be exposed in the same way as others to the uniform prerogatives of the market. The capitalist logic of the general equivalent and the identitarian and cultural logic of communities or minorities form an articulated whole.   (SP 14)

The logic, here, is that of "democratic materialism", which we discussed in the previous chapter.

Against the oscillation between the false universality of monetary abstraction and the logic of particular identities, Paul constructs a discourse of universal singularity, which has four central components. First, in contrast to any discourse that would base itself on a fixed identity, the Christian subject, for Paul, does not depend on any pre-established particularity. "The Christian subject does not preexist the event he declares", Badiou writes (*ibid.*). Such is, for Badiou, the ultimate sense of Paul's famous claim made in Galatians 3.28, "There is no longer Jew or Greek, there is no longer slave or free, there is no longer male or female; for all of you are one in Christ Jesus." Second, truth is for Paul of the order of the subject, meaning that it is based on a declaration of the event and not on any pre-determined law governing the situation, whether this be the Jewish law or the Greek law, both of which Paul critiques. Third, truth for Paul is based on fidelity to the event (the resurrection of the crucified), meaning that "truth is a process, and not an illumination" (SP 15). Finally, like all truth procedures, Paul's is subtracted from the state of the situation, "the apparatus of opinion" (*ibid.*). In Badiou's words, for Paul a "truth is a concentrated and serious procedure, which must never enter into competition with established opinions" (*ibid.*). According to Badiou, "There is not one of these maxims which, setting aside the content of the event, cannot be appropriated for our situation and our philosophical tasks" (*ibid.*). Let us discuss these points in more detail.

Badiou reads Paul as founding a new theory of the subject, a theory that is non-objective, in the sense that it does not base its thinking of subjectivity on the extrinsic factors that mark and determine the status of individuals. On Badiou's account, Paul accomplishes this through the institution of a "Christian discourse" in contradistinction to the two "regimes of discourse" that govern the world he inhabits, namely "Greek discourse" and "Jewish discourse" (SP 41). Now, as Badiou argues, these two discourses do not immediately refer to any objective set of characteristics but are, rather, "subjective dispositions" (*ibid.*). Greek discourse, and the Greek subject that corresponds to it, bases itself on reason, wisdom and totality. In Badiou's words, "Greek discourse is *cosmic*, deploying the subject within the reason of a natural totality. Greek discourse is essentially the discourse of totality, insofar as it upholds the *Sophia* (wisdom as eternal state) of a knowledge of *phusis* (nature as ordered and accomplished deployment of being)" (*ibid.*, original emphasis). Jewish discourse, along with the Jewish subject, is in contrast primarily a discourse of exception, "because the prophetic sign, the miracle, election, designate transcendence as that which lies behind the natural totality" (SP 42).

Badiou argues that Paul's "profound idea" is that both of these discourses are, in the end, two sides of the same coin, in that they presuppose each other in order to function. Greek discourse and Jewish discourse, in this sense, "are the two aspects of the same figure of mastery". It is worth quoting Badiou at length on this point:

> For the miraculous exception of the sign is only the "minus-one", the point of incoherence, which the cosmic totality requires in order to sustain itself. In the eyes of Paul the Jew, the weakness of Jewish discourse is that its logic of the exceptional sign is only valid *for* the Greek cosmic totality. The Jew is in exception to the Greek. The result is, firstly, that neither of the two discourses can be universal, because each supposes the persistence of the other; and secondly, that the two discourses share the presupposition that the key to salvation is given to us within the universe, whether it be through direct mastery of the totality (Greek wisdom), or through mastery of a literal tradition and the deciphering of signs (Jewish ritualism and prophetism). For Paul, whether the cosmic totality be envisaged as such or whether it be deciphered on the basis the sign's exception makes, institutes in every case a theory of salvation tied to mastery (to a law), along with the grave additional inconvenience that the mastery of the wise man and that of the prophet, necessarily unaware of their identity, divide humanity in two (the Jew *and* the Greek), thereby blocking the universality of the Announcement.
>
> (*Ibid.*, original emphasis)

Although seemingly opposed on the surface, Greek discourse and Jewish discourse depend on each other for their viability. Another way to put this is to say that this figure of mastery at work in Greek discourse and Jewish discourse indicates that both are "discourses *of the Father*", binding their respective communal targets to obedience to either the cosmos or the law (*ibid.*, original emphasis). The mutual implication of Greek discourse and Jewish discourse, an implication that allows both to function in tandem, is analogous to the relationship between the abstract universality of capital, the reign of general equivalence, and the logic of particularism: capital depends on the proliferation of differences and differences, in turn, only count in light of their exposure to monetary abstraction.

Paul institutes a third discourse – Christian discourse – that cuts through or suspends the functioning of Greek discourse and its cosmic totality and Jewish discourse and its exceptional particularity. Based neither on the whole and its exception nor on a synthesis of the two, Paul's discourse proceeds from "the event as such, which is a-cosmic and illegal, refusing integration into any totality and signaling nothing" (*ibid.*). The event in question is, of course, the resurrection of Christ, and Badiou argues that, for Paul, it serves as the foundation for something "absolutely *new*", a discourse not of the father but of the son:

> The formula according to which God sent us his Son signifies primarily an intervention within history, one through which it is, as Nietzsche will put it, "broken in two," rather than governed by a transcendent reckoning in conformity with the laws of an epoch. The sending (birth) of the son names this rupture. That it is the son, not the father, who is exemplary, enjoins us not to put our trust any longer in any discourse laying claim to a form of mastery. (SP 43)

To claim that Christian discourse is a discourse of the son, not the father, is to claim that truth for Paul is of the order of the subject, meaning that its operations cannot be subsumed under the existing knowledge or law of the situation. The "radical novelty" instituted through the resurrection of the crucified entails that the truth of Christian discourse proceed without any external support, without appeal to any supposed objective markers that would claim to confirm it. The purely subjective character of Christian discourse is seen, on the one hand, in Paul's famous Damascus road encounter with the risen Christ, an encounter that "mimics the founding event" (SP 17). What is important for Badiou is the immediacy of this encounter, the fact that nothing prepares for, helps along, or confirms Paul's "conversion". Thus Badiou emphasizes that Paul's "conversion" "was a thunderbolt, a caesura, and not a dialectical reversal. It was a conscription instituting a new subject" (*ibid.*). Paul's "conversion" "isn't carried out by anyone: Paul has not been converted by representatives of 'the Church'; he has not been won over. He has not been presented with the gospel" (SP 17). Likewise, after his "conversion", Paul does not go directly to Jerusalem "to see the authorities, the institutional apostles, those who knew Christ. He does not seek 'confirmation' for the event that appoints him in his own eyes as an apostle. He leaves this subjective upsurge outside every official seal" (SP 18).

Paul's authority and the authority of his gospel, then, come directly from the event itself, his conversion to the event. As Paul puts it in Galatians 1:11–12, which Badiou quotes approvingly, "For I want you to know, brothers and sisters, that the gospel that was proclaimed by me is not of human origin; for I did not receive it from a human source, nor was I taught it, but I received it through a revelation of Jesus Christ" (quoted in SP 44).

The subjective character of Paul's discourse and its truth is seen, on the other hand, in the manner in which Paul articulates the novelty of his nascent form of Christianity vis-à-vis the other two discourses operative in his situation, Greek discourse and Jewish discourse. As mentioned above, Badiou reads Paul as understanding the resurrection as something "absolutely new": "It is pure event, opening of an epoch, transformation of the relations between the possible and the impossible" (SP 45). Because of this, it cannot be justified or confirmed through any available means in the established discourses. Otherwise put, the event of Christ's resurrection, along with the truth that proceeds from it, cannot coincide with the knowledge or language of the situation, meaning that it can only look absurd from the perspective of that knowledge or language. Badiou quotes from Paul's First Letter to the Corinthians to make the point:

> For Christ did not send me to baptize but to preach the gospel, and not with eloquent wisdom, lest the cross of Christ be emptied of its power. For the preaching of the cross is folly to those who are perishing, but to us who are saved it is the power of God. For it is written, "I will destroy the wisdom of the wise, and thwart the cleverness of the clever". Where is the wise man? Where is the scribe? Where is the debater of this age? Has not God made foolish the wisdom of the world? For since, in the wisdom of God, the world did not know God through wisdom, it pleased God through the folly of what we preach to save those who believe. For Jews demand signs and Greeks seek wisdom, but we preach Christ crucified, a stumbling block to Jews and a folly to Gentiles, but to those who are called, both Jews and Greeks, Christ the power of God, and the wisdom of God. For the foolishness of God is wiser than men, and the weakness of God is stronger than men. (Quoted in SP 46)

The evental disjunction between Christian discourse and the existing forms of knowledge or language in the situation explain why, in general, Paul does not rely either on philosophical proofs to establish the validity of the resurrection or appeals to the prophetic tradition to show how Christ is the fulfilment of prophecy. Far from being a weakness of Paul's discourse, "it is precisely the absence of proof that constrains faith, which is constitutive of the Christian subject" (SP 50). Thus, rather than attempting to prove the truth of his gospel through the means considered valid by either Greek or Jewish discourse, Paul says in I Corinthians 2:2 that he preaches nothing "except Jesus Christ, and him crucified" (quoted in SP 60).

Although Paul's is a discourse that is fundamentally without proof, Badiou insists on separating it from a fourth possible discourse, which Badiou refers to as the "subjective discourse of glorification" (SP 51). Badiou describes this discourse as "the discourse of the ineffable, the discourse of nondiscourse. It is the subject as silent and mystical intimacy ... only experienced by the subject who has been visited by a miracle" (*ibid*.). Now, as Badiou makes clear, Paul does not deny the existence of such a discourse, and Paul himself claims to have experienced such "mystical intimacy", when he describes his having been "caught up into the third heaven" or "Paradise", where he "heard things that are not to be told, that no mortal is permitted to repeat" (II Cor. 12:1–5; quoted in SP 51). However, on Badiou's account, Paul does not allow this "unaddressed" or "obscurantist" discourse to form the basis of Christian discourse, that is, "the public declaration of the Christ-event" (SP 53). To make the former the basis of the latter would be to lapse back into Jewish discourse, and hence the existing knowledge of the situation. As Badiou puts it:

> Supposing I invoke (as Pascal does) the fourth discourse ("joys, tears of joy ..."), and hence the private, unutterable utterances, in order to justify the third (that of Christian faith), *I relapse inevitably into the second discourse*, that of the sign, the Jewish discourse. For what is a prophecy if not a sign of what is to come? And what is a miracle if not a sign of the transcendence of the True? By granting the fourth discourse (mysticism) no more than a marginal and inactive position Paul keeps the radical novelty of the Christian declaration from relapsing into the logic of signs and proofs. (*Ibid*., original emphasis)

It is worth pointing out that, although Paul is, as we have said, an anti-philosopher, his refusal to put Christian discourse at the service of an "unaddressed" discourse separates him from some other anti-philosophers. For this reason, despite the fact that Paul remains an anti-philosopher, there remains in him and his thought "an ethical dimension of antiobscurantism" (SP 52).

Having discussed how Christian discourse formally relates to the other discourses operative in its milieu, we can now go on to delineate the specific subjective features of the Christian declaration for Paul. The event of Christ's resurrection, Badiou insists, "bears an absolutely new relation to its object" (SP 55). Badiou goes on to delineate the contours of Paul's Christian subject through a discussion of a series of oppositions or "two subjective paths" in

Paul's thought, namely the interrelated divisions between flesh and spirit, death and resurrection, law and love. Badiou treats each of these oppositions as largely synonymous: flesh, death and law all correspond to each other, as do spirit, resurrection and love. Badiou reads the relation between each term in the opposition in a putatively non-dialectical manner, meaning that the evental rupture retroactively configures the subject in the form of "not … but": not flesh but spirit, not death but resurrection, not law but love (SP 64).

The form of the "not … but" constitutes the novelty of Paul's discourse, indicating its universality:

> We shall maintain, in effect, that an evental rupture always con-
> stitutes its subject in the divided form of a "not … but", and that
> *it is precisely this form that bears the universal*. For the "not" is
> the potential dissolution of closed particularities (whose name is
> "law"), while the "but" indicates the task, the faithful labor, in which
> the subjects of the process opened up by the event (whose name
> is "grace") are the coworkers. The universal is neither on the side
> on the flesh as conventional lawfulness and particular state of the
> world, nor on the side of the pure spirit, as private inhabitation
> of grace and truth. The Jewish discourse of the rite and the law is
> undermined by the event's superabundance, but, equally, the arro-
> gant discourse of internal revelation and the unutterable is abol-
> ished. The second and fourth discourses must be revoked because
> they *unify* the subject. Only the third discourse holds to its divi-
> sion as a guarantee of universality. If the event is able to enter into
> the constitution of the subject declaring it, it is precisely because
> throughout it, and irrespective of the particularity of persons, it
> ceaselessly redivides two paths, distributing the "not … but", which,
> through an endless process, sets aside the law the better to enter
> into grace.   (*Ibid.*, original emphasis)

To use the language of *Being and Event*, this form of the "not … but", this setting aside of the law to enter into grace, amounts to an enquiry into the terms of the situation, so as to determine what belongs to the evental mul-tiple and what does not. The form of the "not … but" organizes a fidelity, "a chain of positive or negative atoms, which is to say the reports that such and such existing multiples are or are not connected to the event" (BE 234).

As a way into understanding in more detail this form of the "not … but" that Badiou takes as the organizing principle behind Paul's articulation of the Christian subject, it is helpful to begin with some criticisms of Badiou's reading of Paul on this issue. Doing so will help to orient the discussion that follows around the core issues in Badiou's reading of Paul, without adding any unnecessary repetition in the presentation of those issues.

One of the most common criticisms of Badiou's reading of Paul is that it is more Marcionite than Pauline. Thus, as Dominik Finkelde argues, when Badiou attributes to Paul "a radical break with Jewish tradition" in light of the resurrection, Badiou "arrives ... *not* at Paul, but at Marcion, that is, to the leader of the Marcionites, the man whom the church declared a heretic in the second century" (2007: 36). Simon Critchley makes a similar argument. Critchley rightly notes that Badiou attempts to separate his reading of Paul from Marcionism, which latter Badiou takes as a manipulation of Paul's discourse. Nevertheless, Badiou's insistence that the resurrection-event rely on sheer faith rather than proof, that the resurrection-event take the form of a "pure beginning", seems to point in the direction of Marcion, Badiou's qualifications notwithstanding. Indeed, Badiou's apparent proximity to Marcion is not merely a feature of his reading of Paul but endemic to the ontological structure of his philosophy as a whole. In Critchley's words, "Might we not conclude that Badiou's ontological dualism of being and the event, where the latter is always described as the absolutely new and where Badiou sees his project as the attempt to conceptualize novelty, is a Marcionite radicalization of Paul?" (2012: 200–201).

Even when Badiou's take on Paul is not explicitly labelled as Marcionite, the association of Badiou with some form of Marcionism is clear. Take Daniel M. Bell, Jr's criticism of Badiou, for instance. Based on an interpretation of Badiou's event that associates the latter with a "complete break", "an absolute beginning, a creation *ex nihilo*, the emergence of a naked singularity", his putatively one-sided emphasis on Paul's critique of the law, and his claim that the universality of truths renders differences indifferent, Bell asks rhetorically, "What is left of the Jews by the time Badiou's indifference has passed through their particularity, their difference?" (2007: 102). Bell answers, "What remains is a Judaism whose law is love, where everything is permitted, and subjective commitment is the cornerstone of the gospel. In other words, what remains is modern Protestantism, and the hope that real Jews will come to their senses and realize that they are just like everyone else" (*ibid.*). Indeed, Bell even suggests that "Badiou's Paul and Badiou's universalism are anti-Jewish, Badiou's protestations notwithstanding. Yes, Jews remain; but they are deracinated. They are Jews like a food court taco is a taco" (*ibid.*). In contrast to what he sees as Badiou's tendency to read Paul as advocating an absolute break with Judaism, which implies a devaluation of Judaism itself, Bell emphasizes the continuity between Judaism and Christianity. For Bell, the Christ-event does not institute an irretrievable break with Judaism, from its particularity and its law; rather, following Paul's statements in Romans 11, the Christ-event grafts Gentiles into the particularity of God's election of the Jewish people. Paul's soteriology, for Bell, is about "the Jewish Messiah and everyone's inclusion in Israel's election" (*ibid.*: 108).

Although Adam Kotsko does not explicitly label Badiou's reading of Paul "anti-Jewish", the substance of his critique is, on the whole, similar to Bell's. Kotsko begins his critique of Badiou's reading of Paul by focusing on the oppositions that Badiou draws from the Pauline corpus between faith and works, grace and law, spirit and flesh, life and death, and universality and particularity. Badiou and Badiou's Paul, of course, favour the former term in each pair over the latter. As Kotsko correctly points out, the terms in each pair are, to a certain extent, interchangeable, so that, for instance, "law is opposed to grace first of all because grace is necessarily universal" (2008: 43). That said, what primarily attracts Kotsko's attention, as the last quotation indicates, is the opposition between grace and law, specifically Badiou's characterization of the law in what seems to be purely negative terms, as irremediably linked to works, flesh, death and particularity. Essential for Kotsko is Badiou's statement that "the Christ-event is essentially the abolition of the law, which was nothing but the empire of death" (quoted in *ibid.*: 45). For Kotsko, this statement, coupled with Badiou's emphasis on the transliteral law of love as the end of the law itself, points to a major problem in Badiou's reading of Paul:

> While Badiou is implicitly arguing that Paul's statements would hold for every culture's legal code, he clearly believes that Paul's primary target is the law of his own people and excludes the possibility that Paul could, on principle, say anything positive about the Jewish law – for instance, Badiou seems to regard the inclusion of the love commandment in the Old Testament as a fortunate accident that Paul exploits for political purposes, rather than taking seriously the idea that "love is the fulfillment of the law". Overall, Badiou envisions a break with the law that allows for an overcoming of the division of the subject. (*Ibid.*)

Against Badiou, Kotsko commends Žižek's reading of Paul, which, instead of focusing on the abolition of the law, seeks to found a new relationship to the law, a new relationship already found in Judaism itself. Thus according to Kotsko, Žižek's reading "takes seriously Paul's self-understanding as apostle to the Gentiles, but precisely *from the Jews*, whereas for Badiou Paul's reference to Judaism is a superficial and instrumental one" (*ibid.*: 52, original emphasis).

In light of such criticisms, it is important to emphasize that Badiou does briefly discuss Marcion in *Saint Paul*, but the discussion is on the whole critical of Marcion's position. Immediately after discussing the "radical novelty" of Paul's proclamation, Badiou notes that "it is essential to take into account the upsurge of a heresy that one could call ultra-Pauline, that of Marcion, at the beginning of the second century" (SP 34). As Badiou points out, Marcion posits the evental break between Christianity and Judaism "as absolute in the precise sense: *it is not the same God who is in question in these two religions*" (*ibid.*, original emphasis). For Marcion there is an absolute disjunction between the old and the new, between what he saw as the malevolent creator God of Judaism and the benevolent, fatherly God of Christianity, who is known exclusively through the coming of the Son. Although Marcion took Paul as his guide in positing this ultimately Manichean rupture, Badiou notes that he pushed too far in thinking that "the new gospel is an absolute beginning" (SP 35). Indeed, according to Badiou, Marcion's position is a "manipulation" of the Pauline doctrine of the resurrection-event:

> There is no text of Paul's from which one could draw anything resembling Marcion's doctrine. That the God whose son is Jesus Christ is the God spoken of in the Old Testament, the God of the Jews, is, for Paul, a ceaselessly reiterated and obvious fact. If there is a figure with whom Paul feels an affinity, and one whom he subtly uses to his own ends, it is that of Abraham. That Paul emphasizes rupture rather than continuity is not in doubt. But this is a militant, and not an ontological thesis. Divine unicity bridges the two situations separated by the Christ event, and at no moment is it cast into doubt. (*Ibid.*)

Paul certainly holds that the resurrection-event constitutes a break in and with the situation; however, Badiou notes that this break is not absolute: divine unicity provides a link between past and present. Marcion's error, in this sense, is to mistake the militant features of Paul's discourse for an ontological claim.

I will return to this distinction between militancy and ontology below, where I will suggest that it largely maps onto the distinction between antiphilosophy and philosophy. Nevertheless, and returning to the criticisms mentioned above, Bell at least acknowledges Badiou's attempt to distance himself and his reading of Paul from Marcion's ultra-Paulinism. But Bell suggests that Badiou is being "disingenuous" (2007: 102). The problem, however, with Bell's suggestion and his criticisms of Badiou's reading of Paul, is that they are based on a reading of *Saint Paul* that isolates the latter work, turning it into the definitive statement of Badiou's philosophy as a whole. Now, it is certainly legitimate to read a text, such as Badiou's *Saint Paul*, on its own, taking it as significant in its own right. Indeed, the understandable emphasis placed on *Saint Paul* by theologically minded readers of Badiou serves as an important corrective to the relative lack of attention that has been paid to this text by many of Badiou's most faithful interpreters. That said, isolating one text among others as the key to the whole, turning one text into a synecdoche for the *oeuvre*, runs the risk of misunderstanding and misappropriation. Ironically, the tendency to read Badiou's *Saint Paul* in isolation from the rest of his philosophy repeats at a formal level some of the very criticisms levelled at Badiou. As we have indicated, critics of Badiou's reading of Paul take Badiou to task for not taking seriously Paul's relation to Judaism, for emphasizing Paul's supposed rupture with the content of the latter. In short, Badiou's reading of Paul is at best one-sided, at worst Marcionite, in that it fails to take account of the continuity that Paul sees between Judaism and the universal import of the death and resurrection of Christ. Certainly, for Paul the Christ-event indicates something new, but this newness is only such in light of the tradition out of which it emerges and its expectations. Something similar could be said of the way in which Badiou's theological critics read *Saint Paul*: no attempt is made to connect this novel piece of work with the context in which it occurs, with Badiou's philosophy as a whole. In sum, the charge of Marcionism levelled against Badiou's reading of Paul is, in a sense, Marcionite.

Although such criticisms do, as we will see, have some merit, there is good reason to question this all-too-easy association of Badiou's position with that of Marcion, especially if we consider it in light of other elements of Badiou's philosophy. For example, in the opening chapters of *Theory of the Subject*, Badiou attempts to complicate the notion of the closure of a dialectical sequence, which for Hegel is the irreducible point of action. A dialectical process reaches its completion when the absolute appears as the coincidence of concept and object or when a practical process attains knowledge of its own history. Badiou notes, however, that this moment of closure or completion can be taken in two distinctly different senses. On the one hand, it can be represented as a circularity, which sees the end of the dialectical process as a return to its starting point. From this perspective, the entire process is contained "in the seeds of the beginning, [and] leads back to this very beginning once all the stages of its effectuation, its alienation, its going-outside-itself, and so on, are unfolded" (TS 19). On the other hand, the completion of a dialectical process can be taken as the moment of disjunction between the end of one series and the beginning of another, in which the former serves as the condition of the latter without, however, predetermining it. Understood in this sense, the end point of a dialectical process does not represent the moment of return but "the pure passage from one sequence to the other, in an irreconcilable, unsuturable lag, where the truth of the first stage gives itself to begin with only as the condition of the second as fact, without leading back to anything other than the unfolding of this fact" (*ibid.*).

Badiou favours the second model, and it is at the point of passage from one dialectical sequence to another that Badiou attempts in *Theory of the Subject* to locate the subject as the torsion of historical change. What interests us for the moment, however, is Badiou's characterization of the first model, the representation of the dialectic as circularity. According to Badiou, this understanding of the dialectic is resolutely theological, particularly since it bases itself, implicitly or explicitly, on a specific understanding of Christian doctrine. That is, if we take the dialectic, as does Badiou, as a process of scission, in which the dialectic proceeds and repeats itself as difference through the contradiction between an initial term taken in itself, what Badiou calls the outplace, and its placed or indexed identity for itself, what Badiou calls the splace, then the doctrine of the incarnation provides what is perhaps the most exemplary model of such a process, at least when understood along Hegelian lines. Badiou notes that what gives the contradiction between the infinite and the finite meaning in Christianity is:

> its historicization in scission, which makes the infinite ex-sist in the finite. Therein lies the necessary stroke of genius of Christianity. For this to happen, God (A) is indexed (A_p) as specific outplace of the splace of the finite: this is the principle of the Incarnation. God becomes man. God divides himself (the Father) and himself-placed-in-the-finite (the Son). A is the Father, and A_p, the Son, that historic son by whom God ex-sists. God thus occurs as scission of the outplace, $A = AA_p$, God = Father/Son, a scission that the council of Nicea, the first of the great modern politico-ideological conferences in history, will designate as sole existence – as unity of opposites – in the well known dialectical axiom: "The Son is consubstantial with the Father". (TS 16)

Badiou's problem with this model is that it stops short of allowing for any substantial notion of historical change, since the death of the Son only serves as the means through which the infinite returns to itself in resurrection. The death of the Son in this scheme serves only as a moment, albeit an essential one, for the auto-development of redemption, which through the ascension of the resurrected Christ "redistributes the splace and the outplace in the fusion of Glory. Seated to His own right side, God (the Son) is no more than the immutable intercessor for the tribunal of God (the Father). The revolution is dissolved into the State" (*ibid.*).

Immediately after outlining the dialectic in terms of Hegel's speculative reading of the incarnation, Badiou goes on to discuss "heretical" versions of the incarnation, particularly the general positions of Arianism and Gnosticism. According to Badiou, Arianism, with its emphasis on the distinction-without-equality between the Father and the Son, ruins "the essence of the Christian dialectical proposition" (TS 17). More important for our purposes, however, is Badiou's characterization of the Gnostic position, which emphasizes the divine nature of the Son over against his merely ephemeral earthly existence, an emphasis that amounts to an idealization of the infinite at the expense of the finite. In Badiou's words, "Gnostic radicality maintains an ironclad divergence between the original purity of the divine Father and the blemishes of sex, the world, and death. If God comes to *haunt* the world in order to indicate the true way, he cannot establish himself therein in his essence" (*ibid.*, original emphasis). The sharp division between the divine and the human, the idealization of the infinite at the expense of the finite is, for Badiou, a type of leftist "fanaticism" that obstructs "the path of the new": "Obsessed by the pure and the original and violently inclined toward Manichaeism, this ultra-leftist heresy blocks the dialectical fecundity of the message just as much as the rational and peaceful hierarchical ordering proposed by the Arians" (*ibid.*).

In *Saint Paul* Badiou attempts to distance his own reading of the incarnation from Hegel's, while also avoiding the type of Gnostic radicality mentioned above. This is particularly clear in Badiou's discussion of the relationship between death and resurrection in Chapter 6 of *Saint Paul*, under the title "The Antidialectic of Death and Resurrection". As the title of this chapter suggests, and as Badiou makes explicitly clear in the opening paragraphs to it, the target here is Hegel, specifically his speculative reading of the death of God. According to Badiou, and in line with his reading of Hegel in the opening chapters of *Theory of the Subject*, the Hegelian reading of Christ's death and resurrection "effects a capture of the Christ-event". To quote Badiou more fully:

> If the theme of resurrection becomes caught up in the dialectical apparatus, it must be conceded that the event as supernumerary givenness and incalculable grace is dissolved into an auto-foundational and necessarily deployed rational protocol. It is certainly true that Hegelian philosophy, which is the rational edge of German romanticism, effects a capture of the Christ-event. In Hegel, grace becomes a moment in the self-development of the Absolute, and the material of death and suffering is the due required so that spirituality, externalizing itself in finitude, can return into itself through the experienced intensity of self-consciousness. (SP 65–6)

In opposition to this Hegelian reading of the Christ-event, Badiou maintains that "Paul's position is antidialectical, and that for it death is in no way the obligatory exercise of the negative's immanent power. Grace, consequently, is not a 'moment' of the Absolute. It is affirmation without preliminary negation; it is what comes upon us in caesura of the law. It is pure and simple *encounter*" (SP 66, original emphasis).

Badiou's emphasis on grace against the dialectic of death does not, however, mean that death and resurrection and its counterparts (flesh and spirit, law and love) are entirely unrelated, as critics who associate Badiou's position with Marcionism often assume. Although the relation is, technically speaking, disjunct, it corresponds to the relation between the evental site and the event itself, which we examined in Chapter 2. Recall that the evental site is "only ever a *condition of being* for the event" (BE 179, original emphasis). Although there can be no event without an evental site, the existence of an evental site in a situation does not inevitably entail the emergence of an event for that situation. On Badiou's reading of Paul, death, understood not in biological terms but as a subjective destination, names the evental site. More specifically, the death of Christ "functions as a condition of immanence. We conform to Christ insofar as he conforms to us. The cross (we have been crucified with Christ) is the symbol of that identity" (SP 70). This immanentization or, in other words, reconciliation with God, is necessary if there is to be resurrection, since resurrection names the overcoming of death; but, death itself, qua evental site, does not inevitably entail resurrection, since the function of death only creates the conditions for resurrection. Resurrection remains, on Badiou's account, of the order of grace, meaning that it does not follow dialectically from death, as it does for Hegel. To quote Badiou at length on this point:

> Ultimately, to understand the relation between *katallagē* [or reconcilation] and *sotēria* [or salvation], which is just as much the relation between death and life, is to understand that, for Paul, there is an absolute disjunction between Christ's death and his resurrection. For death is an operation in the situation, an operation that immanentizes the evental site, while resurrection is the event as such. Hence the fact that Paul's argument is foreign to all dialectics. Resurrection is neither a sublation, nor an overcoming of death. They are two distinct functions, whose articulation contains no necessity. For the event's sudden emergence never follows from the existence of an evental site. Although it requires conditions of immanence, that sudden emergence nevertheless remains of the order of grace. (SP 70–71)

Resurrection is thus not of the order of the negation of the negation, as it is for Hegel, but rather of the order "subtraction" or "extraction": "Resurrection suddenly comes forth *out from* the power of death, not through its negation" (SP 73, original emphasis). It is in this sense that resurrection names the contingency of grace, and thereby cannot be subsumed under any preexisting plan, any auto-development of the absolute. The resurrection says "no" to death, so as to allow the subject to "be carried away by the exceptional 'but' of grace, of the event, of life" (*ibid.*). It is "affirmative subtraction from the path of death" (*ibid.*).

However, the subtraction of the resurrection from death does not annul death once and for all, creating a sphere of pure life. As Badiou emphasizes, the separation of the resurrection from death – or, what basically amounts to the same thing, from works, law, flesh, and so on – is an "endless process" (SP 64). Badiou's claim, here, is based on his reading of the Pauline subject as a "divided subject", that is, as a subject constituted through the "weaving together of two subjective paths, which Paul names flesh (*sarx*) and spirit (*pneuma*)" (SP 55). On Badiou's account, these do not correspond to the more substantial notions of body and soul but rather indicate the "two paths that affect every subject in thought" through "its fidelity to the Christ-event" (SP 56). To quote Badiou at length:

> As subject to the ordeal of the real, we are henceforth constituted by evental grace. The crucial formula – which, it must be noted, is simultaneously a universal address – is: *ou gar este hupo nomon all' hupo kharin*, "for you are not under the law, but under grace" (Rom. 6.14). A structuring of the subject according to the "not … but" through which it must be understood as becoming rather than a state. For the "not being under the law" negatively indicates the path of the flesh as suspension of the subject's destiny, while "being under grace" indicates the path of the spirit as fidelity to the event. The subject of the new epoch is a "not … but". The event is at once the suspension of the path of the flesh through a problematic "not", and the affirmation of the path of the spirit through a "but" of exception. Law and grace are for the subject the name of the constituting weave through which he is related to the situation as it is and to the effects of the event as they have to become.
>
> (SP 63)

The potential universality of the truth instigated through the resurrection-event depends upon this divided subject, whose form is the "not … but". The activity of the divided subject, under the pressure of the event, distributes the terms of the situation according to this formula. That is, the divided subject, constituted through the event, wrests the truth of the event from the particularity of the law and pushes it towards the universal, without, however, abolishing the law and all that is associated with it in the process. Indeed, to abolish the law and its analogues (sin, death, flesh) would be to lapse back into the "fourth discourse", discussed above:

> The universal is neither on the side of the flesh as conventional lawfulness and particular state of the world, nor on the side of the pure spirit, as private inhabitation by grace and truth. The Jewish discourse of the rite and the law is undermined by the event's superabundance, but, equally, the arrogant discourse of internal revelation and the unutterable is abolished.   (SP 64)

For this reason, the activity of the divided subject "ceaselessly redivides the two paths, distributing the 'not ... but,' which, through an endless process, sets aside the law to better enter into grace" (*ibid.*).

The activity of the divided subject, in this sense, constitutes a fidelity. In Badiou's reading of Paul, fidelity to the resurrection-event takes place through what theologians normally refer to as the theological virtues: faith, hope and love. As we have said above, it is necessary to tear away from the law to enter into grace. This is necessary because "considered in its particularity, that of the works it prescribes, the law blocks the subjectivization of grace's universal address as pure conviction, of faith. The law 'objectifies' salvation and forbids one from relating it to the gratuitousness of the Christ-event" (SP 75). The law ties salvation to particularity and difference, to finitude and limit. The law, both ontologically and politically, is "statist" in orientation, in that it "enumerates, names, and controls the parts of the situation" (SP 76). Grace, in contrast, is "nondenumerable, impredictable, uncontrollable"; it is "that which occurs without being couched in any predicate, that which happens to everyone without an assignable reason. Grace is the opposite of law insofar as it is what comes *without being due*" (SP 76–7, original emphasis).

Absent the support of the law and suspended in grace, the divided subject can only act on the basis of faith, which Badiou primarily understands in terms of "a declared conviction" (SP 87). In the more formal language of *Being and Event*, faith names "the incorporation of the event into the situation in the mode of a generic procedure" (BE 393). The primacy of faith entails that the "subject *is* subjectivization" (SP 81, original emphasis), meaning that, absent the law, the subject is constituted in its intervention and through its adherence to the potential universality of the truth opened up by the Christ-event. However, the constitution of the subject through faith does not mean that the newly constituted Christian subject is absolutely lawless. Faith, in providing the avenue for the subject to separate from the law, implies the existence of a new law, a law of love. Badiou thus distinguishes between:

> a legalizing subjectivization, which is a power of death, and a law raised up by faith, which belongs to the spirit and to life ...
>
> Under the condition of faith, of a declared conviction, love names a nonliteral law, one that gives to the faithful subject his consistency, and effectuates the postevental truth in the world.
>
> (SP 87)

If faith names the declaration or intervention that founds the subject, love names the power of the declaration to sustain the subject in the production of post-evental truth. Love names the work of truth, which means that on Badiou's account, "salvation" for Paul occurs through love alone. As Badiou puts it, there is "no instantaneous salvation; grace itself is no more than the indication of a possibility. The subject has to be given in his labor, and not only in his sudden emergence. 'Love' is the name of that labor. Truth for Paul is never anything but 'faith working through love' (Gal. 5.6)" (SP 91–2). Hope, in turn, sustains the work of love. As Badiou summarizes the relationship between hope and the other two virtues, "Faith would be the opening to the true; love, the universalizing effectiveness of its trajectory; hope, lastly, a maxim enjoining us to persevere in its trajectory" (SP 93). Hope, in this sense, does not take an objective form, in the sense that it has a specific target towards which it tends. Hope is rather of the order of the subject: "Hope is 'enduring fidelity,' tenacity of love through the ordeal, and in no way vision of a reward or punishment. Hope is the subjectivity of a victorious fidelity, fidelity to fidelity, and not the representation of its future outcome" (*ibid.*).

To conclude this discussion of Badiou's reading of Paul, we mentioned previously that, although Paul provides a way to articulate the relationship between truth and the subject, Paul's intervention falls outside the realm of effective truth procedures, since its impetus is, on the whole, mythological. Paul's discourse, in this sense, pertains not to the production of an actual universality but to "the laws of universality in general" (SP 108). Nevertheless, although Paul's discourse cannot be said to constitute an actual truth procedure, in so far as it pertains to the laws of universality in general, its formal elements apply to each of the four truth procedures as such and their philosophical articulation. More specifically, Paul, that great anti-philosopher, "warns the philosopher that the conditions for the universal cannot be conceptual, either in origin, or in destination" (*ibid.*). Paul reminds the philosopher that truth is supernumerary, of the order of the event, its destination constituted through the militant activity of the subject. What this anti-philosopher offers to the philosopher is "a materialism of grace" (SP 81). How should we understand this in light of Badiou's philosophy as a whole? To this we now turn.

BADIOU'S THEOLOGY

Bruno Bosteels has recently suggested that there is an "antiphilosophical temptation at work in Badiou's philosophy" (2008: 179). Although this "temptation" is evident throughout Badiou's writings, it is particularly evident in his reading of Paul in *Saint Paul*. It is worth quoting Bosteels at length:

> Indeed, I would say that there is a profound oscillation that runs through this study between, on one hand, an effort to delimit Paul's antiphilosophy as a discourse to be traversed and yet kept at a distance, and, on the other, a deep fascination with the ultraradicalism

> of this discourse, whose traits – including stylistic ones – as a result come to be transferred onto Badiou's own philosophy as well, both in this book and elsewhere. It thus becomes frequently impossible in *Saint Paul* to discern whether general statements regarding truth, the act, the subject, and so on, belong to the antiphilosophical aspect of the Apostle's doctrine, which therefore would have to be rejected, or whether they can in addition be attributed, as if written in a free, indirect style, to Badiou's own theory of the event. This theory, in fact, is by no means impeded but thrives on such indiscernibility. (*Ibid.*)

Now, as Bosteels points out, Badiou claims to be able to separate the formal aspects of Paul's discourse that interest him from the religious content of that discourse, which, if we associate anti-philosophy with religion, would allow Badiou to keep the anti-philosophical elements of Paul's theology at bay, at least in principle. However, Bosteels argues that what constitutes anti-philosophy is not merely an association with religion but its anti-dialectical nature. The tendency of all anti-philosophy, according to Bosteels, is an emphasis on "the unmediated, disconnected, and wholly subjective nature of the truth of an event" (*ibid.*: 182). As we have seen, it is precisely through such an anti-dialectical lens that Badiou reads Paul. Hence, it is not just the content of Paul's discourse that is anti-philosophical but the form of that discourse itself, based as it is on "the pure event", and it is exactly this that Badiou finds so attractive in Paul (*ibid.*: 180).

Despite noting the ambivalence regarding philosophy and anti-philosophy in Badiou's reading of Paul, it seems that Bosteels backs off a bit from this insight in the end. Bosteels rightly notes that the relationship between anti-philosophy and philosophy is one of "mimetics" and "rivalry" and that "the philosopher actually thrives on the endless sparring matches with the most illustrious antiphilosophers" (*ibid.*: 185, 186). Hence Badiou's evaluations of anti-philosophy, his various and sustained attempts to think with and through the discourses of the great anti-philosophers. Nevertheless, for Bosteels, anti-philosophy remains external to Badiou's philosophy, a necessary "temptation" but one that, in the end, must be and eventually is overcome. So much is evident, when Bosteels concludes, "For Badiou, the task is more straight-forward. The philosopher, he will always state, must stay in the closest proximity to the antiphilosopher, who alone keeps him on guard against the temptations of religion, disaster, or the 'service of goods' pure and simple" (*ibid.*: 186). This avoidance of ascribing to Badiou anti-philosophical traits is, on the whole, in keeping with Bosteels's more dialectical interpretation of Badiou (Bosteels 2005a; 2005b; 2011). However, it seems that, at least in part, it is precisely this anti-philosophical element – the "pure event", the "absolutely *new*" – that Badiou finds so compelling in Paul's discourse.

Indeed, I want to suggest that the reason anti-philosophy remains a "temptation" for Badiou is because anti-philosophy is internal to Badiou's philosophy itself.

As a way into substantiating this claim, let us return to Badiou's notion of the event. For Badiou an event is the source of novelty for a situation, that which carries within itself the potential to radically alter the situation or world to which it belongs. In Badiou's words, events are "irreducible singularities, the 'beyond-the-law' of situations" (E 44). An event is a "supplement ... committed to chance. It is unpredictable, incalculable. It is beyond what is" (IT 62). Badiou thus variously describes the event as a "radical novelty" (SP 33) or something "absolutely new" (SP 43), a "pure beginning" (SP 49) or "absolute beginning" (D 90), "a pure cut in becoming" (LW 384), an "exception" (LW 360) to what there is. All these descriptions of the event lend support to the claim made in *Being and Event* that the event falls on the side of "what-is-not-being-qua-being" (BE 173). Because the event is undecidable from the perspective of the situation, an interventional decision is required to name the event, making it available for thought and the subsequent development of truth through fidelity.

Given the terms Badiou uses to describe the event and what it requires, it is not surprising that his doctrine of the event has been subject to some criticism concerning the seemingly quasi-religious character of it. For instance, according to Gilles Deleuze, despite Badiou's attempt to erect an ontology of immanent multiplicity founded only on the void, his combination of the latter with the separation of the event from being qua becoming leads him to reintroduce transcendence into philosophy (D 90).[6] Echoing Deleuze, Daniel W. Smith notes that, no matter how much emphasis Badiou places on the necessity of immanence, the very notion that something can be thought in addition to being harbours "an inevitable appeal to transcendence: the eruption, within Being itself, of a supplemental event that is *not* Being-as-being" (2004: 93). Moreover, Badiou's putative reintroduction of transcendence has a quasi-religious ring to it, in so far as the event seems eerily similar to, if not a complete secularization of, divine fiat, creation out of nothing. In Smith's words, "Though Badiou is determined to expel God and the One from his philosophy, he winds up reassigning the event, as if through the back door, the very characteristics of transcendence that were formerly assigned to the divine (as Badiou declares triumphantly, 'I conceptualize absolute beginnings')" (*ibid.*).

Going even further, Daniel Bensaïd suggests that Badiou presents us with "a philosophy haunted by the sacralization of the evental miracle" (2004: 97). The rarity of the event, its exceptional and indeterminate character, its pure break with the past, the voluntarism of decision, and the apparent dogmatism with which Badiou seems to associate the resulting process of truth all coincide to produce "a philosophy of majestic sovereignty, whose decision seems to be founded upon a nothing that commands a whole" (*ibid.*: 105). To quote Bensaïd at length:

> If the future of truth "is decided by those who carry on" and who hold to this faithful decision to carry on, the militant summoned by the "rare" if not exceptional idea of politics seems to be haunted by the Pauline ideal of saintliness, which constantly threatens to turn into a bureaucratic priesthood of Church, State or Party. The absolute incompatibility between truth and opinion, between philosopher and sophist, between event and history, leads to a practical impasse. The refusal to work within the equivocal contradiction and tension which bind them together ultimately leads to a pure voluntarism, which oscillates between a broadly leftist form of politics and its philosophical circumvention. In either case, the combination of theoretical elitism and practical moralism can indicate a haughty withdrawal from the public domain, sandwiched between the philosopher's evental truth and the masses' subaltern resistance to the world's misery.
>
> (*Ibid.*: 101)

Echoing Bensaïd's concerns, Simon Critchley worries that "the idea of the rarity of the political event … makes politics into this heroic act, which we await. It worries me because of its Heideggerian and national aesthetic connotations in the German tradition" (2005a: 297).[7]

What these and similar criticisms seem to have in common is the association, stated or not, of Badiou's event with Carl Schmitt's exception, which latter is, according to Schmitt, "analogous to the miracle in theology" (1985: 36).[8] Indeed, Badiou's notion of the event does bear certain formal similarities to Schmitt's logic of the exception, as Colin Wright has discussed at length in an article entitled "Event or Exception?: Disentangling Badiou from Schmitt, or, Towards a Politics of the Void". First, just as Schmitt's exception occurs in excess of the established law, Badiou's event occurs in excess of the established knowledge of the situation. Because of this excess, both the exception and the event can be said to "evade every calculus of prediction" (Wright 2008a: 4). Second, as a result of this excess, the incompatibility between exception and law for Schmitt and event and knowledge for Badiou, "both thinkers appeal to the figurative power of a secularized version of the Christian concept of 'grace' in order to articulate the event and the exception as bolts from the blue without prior sign or portent" (*ibid.*). For Schmitt such an appeal is all too evident, in his claim that "[t]he exception in jurisprudence is analogous to the miracle in theology" (quoted in *ibid.*: 5). For Badiou the correspondence between the event and grace is most clearly on display in his "reactivation of Paul" in *Saint Paul: The Foundation of Universalism*, where, among other things, he states that "the event's sudden emergence never follows from the existence of the evental site. Although it requires conditions of immanence, that sudden emergence remains of the order of grace" (quoted in *ibid*.: 5). Third, because of the excessive character of Schmitt's exception and Badiou's event, both require a radical decision, a decision that cannot be accounted for from within established law or knowledge. Indeed, as Wright points out, for Schmitt the decision is, in a certain sense, more important than the issue involved, hence Schmitt's decisionism; likewise, for Badiou it is the interventional decision that makes the event available for the production of truth, and at times this decision appears "pure, auto-referential, and singular" (*ibid*.: 6). Finally, both Schmitt and Badiou rely on a performative naming that declares the existence of the exception or event. As Wright puts it, "Just as the name of the event cannot be incorporated into the world of facts within the situation and remain an event, so the Schmittian exception cannot submit itself to protocols of proof and remain truly exceptional. Evental and exceptional nominations, then, share a fragile bridging function: they interweave the old and the radically new, the normal and the abnormal, the legal and the illegal" (*ibid*.: 8).

However, despite the apparent formal similarities between Schmitt's exception and Badiou's event, Wright goes on to note some crucial differences between them. To begin with, although, as Wright points out, both Schmitt and Badiou share "a venomous critique of parliamentary liberalism", they come out against the latter from completely opposite directions: "Schmitt appeals to a conservative tradition of authoritarian absolutism, whereas Badiou's inspiration is drawn from the Jacobin tradition of radicalism" (*ibid*.: 8). Schmitt's theory of the exception ultimately serves to buttress the authority of the state, while Badiou's theory of the event is at root anti- or counter-statist in its orientation. For this reason, although Schmitt's exception is, on the surface, associated with novelty, the end result is largely conservative: the exception must always be brought under the control of the state, so as to maintain sovereign power. In Wright's words, "The logic of the exception always mortgages itself to the *perpetuation* of a configuration of power which preceded the declared state of exception, even if, on a discursive level, a 'new paradigm' may be posited precisely in order to pursue and intensify the hegemonic maintenance of an 'old' social formation" (*ibid*.: 9, original emphasis). In contrast, because Badiou's event evades the count of the state, the metastructure, it has as its goal the real production of something new, against the established order. Wright thus argues that Schmitt's "infamous aphorism" with which he begins *Political Theology* ("sovereign is he who decides on the exception") is "exactly asymmetrical to evental naming" (*ibid*.: 10; cf. Schmitt 1985: 5). For Schmitt, the power to name the exception is concentrated in the pre-given authority of the sovereign, whereas for Badiou, "the event is radically egalitarian because extracted from all specific interests by virtue of its universality" (*ibid*.: 10). Moreover, the interventional nomination of the event for Badiou always takes place in light of evental recurrence, which prevents "evental grace from being simply ineffable, from inducing, at best, dumb and useless piety" (*ibid*.: 12). To sum up, we could say that Schmitt's exception takes place within a logic of transcendence, while Badiou's event takes place within a logic of immanence.

Nevertheless, these differences do not negate the similarities, even if they do put Badiou's event on a different footing from Schmitt's exception. Whether we ground it in a logic of immanence or a logic of transcendence, an exception to what there is is still an exception, political differences not-withstanding. The formal similarities that Badiou's event maintains with Schmitt's exception would seem to leave Badiou open to the criticisms that we have discussed. Moreover, it would seem to bring Badiou closer to an anti-philosophical position, in so far as the latter understands the event in primarily unmediated and volitional terms. Complicating matters even more is the fact that, in *Peut-on penser la politique?*, in which Badiou first begins to develop explicitly the concept of the event, he traces the lineage of the event, intervention and fidelity through a group of anti-philosophers, namely Pascal, Rousseau, Mallarmé and Lacan (PP 84–91). This association continues in *Being and Event*, where the doctrine of the event bears com-parison with Mallarmé's dice-throw and Pascal's wager (BE 191–8, 212–22). Because Schmitt also relied on him, perhaps most striking is Badiou's use of Kierkegaard in *Logics of Worlds* to develop a notion of choice or decision as it relates to the theory of points (Schmitt 1985: 15).[9]

If, according to Badiou, Wittgenstein and Lacan count as the preemi-nent anti-philosophers of the twentieth century, Kierkegaard counts as one of the most important of the nineteenth century. Although Kierkegaard is "the most garrulous among the anti-philosophers", he nonetheless remains "an unsurpassable master when it comes to choice, anxiety, repetition, and the infinite" (LW 557). What interests Badiou in Kierkegaard is largely what interests him in Paul: the relationship between truth and the subject. Spe-cifically, Badiou turns to Kierkegaard for the "connection that Kierkegaard establishes between choice as a cut in time and the eternity of truth as sub-jective truth" (LW 425). Badiou refers to this encounter with the eternal in time as "the Christian paradox", and it is "one of the possible names for the paradox of truths" (LW 428).

Badiou reads Kierkegaard, in this sense, in contrast to Hegel, as Hegel's anti-philosopher. Hegel and Kierkegaard, as Badiou emphasizes, both agree that Christianity is, in essence, concerned with paradox: the appearance of the eternal in time, the incarnation of the absolute in history. Where they diverge is over the interpretation of this paradox. For Hegel, the absolute appears in history through the becoming-other of itself, through the expo-sure of the absolute to finitude and its mediation in time. Hegel condenses the mediation of the paradox between eternity and time, between the absolute and history in the Christian dogma of the death and resurrection of Christ. Kierkegaard, however, in a move correlative to the one Badiou finds in Paul, radically subjectivizes this paradox and rejects mediation: "It is a challenge addressed to the existence of each and everyone, and not a reflective theme that a deft use of dialectical mediations would externally enlist in the spectacular fusion of time and eternity" (LW 426). Whereas for Hegel the appearance of the absolute in history is a rational process, and thus knowable in principle through philosophical speculation, for Kierkegaard it is absurd and irrational, a paradox that cannot be known in the strict sense but only experienced as "subjective inwardness" (LW 427). It is this focus on subjective inwardness as the truth of Christianity, against Hegel's pretentions to systematicity, that in part characterizes Kierkegaard as an anti-philosopher:

> That is why, for Kierkegaard, there cannot exist a moment of knowledge ("absolute knowledge", in Hegel's terms) where truth is complete or present as result. Everything commences, or recommences, with each subjective singularity. We can recognize here the pointed thrust of anti-philosophy: the philosopher imagines that he has settled the question, because he approaches the relation between time and eternity the wrong way around. The philosopher reconstructs time on the basis of eternity, while Christianity commands us to encounter eternity in our own time. The philosopher claims to know the game of life because he knows its rules. But the existential question, that is the question of truth, is not that of knowing and reproducing the rules of the game. The point is to play, to partake in the contest, and this is what the (Hegelian) philosopher avoids: "For the philosopher, world history is ended, and he mediates ... He is outside; he is not a participant. He sits and grows old listening to the songs of the past; he has an ear for the harmonies of mediation." (*Ibid.*)

Despite Badiou's association of Kierkegaard with anti-philosophy and his insistence that Kierkegaard's discourse suffers from "a kind of Christian limitation" (LW 433), this does not stop him from drawing two important things from Kierkegaard.

First, according to Badiou, since for Kierkegaard truth is found in the subjective encounter of eternity in time, Kierkegaard proposes a generic conception of truth that, despite its heavy theological leanings, corresponds to Badiou's own. That is, for Kierkegaard, "the experience of the True in the existential singularity of a world is possible for everyone, without any predicative condition; and, moreover, ... it takes the form of a relation, which for us is the incorporation into the becoming of a postevental truth" (LW 429).

Moreover, what Badiou finds important in Kierkegaard for his own theory of truth is Kierkegaard's grounding of subjective truth in sheer belief, a belief that allows the subject to abide in the paradox of time and eternity beyond its simple, existential encounter. This passage from encounter to abiding is, for Kierkegaard, the passage from the ethical to the religious, and it marks "the sole form of authentic existence, existence in faith" (LW 430). Badiou quotes the following statement from Kierkegaard's *Concluding Unscientific Postscript* approvingly:

> *To believe* is specifically different from all other appropriation and inwardness. Faith is the objective uncertainty due to the repulsion of the absurd held fast by the passion of inwardness, which in this instance is intensified to the utmost degree. This formula fits only the believer, no one else, not a lover, not an enthusiast, not a thinker, but simply and solely the believer who is related to the absolute paradox.   (*Ibid.*, original emphasis)

Belief thus is, on Badiou's account, "the subjective form of the True, whose proper pathos is that of the absurd as the holding fast of objective uncertainty" (*ibid.*).

This leads to the second thing that Badiou draws from Kierkegaard, the doctrine of the point, which for Kierkegaard is condensed in his grounding of the importance of choice or decision as constitutive of belief. In *Logics of Worlds*, a point functions as "a topological operator – a corporeal localization with regard to the transcendental – which simultaneously spaces out and conjoins the subjective (a truth-procedure) and the objective (the multiplicities that appear in a world)" (LW 399). That is, a point in a world allows the complexity of the world, its various degrees of intensity and its network of identities and differences, to be submitted to the Two, to a "yes" or "no", to an affirmation or negation. A point, "as the reduction of infinite multiplicity to the Two localizes the action of that truth to which an event has given the chance to appear in a world" (LW 401). Badiou's doctrine of the point in *Logics of Worlds* thus corresponds to the enquiry and the operator of faithful connection in *Being and Event* and the form of the "not ... but" in Paul's letters. Badiou sees something similar operative in Kierkegaard: for Kierkegaard, the moment of choice, of the absolute choice for the eternal in time, cuts through the abstraction of the laws of the world, putting the subject in the face of an either/or. Indeed, as Badiou puts it, "Kierkegaard understands just as we do that the decision imposed by the treatment of a point – the occurrence of the choice – is truly the moment when one has a chance of incorporating oneself into a process of truth" (LW 432). Thus it can be said that "Kierkegaard anchors the existential contingency of eternal truths to the encounter and to the treatment of special points" (LW 433).

In *Being and Event*, this sort of radical decision that Badiou adopts from Kierkegaard and, we should add, Saint Paul, is tempered with Badiou's statements against associating it with the brute heroism of speculative leftism. As Badiou states, "What the doctrine of the event teaches us is rather that the entire effort lies in following the event's consequences, not in glorifying its occurrence. There is no more an angelic herald of the event than there is a hero. Being does not commence" (BE 210–11). Nonetheless, recently Badiou has begun to associate fidelity more explicitly with the virtue of courage, which he defines as "endurance in the impossible" (MS 72). In contrast to heroism, which puts sole emphasis on the act of confronting the impossible in a sublime encounter, courage is a discipline that must be constructed: it "is displayed in practices that construct a particular time, regardless of the laws of the world or the opinions that support these laws" (*ibid.*). Courage, however, is not absolutely distinct from heroism, but only works in so far as it maintains heroism dialectically. That is, courage is attendant upon a prior act of "dialectical conversion" or "heroic conversion":

> Courage, in the sense in which I understand it, has its origin in a heroic conversion, and is oriented towards a point that was not there, a Real woven out of the impossible. Courage starts at a point, a heroic turn that cuts through established opinions and does not tolerate any nostalgia, even if, in its essence, courage is the disciplined holding on to the consequences of the encounter with this point. (MS 75)

Thus Badiou states that "the message of courage always brings with it a dose of heroism" (MS 73).

Although it might be possible in theory to separate "heroic conversion" and "heroism" from the figure of the "hero", it is not at all clear that Badiou does this. For instance, in *The Communist Hypothesis*, Badiou notes that emancipatory politics is, in essence, a politics of the "anonymous masses", the "victory of those with no names, of those who are held in a state of colossal insignificance by the State" (C 249–50). However, in so far as these masses are anonymous, they must be represented historically by a series of "proper names", a "glorious Pantheon of revolutionary heroes", whose names include "Spartacus, Thomas Müntzer, Robespierre, Toussaint Louverture, Blanqui, Marx, Lenin, Rosa Luxemburg, Mao, Che Guevara, and so many others" (C 250). Badiou describes their role as follows:

> Why is there this long series of proper names? Why this glorious [*glorieux*] Pantheon of revolutionary heroes? … The reason is that all these proper names symbolize historically – in the guise of an individual, of a pure singularity of body and thought – the

> rare and precious network of ephemeral sequences of politics as truth. The elusive formalism of bodies-of-truth is legible here as empirical existence. In these proper names, the ordinary individual discovers glorious [*glorieux*], distinctive individuals as the mediation for his or her own individuality, as the proof that he or she can force its finitude. The anonymous action of millions of militants, rebels, fighters, unrepresentable as such, is combined and counted as one in the simple, powerful symbol of the proper name. (C 250)

It would seem, then, that there are indeed, heroes of the event, a series of grand figures whose task is to mediate and represent sequences of truth, especially political truth.

I am tempted to go even further and say that this heroic figure who represents the anonymous masses dovetails with the Christian conception of the saint.[10] A few pages prior to the previous quotation, Badiou notes that what he refers to as a "body" of truth, which, in terms of politics, is the collective subject organized around the consequences of an event, relies on religious metaphor for its conceptualization. As Badiou puts it:

> Making unabashed use of a religious metaphor, I will say that the body-of-truth, as concerns what cannot be reduced to facts within it, can be called a glorious [*glorieux*] body. With respect to this body, which is that of a new collective Subject in politics, of an organization composed of individual multiples, we will say that it shares in the creation of political truth. (C 244–5)

Moreover, is it not precisely in the saint that "the ordinary individual discovers glorious [*glorieux*], distinctive individuals as the mediation for his or her own individuality"? It is hard not to hear behind Badiou's "Pantheon of revolutionary heroes" the words of Hebrews 12:1, which combine the figure of the saint, the hero of faith, with perseverance or, to use Badiou's words, courage or fidelity: "Therefore, since we are surrounded by so great a cloud of witnesses, let us also lay aside every weight and the sin that clings so closely, and let us run with perseverance the race that is set before us."

In light of this discussion, it seems that Badiou's critics do have a point: Badiou's philosophy is, it seems, "a philosophy haunted by the sacralization of the evental miracle" (Bensaïd 2004: 97). It seems to me that this element of Badiou's philosophy, pointed out in numerous ways by his critics, corresponds to what Feltham identifies as the voice of the eagle, the more voluntarist and idealist voice which associates change with a radical break in the situation, an excessive rupture that converts the impossible into the possible (Feltham 2008: 53–67, 110–23). The voice of the eagle is, likewise, the voice of Marcion in Badiou, the voice of the speculative leftist, the militant. Although Feltham himself does not make this identification, the voice of the eagle is the voice of the anti-philosopher in Badiou. Is it not precisely the anti-philosopher who desires a radical beginning, a desire borne out by the language of rupture that he/she uses? The identification of anti-philosophy as internal to Badiou's philosophy is, in this sense, evident in the language Badiou uses to describe the event and its consequences ("absolutely new", "pure beginning", "absolute beginning", "a pure cut in becoming", "exception", "heroic conversion", "endurance in the impossible") and the intimate link that such language has with the conceptual activity of the anti-philosophers. Moreover, Badiou's reliance on anti-philosophy is irretrievably crossed with the discourse of theology. We have already mentioned that, at a general level, anti-philosophy remains close to religion, and in particular Christianity. The link between anti-philosophy and religion becomes specific in Badiou's philosophy in his reliance on the language and concepts of Christian theology to articulate his own philosophical positions, which we have analysed in detail above. Although such reliance can be found throughout his writings, it is condensed in an extraordinary way in his reading of Paul in *Saint Paul*, a reading that is more than just an example: it is a "reactivation", a resurrection of an eminent anti-philosophical theologian for a philosophical purpose. When all is said and done, Paul offers the philosopher an understanding of the relationship between truth and the subject that rests on "a materialism of grace" (SP 81). In sum, the heart of Badiou's philosophy appears determined by an internal anti-philosophical element, an element that is inseparable from theology.

Why does Badiou retain this voice of the anti-philosopher? Given the fact that the anti-philosopher institutes a discourse of rupture, I would suggest that it is a necessity, given Badiou's understanding of the advent of truth as evental. The language of rupture, of absolute novelty against the status quo, lends support to a corresponding notion of change. It is worth recalling, here, a distinction Badiou makes in reference to Marcion in *Saint Paul* between militancy and ontology:

> There is no text of Paul's from which one could draw anything resembling Marcion's doctrine. That the God whose son is Jesus Christ is the God spoken of in the Old Testament, the God of the Jews, is, for Paul, a ceaselessly reiterated and obvious fact. If there is a figure with whom Paul feels an affinity, and one whom he subtly uses to his own ends, it is that of Abraham. That Paul emphasizes rupture rather than continuity is not in doubt. *But this is a militant, and not an ontological thesis.* Divine unicity bridges the two situations separated by the Christ event, and at no moment is it cast into doubt.   (SP 35; emphasis added)

Like Paul's own discourse, Badiou's internalization of anti-philosophy, an internalization that brings the language and content of theology into Badiou's philosophy, is militant. Where Badiou's critics go wrong is in their overemphasis on this militancy, this anti-philosophical or theological element in Badiou's philosophy. Ironically, as I have said above in another context, this overemphasis repeats Marcion's error. By pushing a little too much, by isolating this element of Badiou's philosophy from the whole, we overlook the other voice present in Badiou's philosophy, what Feltham refers to as the old mole, which is the "the dialectization of the eagle" (Feltham 2008: 122). I want to suggest, however, that this voice itself is theological, albeit in a different register: it is eschatological.

We should note from the outset that the identification of Badiou's philosophy with the structure of Christian eschatology is far from self-evident, at least at first glance. Indeed, if anything, the opposite would seem to be the case. Arguing on the assumption of a break between Badiou's earlier, Maoist-influenced philosophy and his later, mathematical ontology found in particular in *Being and Event*, Peter Hallward argues that any notion of a "historical eschatology" is absent from Badiou's mature philosophical system. According to Hallward, the "impasse of Badiou's early work … lay in its partial delegation of philosophical autonomy to historical development" (2003: 49)· Much like Hegel and Marx, Badiou, in his earlier work, adopts a cumulative conception of truth, which is guided by "the singular movement of History as a whole" (*ibid.*: 49). In place of the "objective mediation" of History, Badiou's later work, based as it is on the mathematical ontology formulated in *Being and Event*, attempts to work out a subtractive theory of truth and the subject. Hallward summarizes this shift in Badiou's thinking as follows:

> From now on *confiance dans la confiance* will be carried by the rigor of a self-sustaining prescription with a minimum of direct historical mediation. For a more conventionally materialist ontology, Badiou has substituted the mathematical manipulation of the void, which has become the exclusive basis for his articulation of a be-ing without substance, without constituent relation to material existence; for a historical eschatology, he has substituted a "politics of the impossible," a politics purged of dialectical *liens*. Truth is what happens in history, but as a subtraction from history. (*Ibid.*: 50)

Hallward is certainly correct, here, at least in part. As Badiou puts it in *Theory of the Subject* with reference to eschatological character of Marxism, "[H]istory does not exist (it would be a figure of the whole). Only historical periods or historicizations (figures of the One-of-the-two) exist. This is why we communists postulate no halting point" (TS 92). The same claim is repeated in *Being and Event*, where it is treated in a more formal manner: "there are in situation evental sites, but there is no evental situation. We can think the *historicity* of certain multiples, but we cannot think *a* History" (BE 176, original emphasis). Badiou repeats the same claim in *The Communist Hypothesis*, in which he notes that, in order to combat the subordination of truths to historical meaning, he has had "to insist that History does not exist, which is in keeping with my conception of truths, namely, that they have no meaning, and especially not the meaning of History ... [T] here is no real of History and it is therefore true, transcendentally true, that it cannot exist" (C 241). The denial of the singular movement of history, of a History, is, of course, in keeping with Badiou's claim concerning the ontological inexistence of the One and the Whole, and in this sense it dovetails with the anti-theological emphasis of Badiou's ontology and philosophy.

Yet it seems that the issue is not as straightforward as Badiou would like it to be. For instance, as Oliver Feltham notes, although *Being and Event* is often read "as effectuating a pulverization of the Marxist conception of history as an oriented totality", Badiou does allow for "sequences of historical situations that closely resemble the historicized dialectic of [*Theory of the Subject*]" (2008: 104). That is, although Badiou denies an overarching sense to the sequences of historical situations, any totalization of the latter as History, there is in his thought "a conception of long historical series, of histories that are not just local, but *regional*" (*ibid.*, original emphasis).

We see this most clearly, perhaps, in the Preface to *Logics of Worlds*, where Badiou calls for "a didactics of eternal truths" (LW 9). As Badiou makes clear, to speak of truths as eternal does not mean that they exist in some immaterial, transcendent realm, apart from their material instantiation in worlds. Badiou emphasizes that his "didactics of eternal truths" presupposes "an ideology of immanence" (*ibid.*), and he maintains that truths are "real processes which, as subtracted as they may be from the pragmatic opposition of bodies and languages, are nonetheless in the world" (LW 10). Nevertheless, to speak of truths as eternal does suggest that all truths, precisely because they are truths, do have a certain degree of timelessness to them, certain qualities that subsist above and beyond their contingent appearances. In Badiou's words, truths have an "invariance existing across otherwise disparate worlds" (LW 9). To speak of truths as eternal is to speak of them as "universal" and "trans-worldly", as composing "an atemporal meta-history" (*ibid.*).

Badiou goes on to illustrate his conception of eternal truths in reference to the four truth procedures: mathematics, art, politics and love. Badiou attempts, in each case, to show how an Idea subsists among disparate truth procedures, linking them together across disparate times and places. Badiou discusses numbers in mathematics; the images of horses in the Chauvet caves and Picasso; revolutionary politics in China in 81 BCE and 1975 CE; and love from Virgil to Berlioz (LW 10–33). What Badiou means by "Idea" as the trans-worldly aspect of truths, in these contexts, does not immediately correspond to History, understood as a totalizing, progressive movement towards an end. We can see the distinction between Idea and History in the following quotation, in which Badiou discusses the invariance of the communist Idea:

> Of course, there is no real of History and it is therefore true, transcendentally true, that it cannot exist. Discontinuity between worlds is the law of appearance, hence of existence. What *does* exist, however, under the real condition of organized political action, is the communist Idea, an operation tied to intellectual subjectivation and that integrates the real, the symbolic and the ideological at the level of the individual. We must bring this Idea back, by uncoupling it from any predicative usage. We must rescue the Idea, but also free the Real from any immediate fusion with it. Only political sequences that it would ultimately be absurd to label as communist can be recovered by the communist Idea as the potential force of the becoming-Subject of individuals. (C 242)

Although there is no real History, no real to History, there is nonetheless a role for History at the symbolic level. Drawing on Lacan's three registers, Badiou splits the Idea of communism in three regarding its operation: "politics-real, history-symbolic and ideology-imaginary" (*ibid.*). It is in this sense that History can play a role as a "symbolic fiction" that supports political sequences and the subjects of them. As Badiou explains:

> A truth is the political real. History, even as a reservoir of proper names, is a symbolic place. The ideological operation of the Idea of communism is the imaginary projection of the political real into the symbolic fiction of History, including in its guise as a representation of the action of innumerable masses via the One of a proper name. The role of this Idea is to support the individual's incorporation into the discipline of a truth procedure, to authorize the individual, in his or her own eyes, to go beyond the Statist constraints of mere survival by becoming a part of the body-of-truth, or the subjectivizable body. (C 252)

History is thus not entirely absent for Badiou. It returns as an essential symbolic fiction, allowing individuals to become subjects of a truth procedure.

We can see this in particular if we return to Badiou's notion of the event, situating it in light of the notions of intervention and eventual recurrence. Our discussion of the event above focused on it as a sort of *creatio ex nihilo*, the irruption of something absolutely new, which allowed us to identify an anti-philosophical and theological element at work in Badiou's theory of the event. However, we should not lose sight of the role that evental recurrence plays in Badiou's theory of the event. Recall from our discussion in Chapter 2 that the interventional naming of a new event always depends on its being placed in relation to another, already named event in circulation. According to Badiou:

> [F]or there to be an event, one must be able to situate oneself within the consequences of another. The intervention is a line drawn from one paradoxical multiple, which is already circulating, to the circulation of another, a line which scratches out. It is a *diagonal* of the situation.   (BE 210, original emphasis)

Intervention in light of a previous evental multiple makes that multiple available for the production of another evental multiple. Neither a matter of mere repetition nor an absolute rupture, the between-two of intervention "evokes the previous situations and uses them precisely to create its own rationality" (Badiou 2006a: 185). This notion of evental recurrence is one of the ways in which Badiou attempts to guard his notion of the event from any hint of "speculative leftism", that is, "any thought of being which bases itself upon the theme of an absolute commencement" (BE 210; cf. Bosteels 2005b).

What is significant for our purposes is that, after introducing the idea of evental recurrence in Meditation 20 of *Being and Event*, Meditation 21 goes on to illustrate this idea in light of the "truth" of Christianity. Importantly, Badiou invokes a pared-down eschatological scheme to discuss the manner in which he takes Christianity to be "structured from beginning to end by evental recurrence":

> The intervention is based upon the circulation, within the Jewish milieu, of another event, Adam's original sin, of which the death of Christ is the relay. The connection between original sin and redemption definitively founds the time of Christianity as a time of exile and salvation. There is an essential historicity to Christianity which is tied to the intervention of the apostles as the placement-into-circulation of the event of the death of God; itself reinforced by the promise of a Messiah which organized the fidelity to the initial exile. Christianity is structured from beginning to end by evental recurrence; moreover, it prepares itself for the divine hazard of the third event, the Last Judgement, in which the ruin of the terrestial situation will be accomplished, and a new regime of existence will be established.   (BE 213)

What this rough eschatological scheme organizes, according to Badiou, is a "periodized time ... in which the connection to the chance of the event of the regulated consequences it entails remains discernible due to the effect of an *institutional fidelity*" (BE 214, original emphasis).

It is significant that in *Being and Event* Badiou refers to the eschatological time of Christianity, a time that connects the movement of history through retroaction and prolepsis, as a periodized time. To label this time as periodized recalls Badiou's *Theory of the Subject*, the goal of which is, at least in part, to think the notion "periodization" or the "materialist" dialectic against the "circularity" of the Hegelian dialectic (TS 18). As mentioned above, the Hegelian dialectic, on Badiou's reading, is circular, in the sense that the end is correlated to the beginning as the latter's necessary outcome. The structure of this dialectical sequence, in which the absolute deploys itself only to return to itself, is, as we have mentioned, theological, in that Hegel articulates it in light of his understanding of salvation history. In Badiou's words, this:

> theological circularity ... presupposing the absolute in the seeds of the beginning, leads back to this very beginning once all the stages of its effectuation, its alienation, its going-outside-itself, and so on, are unfolded. Thus, the dead Son reintegrated into the divisible immanence of the Father *completes* the world-concept of the Christian God, which is the holiness of the Spirit.
>
> (TS 19, original emphasis)

Against this ultimately circular and idealist conception of the dialectic, Badiou proposes one that is periodized and materialist. Rather than taking the unfolding of the dialectic as an auto-development, Badiou stresses that it is necessary to understand dialectical sequences "in the sense of the passage from one sequence to the other, in an irreconcilable, unsuturable lag, where the truth of the first stage gives itself to begin with only as the condition for the second as *fact*, without leading back to anything other than the unfolding of this fact" (*ibid.*). That is, in the periodizing, materialist view, there are only contingent passages between distinct dialectical sequences, where a former sequence serves as the condition for a latter and, in turn, the latter sums up or periodizes the former. In contrast to the idealist conception of the dialectic which, because it loops back to itself, cannot provide a real theory of change, the periodized view, as Feltham points out, "ensures that the process produces something different from what it starts with, and consequently that one dialectical process distinguishes itself from another" (TS 43). Otherwise put, in *Theory of the Subject* periodization ostensibly delivers historicity without History.

We should note two things, here. First, periodization is still a mode of dialectical thought and practice. The goal is not to get rid of dialectical thought and practice but to put it on more stable ground, so to speak, where it can function as a materialist principle for the analysis of real change. Second, although by the time of *Being and Event* Badiou to a large extent drops the Marxist framework of analysis found in *Theory of the Subject* and earlier works, he does not, it seems, drop the notion of periodization. For instance, in *Peut-on penser la politique?*, Badiou declares the crisis of Marxism as complete, and goes on to begin to develop an entire new series of concepts that will make up the substance of *Being and Event*.[11] However, noting that common opinion holds that we should be done with the dialectic and speculative thought in general, Badiou goes on to indicate that "the concepts of the event, structure, intervention, and fidelity are the same concepts of the dialectic, so long as this is not returned to the flat image, inadequate already for Hegel, of the totalization of the work of the negative" (PP 84). The point is not to jettison dialectical thought and practice as such, but to base it on "a doctrine of the event, and not an adventure ruled by Spirit" (*ibid.*). So understood, dialectical thought "does not commence from the law, but from the exception" (PP 90).

Key to making sense of the relationship between the exception and the dialectic is the notion of eventual recurrence, which we discussed in detail in Chapter 2. If the event as such, understood as a radical beginning, institutes a fidelity through intervention, the process of fidelity, the working out of truth, takes place between events, drawing the truth of one sequence towards its consummation, a consummation that is, in actuality, a prolepsis towards another event. Fidelity, in light of the notion of eventual recurrence, works between events, between retroaction and anticipation, situating the history of events on a continuum. Otherwise put, to borrow from Feltham, it is the old mole dialecticizing the eagle. However, this dialecticization is eschatological in form, in the sense that eschatology depends upon a series of unique "events" and the relationship among them (in the terms Badiou evokes in reference to Pascal, sin, redemption, judgement) which constitute the trajectory of truth.

The eschatological form of fidelity within the production of specific truths, then, appears in Badiou's reliance on the future anterior as its mode of discernment. Theologically speaking, eschatology has, of course, traditionally been associated with "the last things" (Moltmann 1993: 15). At a more structural level, eschatology refers to a teleological form of thought that finds the truth of the present in its relationship to the past and its confirmation in the future. Indeed, for eschatological thinking, the present only makes sense in light of an anticipated future, a future that makes rational the contingency of the present and the past. For this reason, eschatological time is structured through and through by "expectation and hope" (Löwith 1957: 6).

We can see this structure in the notions of periodized time and eventual recurrence, in which the past, present and future are linked together through retroaction and anticipation. But it is also present, I want to suggest, in Badiou's use of the idea of forcing in relation to the production of truths, since it relies on the modality of the future anterior to discern the value of a truth in the present. Recall from our discussion in Chapter 2 that, with respect to the production of truths, forcing names the being of the subject of truth · as constituted through what it will have been. For Badiou there can be no direct or immediate correspondence between the subject and the generic procedure itself. The subject, to be sure, is the local status of the generic procedure; the subject is what makes truth possible in a situation. However, because the generic procedure is, by definition, infinite, the subject can in no way exhaust the possibilities of the generic procedure itself. The generic procedure, because it is infinite, is in excess over its local, subjective configuration, meaning that the subject can only ever approximate truths in situations. "Every truth is transcendent to the subject," Badiou writes, "precisely because the latter's entire being resides in supporting the realization of truth" (BE 397). It is here that the notion of the future anterior comes in. Because a truth is infinite, its status is always, to a certain degree, to come, suspended into the future. A truth only exists in the mode of the "future anterior": a truth "will have been presented" (BE 400). Because a generic procedure takes place under the mode of the future anterior, then, conversely and strictly speaking, knowledge of a truth is always retroactive, and it can be partially grasped through the positing of provisional results. The same goes, as we have seen, for the event itself: an event, as undecidable, "is only recognized in the situation by its consequences", meaning that "there will have been some chance in the situation" (BE 207).

Because the structure of truth is the future anterior, meaning that the truth is always retroactive, determined as truth from its future, the subject must act in the present on the basis of confidence or belief, that is, faith. The following quotation brings these themes together succinctly:

> What does confidence mean? The fidelity operator locally discerns connections and disconnections of multiples of the situation with or from the name of the event. This discerning is an *approximative truth*, for the terms positively connected are yet to come – in a truth. This "yet to come" is the distinctive characteristic of a subject who judges. Belief here is the yet-to-come which goes by the *name* of truth. Its legitimacy derives from the fact that the name of the event, having supplemented the situation with a paradoxical multiple, circulates in the evaluations as that on the basis of which the void – the latent and wandering being of the situation – has been convoked. A finite series of evaluations thus possesses, in a manner at once effective and fragmentary – the being-in-situ of the situation itself. This

fragment materially pronounces the yet-to-come for, though it is locatable by knowledge, it is the fragment of an indiscernible trajectory. Belief consists merely in the fact that the encounters' randomness is not vainly gathered up by the faithful connection operator.   (Badiou: 1988: 97, original emphasis)

Because of the relationship between belief and the structure of truth as "yet to come", we can thus affirm with Quentin Meillassoux that Badiou remains in "extreme fidelity ... – with the structure, if not the contents – of Christian eschatology" (2008).

The eschatological character of Badiou's understanding of the production of truth comes full circle in *Logics of Worlds*, in which he invokes the term "resurrection" to indicate the reactivation of an occulted truth in a new logic of appearing. It should be obvious that there is no term more deeply embedded in Christian theology, particularly in regard to eschatology, than resurrection, and Badiou uses the term similarly to indicate literally the raising of a dead truth to new life. Moreover, I would suggest that resurrection is one of the forms that eventual recurrence can take, since it assumes a connection between truth sequences in different logics. In his review of *Logics of Worlds*, Justin Clemens has pointed out the difficulty in conceptualizing this relationship between truths, since Badiou simultaneously affirms the inconsistency of worlds and denies the existence of the one. Quoting Badiou, Clemens notes:

The difficulty is then to explain how eternality can emerge from *within* a world, and how this eternality then communicates *between* worlds: "I believe in eternal truths and in their fragmented creation in the present of worlds. My position on this point is completely isomorphic to that of Descartes: truths are eternal because they have been created, and not because they have been there forever" [LW 512]. But this is to restate the problem in the guise of a conviction, supported, moreover, by an appeal to authority.   (2006: 307, original emphasis)

Clemens is correct to note the difficulty, here, but I would suggest that, at least in regard to the idea of the resurrection of a truth, the way Badiou attempts to bridge the gap between worlds is theological, in that he relies on a notion of grace. For, as we discussed in reference to Paul above, it is precisely grace that happens in caesura of the law, resurrection that brings life to death without any reason. Indeed, is this not precisely what Badiou does with Paul, resurrecting his discourse to new life? Such is the extent of Badiou's "materialism of grace". Although such an explanation is not likely to be philosophically satisfying to many, it does shore up the extent of Badiou's reliance on theology.

In conclusion, by emphasizing the theological elements at work in Badiou's philosophy, one could suggest that I have ignored the sense in which Badiou's philosophy is conditioned by mathematics against religion. Mathematics is certainly essential to Badiou's entire enterprise, and emphasizing this was the purpose of a good portion of the previous chapters. That we can not ignore the importance of mathematics for Badiou should be evident in my claims concerning the anti-theological thrust of Badiou's ontology and philosophy. Nevertheless, it is also important to emphasize that, particularly when it comes to truth and the subject, Badiou's thought is not just determined mathematically: it requires all four truth procedures and the discourses of sophism and anti-philosophy, as we discussed in Chapter 3. The claim that Badiou's philosophy remains fundamentally linked to theology in the sense outlined above, then, should not be taken as a denial of mathematics; it should, rather, be taken as an attempt to complicate the understanding of Badiou's philosophy, which latter, by definition, can neither be reduced to any one of its conditions nor take leave of anti-philosophy. If, as I have claimed, there is a theological element at work in Badiou's philosophy, then it only shores up the complex character of that philosophy itself, even philosophy in general. Thus we can say that Badiou's philosophy is situated between philosophy and anti-philosophy and, because of this, between theology and anti-theology. God is certainly dead for Badiou, but God's shadow still remains.

NOTES

INTRODUCTION

1. Although one can find this disjunction in nascent form in Paul's letters (cf. I Cor. 2:1–5), Tertullian set down its classical formulation. In *The Prescription Against Heretics*, chapter 7, he declares, "What indeed has Athens to do with Jerusalem? What concord is there between the Academy and the Church? What between heretics and Christians? Our instruction comes from 'the porch of Solomon,' who had himself taught that 'the Lord should be sought in simplicity of heart.' Away with all attempts to produce a mottled Christianity of Stoic, Platonic, and dialectic composition! We want no curious disputation after possessing Christ Jesus, no inquisition after enjoying the gospel! With our faith, we desire no further belief. For this is our palmary faith, that there is nothing which we ought to believe besides" (Tertullian 1885: 246). Badiou's more immediate reference, here, is likely Pascal, who makes use of the distinction throughout his *Pensées* (Pascal 2008).

2. Badiou associates the "nihilism" found in Nietzsche and, later, Heidegger, with a nostalgic longing for presence, a longing that seeks to get behind the Platonic inauguration of philosophy through an appeal to the power of the poem. What separates Badiou from Nietzsche is the former's positive evaluation of Plato and, thus, of philosophy in general. Unlike Nietzsche, then, the death of God does not correspond to the end of philosophy and its concern with truth. Badiou can, however, acknowledge "nihilism" to the extent that it names "the *rupture of the traditional figure of the bond*, un-binding as a form of being of all that pretends to be of the bond" (MP 55, original emphasis). I discuss the notion of un-binding being from the one in Chapter 1, but see (MP 47–77) for a discussion of these issues.

3. Badiou gives extremely condensed versions of this thesis in (TO 21–2) and (TC 165–78). As Badiou puts it in *The Century*, "[T]he God of monotheisms has been dead for a long time, no doubt for the last two hundred years ..." (TC 166).

4. It may seem odd to include analytic philosophy here. But as Badiou points out, "The positivist and empiricist approaches, which have been highly influential during the last two centuries, merely invert the Romantic speculative gesture. The claim that science constitutes the one and only paradigm for the positivity of knowledge can be made only from within the completed disentanglement of philosophy and the sciences. The anti-philosophical verdict returned by the various forms of positivism overturns the anti-scientific verdict returned by the various forms of Romantic philosophy, but fails to interrogate its initial premise. It is striking that Heidegger and Carnap disagree about everything, except the idea that it is incumbent upon us to

169

inhabit and activate the end of metaphysics. This is because for both Heidegger and Carnap, the name 'metaphysics' designates the Classical era of philosophy, the era in which mathematics and philosophy were still reciprocally entangled in a general representation of the operations of thought. Carnap wants to *purify* the scientific operation, while Heidegger wishes to *oppose* to science – in which he perceives the nihilist manifestation of metaphysics – a path of thinking modeled on poetry. In this sense, both remain heirs to the Romantic gesture of disentanglement, albeit in different registers" (TW 23).

1. BADIOU'S ANTI-THEOLOGY

1. Good overviews of this period in the development of Badiou's philosophy can be found in Badiou (2007b: xii–lxv), Feltham (2008: 1–31) and Brassier (2005).
2. The passage is Badiou's own translation of Book 6, 511, c–d.
3. Brassier (2005) suggests that Daniel W. Smith (2004) falls into this trap. John Milbank (2007) makes the same mistake.
4. Although there are other variant systems of axioms, ZF has become standard. For a discussion of this, see Tiles (1989: 118–37).
5. The letter can be found in van Heijenoort (1999: 124–5).
6. A good overview of these can be found in Hallward (2003: 81–106, 323–48).
7. Hallward provides a helpful example: "As a rough analogy, consider the set of all galaxies, with its many millions of elements. Each galaxy may be said to exist as an element of this set, that is, it counts as one member of the set. 'In itself', of course, what makes up a galaxy is a very large set of physical components: stars, planets, parts of planets, and so on, down to subatomic collections of electrons and quarks. But as far as set theory is concerned, such substantial realities are of no consequence: 'There is only one kind of variable ...: everything is a multiple, everything is a set" (2003: 84).
8. Hallward again provides a useful example. If we take the set of all galaxies, "it is possible to establish, within the set of galaxies, an altogether astronomical number of subsets or parts of this set: for example, galaxies grouped according to shape, number of stars, age of stars, presence of life forms, and so on" (2003: 84).
9. Quotations from Frege (1960) refer to paragraph numbers.
10. Kenny (2000: 95) summarizes the procession as follows:
    0 is the number belonging to the concept *non-self-identical*,
    1 is the number belonging to the concept *identical with zero*,
    2 is the number belonging to the concept *identical with 0 or 1*,
    3 is the number belonging to the concept *identical with 0, 1, or 2.*
11. In his letter to Frege, Russell expressed the paradox in the following terms: "Let *w* be the predicate: to be a predicate that cannot be predicated of itself. Can *w* be predicated of itself? From each answer its opposite follows. Therefore we must conclude that *w* is not a predicate. Likewise, there is no class (as a totality) of those classes which, each taken as a totality, do not belong to themselves. From this I conclude that a definable collection does not form a totality."
12. Justin Clemens (2001: 212) summarizes the difference between the Romantic infinite and Badiou's own mathematical infinite: "For Badiou, not only does set-theory strip infinity of all Romantic pathos – infinity is now just a number, not an achievable destiny – but it also unleashes number from the jurisdiction of the One. Infinity, far from being the forever proximate-distant home of sacralised presence, is thus rendered utterly banal and indifferent, and mathematics, in an absolutely literal fashion, can be reactivated by radical philosophy as fundamental ontology."
13. For a brief, yet highly readable, history of the infinite, see Zellini (2005).

14. The examples in this paragraph are taken from Dauben (1979: 122).
15. For discussions of Zeno's paradoxes, see Tiles (1989: 12–20) and Huggett (2010).
16. One could suggest that Badiou falls into a similar trap, with his splitting of being into inconsistent and consistent multiplicity. Although Badiou's move invites some formal comparison to the theological insistence on two regions of being, the key difference in his conception is that it is primarily operational rather than substantial. That is, the split between inconsistent multiplicity and consistent multiplicity in a situation depends upon the one-count of that situation, not any substantial qualities of the multiples in question.
17. There is a sense in which it could be said that Aquinas accepts the notion of an eternal cosmos from Aristotle, in that Aquinas adapts the consequences of Aristotle's arguments for the eternity of motion to the idea of creation, and attempts to show that the eternality of the cosmos is philosophically compatible with the idea of creation. For a discussion of this, see Pegis's Introduction to *The Basic Writings of Saint Thomas Aquinas*, vol. 1 (1945). See also Aquinas (1920: I, Q. 46).
18. The discussion of Cantor's innovation relies on Hallward (2003).
19. Badiou's remarks are consistent with Dauben's (1979: 140–48) analysis of Cantor's understanding of the religious implications of his theory. Indeed, as Dauben notes, "by the end of his life … Cantor saw himself as the servant of God, a messenger or reporter who could use the mathematics he had been given to serve the Church" (*ibid*.: 143).
20. It is certainly possible that one could construct a theology that takes seriously Badiou's presuppositions concerning the infinite and the inexistence of the one, although this would entail either abandoning or seriously reworking the traditional distinction between two regions of being. Such an approach, for instance, can be found in many contemporary process theologies, which draw on the work of A. N. Whitehead. For instance, as Roland Faber notes, Whitehead's ontology "prevents the notion of a layered universe in which everything is gathered toward ever greater unities until everything eventually flows together in the unity of God. In fact, Whitehead explicitly refuses to acknowledge any 'inclusive unity' that might muzzle the universe, as it were, by bracing and layering it" (Faber 2008: 113). When Whitehead does speak of "unity" it is "neither the ground of unfolding nor the highest being (the unity of the universe); instead it consistently represents a *finite moment* within the overall creative process". Within such an ontology, God functions primarily as "that particular power that preserves precisely *this* unity by *keeping it open*. God acts efficaciously as the power of the future (Eros, adventure, harmony) that perpetually prevents the emergence of frozen formal unity" (*ibid*.: 118, original emphasis). Otherwise put, Whitehead's God is on the side of multiplicity, rather than the one.

2. EVENT, TRUTH AND THE SUBJECT

1. Badiou introduces this thesis on the inexistence of History in *Theory of the Subject*: "[H]istory does not exist (it would be a figure of the whole). Only historical periods or historicizations (figures of the One-of-the-two) exist" (TS 92).
2. However, Badiou (BE 179) notes the following: "Strictly speaking, a site is only 'evental' insofar as it is retroactively qualified as such by the occurrence of an event." I will return to this crucial point later on in this chapter and in Chapter 4.
3. This is, of course, not the only reading that could be given of the significance of the incarnation. However, Badiou's reading along these lines is important, in that it shores up the eschatological character of Christianity. I discuss this in more detail in Chapter 4.

4. Deleuze and Guatarri make this criticism in *What is Philosophy?* (1994: 151–3). A good overview of the issues involved can be found in Feltham (2008: 103–7).

5. Justin Clemens and Oliver Feltham note: "The problem with the solution proffered by *Logiques des mondes* is that it results, in Aristotelian terms, in a proliferation of little prime movers; moreover, these sites still emerge from nowhere, so we still have *deus ex machine*; and, insofar as they are self-movers, they are spontaneous and *automata*" (2010: 35).

6. My understanding of this difficult aspect of Badiou's theory is heavily indebted to Hallward (2003), Gillespie (2008) and Tiles (1989).

7. I discuss Badiou's particular understanding of love in detail in the next chapter.

8. For an excellent discussion of the reactive and obscure forms of subjectivity in relation to Badiou's own political trajectory, see Power and Toscano (2009).

9. Hence I disagree with Colin Wright (2008b) that this is a "new concept".

3. PHILOSOPHY AND ITS CONDITIONS

1. The coincidence of science, art, politics and love is classically exhibited in Plato's *Republic*, a work that is, in many ways, seminal for Badiou's own philosophy. Because of this, it is not at all surprising that Badiou has recently published a contemporary translation or "hypertranslation", as he refers to it, of the *Republic*, the express goal of which "is to incorporate Plato into contemporary discourse, to present him to everyone as being absolutely available for the only thing that matters: that thought indeed be the liveliest, most concrete thing in the world" (Badiou 2009a: 55; see also Badiou 2012).

2. As we discussed in Chapter 1, this is also why Badiou does not associate his ontological deployment of mathematics with a philosophy of mathematics.

3. Among interpreters of Badiou, Justin Clemens has, perhaps, done the most to emphasize this point. See, for instance, Clemens (2001, 2003a).

4. For instance, Badiou writes: "It so happens that the main stake, the supreme difficulty, is to de-suture philosophy from its poetic condition. Positivism and dogmatic Marxism now constitute but ossified positions. As sutures, they are purely institutional or academic. On the other hand, what has given potency to the poeticizing suture, thus to Heidegger, is far from having been undone, indeed has never been examined" (M 67).

5. Clemens (2003a) makes this point. Clemens notes, rightly, that politics has been the particular emphasis of many readers. Among major interpreters of Badiou, this is seen most clearly in the work of Bruno Bosteels. However, an emphasis on the mathematical-scientific condition can be seen in the work of Ray Brassier. See Brassier (2005: 97–117).

6. It should also be noted that, given the highly specialized and technical language of mathematics, the issue of expertise makes it difficult for non-mathematicians to engage Badiou's ontology on mathematical terms. This is, perhaps, one of the reasons why mathematics is often treated as little more than an appendage to Badiou's ontology and philosophy in general, rather than as determinative of the latter.

7. For critical discussions of Badiou's understanding of love, see MacCannell (2005) and McNulty (2005).

8. For what is perhaps the most thorough treatment of Badiou's politics, see Bosteels (2011).

9. Badiou refers to Plato's critique of democracy in the *Republic* in (M 78).

10. For a concrete example of this logic in relation to the Headscarf Law in France, see Badiou's "The Law on the Islamic Headscarf" (P 98–114).

11. Methodologically, Badiou overwhelmingly treats the truth procedures as separate. See, for instance, (LW 10–22). Such is also the case in the publication of works devoted to particular truth procedures: *Metapolitics* deals with the specificity of political truths; *Handbook of Inaesthetics* with artistic truths; "What is Love?" and "The Scene of the Two", originally published in the collection *De l'amour*, with amorous truths; and his (first) *magnum opus Being and Event* with scientific or mathematical truths.

12. Notwithstanding Barbara Cassin's work on sophism. Badiou states his appreciation for, but ultimate disagreement with, Barbara Cassin's *L'Effet sophistique* (1995) in a note in *Logics of Worlds*, which reads in part: "In what concerns sophistry, it is obviously necessary to be aware of the role it is accorded by Barbara Cassin, the very opposite of the one I reserve for it. See her great book *L'Effet sophistique* (Paris: Gallimard, 1995). Convinced that philosophy's inception is fettered by a specific rhetoric (the predicative rhetoric that Aristotle transforms into a general logic, or ontology, in Book I of the *Metaphysics*), Cassin makes Gorgias and his successors into the artisans of another path for philosophy, in which, since 'being' is exchangeable with 'being said', the function of non-being (ultimately, of silence) is constitutive, in the stead and place of that of being. Ontology is replaced with logology. We could say that Cassin attempts a synthesis between Heidegger (there is indeed a Greek inception that destines and traverses us) and the linguistic turn (everything is language, and the philosophy closest to the real is a general rhetoric). It is as the hero of this synthesis that Gorgias challenges the hegemony of Parmenides" (LW 541~2).

13. However, as Bruno Bosteels (2008) points out, the term itself has its origin in the *antiphilosophes* of the eighteenth century, where it functions as "a self-applied label that historically refers to the mostly religious and conservative, if not outright reactionary, thinkers who resist the arrival of rationalism, deism, or materialism on the part of the French Enlightenment thinkers, the so-called *philosophes*, such as Diderot, Voltaire, or d'Holbach" (156–7).

14. Slavoj Žižek (1999: 250–51) suggests that the specific target of Lacan's anti-philosophical statements against philosophy is Gilles Deleuze.

4. BADIOU'S THEOLOGY

1. However, since his *Badiou: A Subject to Truth* was published in 2003, it does not include a full discussion of *Logics of Worlds*, published in 2006.

2. The article was originally published as "Demanding Approval: On the Ethics of Alain Badiou", *Radical Philosophy* 100 (2000): 16–27.

3. Stephen Fowl (2010) makes a similar claim: "For Badiou, Paul is simply a cipher for an apocalyptic or evental notion of truth and its attendant procedures. Once that notion has been developed and displayed, there is very little need to retain the figure that provoked or generated the allegory in the first place" (128).

4. Adam Miller (2008) does, however, discuss the relationship between Badiou's ontology and his reading of Paul.

5. Badiou also writes, "The Resurrection, after all, is just a mythological assertion. The claim 'there is a limitless succession of prime numbers' possesses an indubitable universality. The claim 'Christ is resurrected' is as though subtracted from the opposition between the universal and the particular, because it is a narrative statement that we cannot assume to be historical" (SP 107).

6. See also Deleuze and Guattari: "But perhaps we then arrive at a conversion of immanence of the situation, a conversion of the excess of the void, which will reintroduce the transcendent: this is the *event site* that sticks to the edge of the void in the

situation and now includes not units but singularities as elements dependent on the preceding functions. Finally, the *event* itself appears (or disappears), less as a singularity than as a separated aleatory point that is added to or subtracted from the site, within the transcendence of the void or *the* truth of the void, without it being possible to decide on the adherence of the event to the situation in which it finds its site (the undecidable)" (1994: 151–2).

7. Critchley raises the same concern in *Infinitely Demanding* (2007: 48). Kenneth Surin raises a similar concern: "The other problem with a politics of the exceptional event is that it is the right that is now using the category of the exceptional event to mobilize the very considerable resources of power and coercion that are at its disposal after September 11. September 11 is clearly the right-wing obverse of Badiou's 1968 truth-event, as evidenced by such claims as 'things can never be the same again in America' or 'from now on everything is different', used by George Bush and his handlers to mobilize American public opinion not just as a response to al-Qaeda, but also to promote the republican Party's overall right-wing agenda" (2005: 255–6).

8. In an interview entitled "Ontology and Politics", Badiou notes, "Lyotard said that I was an absolute decisionist, a sort of new Carl Schmitt" (IT 172). Colin Wright also notes that "the spectre of Schmitt has haunted Badiou's project since its starkest, and arguably most brilliant, exposition in *L'être et l'événement* (1988)" (Wright 2008a: 1).

9. It is also interesting to point out that in *Homo Sacer*, Giorgio Agamben includes Badiou in a genealogy of the concept of the exception, which includes, among others, Kierkegaard and Schmitt (Agamben 1998: 15–29).

10. Badiou discusses the figure of the saint in reference to Paolo Pasolini in (SP 36–9).

11. Commenting on *Peut-on penser la politique?*, Feltham (2008: 85) notes: "The text that thus seals the almost complete disappearance of Marxist vocabulary – party, dialectic, revolution, proletariat – from Badiou's work is *Peut-on penser la politique?*, the first text of the new period. Without reading this work one can understand neither Badiou's strategy in *Being and Event* nor its context."

BIBLIOGRAPHY

Agamben, G. 1998. *Homo Sacer: Sovereign Power and Bare Life*, D. Heller-Roazen (trans.). Stanford, CA: Stanford University Press.

Althusser, L. 2001. *Lenin and Philosophy and Other Essays*. New York: Monthly Review Press.

Aquinas, T. 1920. *The Summa Theologica of St Thomas Aquinas*, Fathers of the English Dominican Province (trans.). London: Burns, Oates & Washburn.

Aristotle 2001a. *Metaphysics*. See McKeon (2001).

Aristotle 2001b. *On the Heavens*. See McKeon (2001).

Aristotle 2001c. *Physics*. See Mckeon (2001).

Badiou, A. 1985. *Peut-on penser la politique?* Paris: Editions du Seuil.

Badiou, A. 1988. "On a Finally Objectless Subject". *Topoi* **7**: 93–8.

Badiou, A. 1996. "What is Love?", J. Clemens (trans.). *Umbr(a)*: 37–53.

Badiou, A. 1999a. "Definition of Philosophy". See Badiou (1999c): 141–4.

Badiou, A. 1999b. *De l'amour*. Paris: Flammarion.

Badiou, A. 1999c. *Manifesto for Philosophy*, N. Madarasz (trans.). Albany, NY: SUNY Press.

Badiou, A. 1999d. "The (Re)turn of Philosophy Itself". See Badiou (1999c): 113–40.

Badiou, A. 2000. *Deleuze: The Clamor of Being*, L. Burchill (trans.). Minneapolis, MN: University of Minnesota Press.

Badiou, A. 2001. *Ethics*, P. Hallward (trans.). London: Verso.

Badiou, A. 2003a. *Saint Paul: The Foundation of Universalism*, R. Brassier (trans.). Stanford, CA: Stanford University Press.

Badiou, A. 2003b. "The Writing of the Generic". In *On Beckett*, A. Toscano & N. Power (ed. & trans.), 1–36. Manchester: Clinamen Press Ltd.

Badiou, A. 2003c. *On Beckett*. Manchester: Clinamen Press.

Badiou, A. 2004a. *Infinite Thought: Truth and the Return of Philosophy*, O. Feltham & J. Clemens (ed. & trans.). London: Continuum.

Badiou, A. 2004b. "Mathematics and Philosophy: The Grand Style and the Little Style". See Badiou (2004g): 3–20.

Badiou, A. 2004c. "On Subtraction". See Badiou (2004g): 104–18.

Badiou, A. 2004d. "One, Multiple, Multiplicities". See Badiou (2004g): 67–80.

Badiou, A. 2004e. "Philosophy and Mathematics: Infinity and the End of Romanticism". See Badiou (2004g): 21–38.

Badiou, A. 2004f. "Platonism and Mathematical Ontology". See Badiou (2004g): 49–58.

Badiou, A. 2004g. *Theoretical Writings*, R. Brassier & A. Toscano (ed. & trans.). London: Continuum.

Badiou, A. 2004h. "Truth: Forcing and the Unnameable". See Badiou (2004g): 119–33.

Badiou, A. 2005a. *Being and Event*, O. Feltham (trans.). London: Continuum.

Badiou, A. 2005b. *Handbook of Inaesthetics*, A. Toscano (trans.). Stanford, CA: Stanford University Press.

Badiou, A. 2005c. *Metapolitics*, J. Barker (trans.). London: Verso.

Badiou, A. 2006a. "After the Event: Rationality and the Politics of Intervention". *Prelom* **8**: 180–94.

Badiou, A. 2006b. *Briefings on Existence: A Short Treatise on Transitory Ontology*, N. Madarasz (trans.). Albany, NY: SUNY Press.

Badiou, A. 2006c. "Lacan and the Pre-Socratics". In *Lacan: The Silent Partners*, Slavoj Žižek (ed.), 7–16. London: Verso.

Badiou, A. 2006d. *Polemics*, S. Cocoran (trans.). London: Verso.

Badiou, A. 2007a. *The Century*, A. Toscano (trans.). Cambridge: Polity Press.

Badiou, A. 2007b. *The Concept of Model*, Z. L. Fraser & T. Tho (ed. & trans.). Melbourne: re.press.

Badiou, A. 2008a. *Conditions*, S. Cocoran (trans.). London: Continuum.

Badiou, A. 2008b. *The Meaning of Sarkozy*, D. Fernbach (trans.). London: Verso.

Badiou, A. 2008c. *Number and Numbers*, R. Mackay (trans.). Cambridge: Polity Press.

Badiou, A. 2009a. "For Today: Plato!". In *Lacanian Ink* **34**: 53–5.

Badiou, A. 2009b. *L'antiphilosophie de Wittgenstein*. Paris: Nous.

Badiou, A. 2009c. *Logics of Worlds*, A. Toscano (trans.). London: Continuum.

Badiou, A. 2009d. *Pocket Pantheon*, D. Macey (trans.). London: Verso.

Badiou, A. 2009e. *Theory of the Subject*, B. Bosteels (trans.). London: Continuum.

Badiou, A. 2010a. *The Communist Hypothesis*, D. Macey & S. Cocoran (trans.). London: Verso.

Badiou, A. 2012. *La République de Platon*. Paris: Fayard.

Badiou, A. & S. Critchley 2007. " 'Ours Is Not a Terrible Situation'". *Philosophy Today* **51**(3): 357–65.

Badiou, A. & P. Hallward 1998. "Politics and Philosophy: An Interview with Alain Badiou". *Angelaki* **3**(3): 113–33.

Badiou, A. & L. Sedofsky. 1994. "Being by Numbers – Interview with Alain Badiou". www.scribd.com/doc/20243826/Badiou-and-Sedofsky-Being-by-Numbers-Interview-With-Artists-and-Philosopher-Alain-Badiou-I (accessed November 2012).

Bartlett, A. J. & J. Clemens 2010. *Alain Badiou: Key Concepts*. Durham: Acumen.

Bell, Jr D. M. 2007. "Badiou's Faith and Paul's Gospel: The Politics of Indifference and the Overcoming of Capital". *Angelaki* **12**(1): 97–111.

Bensaïd, D. 2004. "Alain Badiou and the Miracle of the Event". In *Think Again: Alain Badiou and the Future of Philosophy*, P. Hallward (ed.), 94–105. London: Continuum.

Berger, P. L. 1999. "The Desecularization of the World: A Global Overview". In *The Desecularization of the World: Resurgent Religion and World Politics*, P. L. Berger (ed.), 1–18. Grand Rapids, MI: William B. Eerdmans Publishing Company.

Boesel, C. & C. Keller (eds) 2010. *Apophatic Bodies: Negative Theology, Incarnation, and Relationality*. New York: Fordham University Press.

Bosteels, B. 2005a. "Post-Maoism: Badiou and Politics". *Positions* **13**(3): 575–632.

Bosteels, B. 2005b. "The Speculative Left". *South Atlantic Quarterly* **104**(4) (Fall): 751–67.

Bosteels, B. 2008. "Radical Antiphilosophy". *Filozofski vestnik* **XXIX**(2): 155–87.

Bosteels, B. 2011. *Badiou and Politics*. Durham, NC: Duke University Press.

Brassier, R. 2005. "Badiou's Materialist Epistemology of Mathematics". *Angelaki* **10**(2): 135–50.

Brassier, R. 2007. *Nihil Unbound: Enlightenment and Extinction*. London: Palgrave Macmillan.

Caputo, J. D. & L. A. Alcoff (eds) 2009. *Saint Paul among the Philosophers*. Bloomington, IN: Indiana University Press.

Cassin, B. 1995. *L'Effet sophistique*. Paris: Gallimard.

Clemens, J. 2001. "Platonic Meditations: The Work of Alain Badiou". *Pli* **11**: 200–229.

Clemens, J. 2003a. "Letters as the Condition of Conditions for Alain Badiou". *Communication & Cognition* **36**(1 & 2): 73–102.

Clemens, J. 2003b. *The Romanticism of Contemporary Theory*. Aldershot: Ashgate.

Clemens, J. 2005. "Doubles of Nothing: The Problem of Binding Truth to Being in the Work of Alain Badiou". *Filozosfki vestnik* **XXVI**(2): 97–111.

Clemens, J. 2006. "Had We But Worlds Enough, And Time, This Absolute, Philosopher …". *Cosmos and History: The Journal of Natural and Social Philosophy* **2**(1–2): 277–310.

Clemens J. & O. Feltham 2010. "The Thought of Stupefaction; or, Event and Decision as Non-ontological and Pre-political Factors in the Work of Gilles Deleuze and Alain Badiou". In *Event and Decision: Ontology and Politics in Badiou, Deleuze, and Whitehead*, R. Faber, H. Krips & D. Pettus (eds), 16–47. Newcastle: Cambridge Scholars Publishing.

Clemens, J. & J. Roffe 2008. "Philosophy as Anti-Religion in the Work of Alain Badiou". *Sophia* **47**: 345–58.

Critchley, S. 2000. "Demanding Approval: On the Ethics of Alain Badiou". *Radical Philosophy* **100**: 16–27.

Critchely, S. 2005a. "'Fault Lines': Simon Critchley in Discussion on Alain Badiou". *Polygraph* **17**: 295–307.

Critchley, S. 2005b. "On the Ethics of Alain Badiou". See Riera (2005): 215–35.

Critchley, S. 2007. *Infinitely Demanding*. London: Verso.

Critchely, S. 2012. *The Faith of the Faithless: Experiments in Political Theology*. London: Verso.

Crockett, C. 2010. "Review of *Badiou and Theology*". *Notre Dame Philosophical Reviews*, http://ndpr.nd.edu/review.cfm?id=19847 (accessed June 2010).

Dauben, J. W. 1979. *Georg Cantor: His Mathematics and Philosophy of the Infinite*. Cambridge, MA: Harvard University Press.

Deleuze, G. & F. Guatarri 1994. *What is Philosophy?*, H. Tomlinson & G. Burchell (trans.). New York: Columbia University Press.

Depoortere, F. 2009. *Badiou and Theology*. London: T & T Clark International.

Derrida, J. 1995. *On the Name*, D. Wood *et al.* (trans.). Stanford, CA: Stanford University Press.

During, E. 2010. "Art". In *Alain Badiou: Key Concepts*, A. J. Bartlett & J. Clemens (eds), 82–93. Durham: Acumen.

Faber, R. 2008. *God as Poet of the World*, D. W. Stott (trans.). Louisville, KY: Westminster John Knox Press.

Faber, R. 2010. "Bodies of the Void: Polyphilia and Theoplicity". See Boesel & Keller (2010): 200–223.

Feltham, O. 2008. *Alain Badiou: Live Theory*. London: Continuum.

Finkelde, D. 2007. *Politische Eschatologie Nach Paulus*. Vienna: Verlag Turia & Kant.

Fowl, S. 2010. "A Very Particular Universalism: Badiou and Paul". In *Paul, Philosophy, and the Theopolitical Vision*, D. Harink (ed.), 119–34. Eugene, OR: Cascade Books.

Frege, G. 1960. *The Foundations of Arithmetic*, J. L. Austin (trans.). New York: Harper & Brothers.

Fukuyama, F. 1992. *The End of History and the Last Man*. New York: Free Press.

Gillespie, S. 2008. *The Mathematics of Novelty: Badiou's Minimalist Metaphysics*. Melbourne: re.press.

Griffiths, P. J. 2004. "Christ and Critical Theory". *First Things* **145**: 46–55.

Hallett, M. 1984. *Cantorian Set Theory and the Limit of Size*. Oxford: Clarendon Press.

Hallward, P. 2000. "Ethics Without Others: A Reply to Critchley on Badiou's Ethics". *Radical Philosophy* **102**: 27–30.

Hallward, P. 2003. *Badiou: A Subject to Truth*. Minneapolis, MN: University of Minnesota Press.

Hallward, P. 2005. "Depending on Inconsistency: Badiou's Answer to the 'Guiding Question of All Contemporary Philosophy'". *Polygraph* **17**: 11–25.

Harink, D. (ed.) 2010. *Paul, Philosophy, and the Theopolitical Vision*. Eugene, OR: Cascade Books.

Heidegger, M. 1969. *Identity and Difference*, J. Stambaugh (trans.). Chicago, IL: Univeristy of Chicago Press.

Heidegger, M. 1988. "Only a God Can Save Us." In *The Heidegger Controversy*, R. Wolin (ed.), 91–116. Cambridge, MA: MIT Press.

Huggett, N. 2010. "Zeno's Paradoxes". *Stanford Encyclopedia of Philosophy*. http://plato. stanford.edu/entries/paradox-zeno (accessed April 2012).

Janicaud, D., J.-F. Courtine, M. Henry, J.-L. Marion & P. Ricoeur 2001. *Phenomenology and the Theological Turn: The French Debate*. New York: Fordham University Press.

Johnston, A. 2009. *Badiou, Žižek, and Political Transformations: The Cadence of Change*. Evanston, IL: Northwestern University Press.

Juergensmeyer, M. 2003. *Terror in the Mind of God: The Global Rise of Religious Violence*. Berkeley, CA: University of California Press.

Keller, C. 2010. "The Cloud of the Impossible: Embodiment and Apophasis". See Boesel & Keller (2010): 25–44.

Kenny, A. 2000. *Frege: An Introduction to the Founder of Modern Analytic Philosophy*. Oxford: Blackwell Publishers Ltd.

Kierkegaard. S. 1992. *Concluding Unscientific Postscript*, H. Hong & E. Hong (trans.). Princeton, NJ: Princeton University Press.

Kotsko, A. 2008. "Politics and Perversion: Situating Žižek's Paul". *Journal for Cultural and Religious Theory* **9**(2): 43–52.

Koyré, A. 1957. *From the Closed World to the Infinite Universe*. Baltimore, MA: Johns Hopkins Press.

Lecercle, J.-J. 1999. "Cantor, Lacan, Mao, Beckett, *même combat*". *Radical Philosophy* **93**: 6–13.

Löwith, K. 1957. *Meaning in History: The Theological Implications of the Philosophy of History*. Chicago, IL: University of Chicago Press.

MacCannell, J. F. 2005. "Alain Badiou: Philosophical Outlaw". See Riera (2005): 137–84.

Maor, E. 1987. *To Infinity and Beyond: A Cultural History of the Infinite*. Stuttgart: Birkhäuser.

Marchart, O. 2007. *Post-Foundational Political Thought*. Edinburgh: Edinburgh University Press.

McKeon, R. (ed.) 2001. *The Basic Works of Aristotle*. New York: Random House.

McNulty, T. 2005. "Feminine Love and the Pauline Universal". See Riera (2005): 185–212.

Meillassoux, Q. 2008. "Histoire et évènement chez Alain Badiou". Intervention au séminaire "Marx au xxiᵉ siècle: l'esprit & la lettre", www.marxau21.fr/index.php?option=com_con tent&view=article&id=83:histoire-et-evenement-chez-alain-badiou&catid=39:badiou-alain&Itemid=62 (accessed April 2012).

Milbank, J. 2007. "The Return of Mediation, or The Ambivalence of Alain Badiou". *Angelaki* **12**(1): 127–43.

Miller, A. 2008. *Badiou, Marion, and St Paul: Immanent Grace*. London: Continuum.

Moltmann, J. 1993. *Theology of Hope*, J. W. Leitch (trans.). Minneapolis, MN: Fortress Press.

Nicholas of Cusa, 1997. *Nicholas of Cusa: Selected Spiritual Writings*, H. L. Bond (ed. & trans.). New York: Paulist Press.

Nietzsche, F. 1967. *The Will to Power*, W. Kaufmann & R. J. Hollingdale (trans.). New York: Vintage Books.

Nietzsche, F. 1974. *The Gay Science*, W. Kaufmann (trans.). New York: Vintage Books.

Pascal, B. 2008. *Pensées and Other Writings*, A. Levi & H. Levi (eds & trans.). Oxford: Oxford University Press.

Pegis, A. C. (ed.) 1945. *Basic Writings of Saint Thomas Aquinas*, vol. 1. New York: Random House.

Plato 2005. *The Republic*. In *The Collected Dialogues of Plato*, E. Hamilton & H. Cairns (eds). Princeton, NJ: Princeton University Press.

Pluth, E. 2010. *Badiou*. Malden, MA: Polity Press.

Power, N. & A. Toscano 2009. "The Philosophy of Restoration: Alain Badiou and the Enemies of May". *boundary 2* **36**(1): 27–46.

Pseudo-Dionysius 1987. *The Divine Names*. In *Pseudo-Dionysius: The Complete Works*, C. Luibheid (trans.). New York: Paulist Press.

Reynhout, K. 2008. "Alain Badiou: Hidden Theologian of the Void?". *The Heythrop Journal* **52**(2): 219–33.

Riera, G. (ed.) 2005. *Alain Badiou: Philosophy and its Conditions*. Albany, NY: SUNY Press.

Schmitt, C. 1985. *Political Theology*, G. Schwab (trans.). Chicago, IL: University of Chicago Press.

Smith, D. 2004. "Badiou and Deleuze on the Ontology of Mathematics". In *Think Again: Alain Badiou and the Future of Philosophy*, P. Hallward (ed.), 77–93. London: Continuum.

Surin, K. 2005. "Rewriting the Ontological Script of Liberation: On the Question of Finding a New Kind of Political Subject". In *Theology and the Political: The New Debate*, C. Davis, J. Milbank & S. Žižek (eds), 240–66. Durham, NC: Duke University Press.

Tertullian 1885. *The Prescription Against Heretics*. In *Ante-Nicene Fathers*, vol. 3, A. Roberts, J. Donaldson & A. C. Coxe (eds). Buffalo, NY: Christian Literature Publishing Co.

Tiles, M. 1989. *The Philosophy of Set Theory: A Historical Introduction to Cantor's Paradise*. Mineola, NY: Dover Publications.

Tillich, P. 1951. *Systematic Theology, Volume 1*. Chicago, IL: University of Chicago Press.

Tomarchio, J. 2002. "Aquinas's Concept of Infinity". *Journal of the History of Philosophy* **40**(2): 163–87.

Toscano, A. 2010. *Fanaticism*. London: Verso.

van Heijenoort, J. (ed.) 1999. *From Frege to Gödel: A Source Book in Mathematical Logic, 1879–1931*. Cambridge, MA: Harvard University Press.

Ward, G. & B. Daniels 2008. "The Academy, the Polis, and the Resurgence of Religion: An Interview with Graham Ward". *The Other Journal* **12**, http://theotherjournal.com/2008/11/18/the-academy-the-polis-and-the-resurgence-of-religion-an-interview-with-graham-ward/ (accessed November 2012).

Wittgenstein, L. 1955. *Tractatus Logico-Philosophicus*. London: Routledge & Kegan Paul.

Wright, C. 2008a. "Event or Exception?: Disentangling Badiou from Schmitt, or, Towards a Politics of the Void". *Theory & Event* **11**(2), http://muse.jhu.edu/login?auth=0&type=summary&url=/journals/theory_and_event/v011/11.2.wright.html (accessed November 2012).

Wright, C. 2008b. "Resurrection and Reaction in Alain Badiou: Towards an Evental Historiography". *Culture, Theory & Critique* **49**(1): 73–92.

Zellini, P. 2005. *A Brief History of Infinity*. New York: Penguin.

Žižek, S. 1999. *The Ticklish Subject: The Absent Centre of Political Ontology*. London: Verso.

INDEX